THE MORAL NATION

Kellogg Institute titles from
The University of Notre Dame Press

Debt and Development in Latin America
Kwan S. Kim and David F. Ruccio, Editors

Profits, Progress and Poverty: Case Studies of
International Industries in Latin America
Richard Newfarmer, Editor

Development, Democracy, and the Art of Trespassing:
Essays in Honor of Albert O. Hirschman
Alejandro Foxley, Michael S. McPherson, and Guillermo O'Donnnell,
Editors

Development and External Debt in Latin America:
Bases for a New Consensus
Richard Feinberg and Ricardo Ffrench-Davis, Editors

The Progressive Church in Latin America
Scott Mainwaring and Alexander Wilde, Editors

The Moral Nation: Humanitarianism and U.S. Foreign Policy Today
Bruce Nichols and Gil Loescher, Editors

THE MORAL NATION: HUMANITARIANISM AND U.S. FOREIGN POLICY TODAY

Edited by Bruce Nichols and Gil Loescher

UNIVERSITY OF NOTRE DAME PRESS
NOTRE DAME, INDIANA

Library of Congress Cataloging-in-Publication Data

The Moral nation : humanitarianism and U.S. foreign policy
   today / edited by Bruce Nichols and Gil Loescher.
      p. cm.
   ISBN 0-268-01372-1
   1. Human rights. 2. United States—Foreign relations—
1945-
I. Nichols, J. Bruce. II. Loescher, Gil.
K3240.4.M6737 1989
342'.085—dc19
[342.285]   88-40323

Manufactured in the United States of America

CONTENTS

ACKNOWLEDGMENTS

We would like to acknowledge and thank the Carnegie Council on Ethics and International Affairs and the Kellogg Institute for International Studies for co-sponsoring the 1986–87 Ethics and Foreign Policy Lecture Series which was held on the campus of the University of Notre Dame. Many of these chapters were part of that lecture series. We want to acknowledge the generous support of the Carnegie Council which paid for the administrative costs of the series. In particular, we would like to thank the following persons for their substantial contributions: Robert J. Myers, president of the Carnegie Council; Denis Goulet, O'Neill Professor of Education for Justice at the University of Notre Dame and one of the co-organizers of the series; Rev. Ernest Bartell, executive director of the Kellogg Institute for International Studies; Pam Putt, secretary to Denis Goulet and the local administrator for the series at Notre Dame; Alex Wilde, formerly associate director of the Kellogg Institute; the Hon. John J. Gilligan, director of the Institute for International Peace Studies at Notre Dame; and Linda Griffin Kean, formerly director of publications at the Carnegie Council.

Finally, we would like to thank John Ehmann and Ann Rice, both of the University of Notre Dame Press, for the keen interest they have shown in this book from the very beginning. The chapters by Gil Loescher and Bruce Nichols have previously been published in somewhat different form in *Political Science Quarterly* (New York: The American Academy of Political Science, 1988) and in *The Uneasy Alliance: Religion, Refugee Work, and U.S. Foreign Policy* (New York: Oxford University Press, 1988).

INTRODUCTION

Gil Loescher and Bruce Nichols

In the editorial pages of the New York *Times* in 1985 Sydney
Schanberg wrote that the United States was "a moral nation." He
claimed that U.S. leaders often appeared lost in "geopolitical
balancing acts" and seemed to lose "the memory of the great
strength that is derived from being a 'moral nation.' " A striking
example of this national conscience is the sense of guilt many
Americans felt when boatloads of Jewish refugees were refused
in the 1930s, or Haitians were turned back in the 1980s. Schanberg insisted that "the humanitarian tradition in the United
States was not a myth," and that many Americans wanted its
ideals reflected in government policy.

Humanitarian activities and tenets form an integral part of
America's dominant ideologies and moral traditions. While these
values compete with self-interest and realpolitik, their importance to many citizens' sense of legitimacy and purpose in foreign policy is such that no definition of the nation's long-term
interests which wholly excludes these values is likely to be adequate. Thus, Americans frequently call upon their political leaders to demonstrate solicitude for the misfortune of outsiders and
to contribute materially to the amelioration of natural and other
disasters which occur in distant nations. Annually tens of thousands of Americans may be found outside the country's borders
working for nongovernmental bodies and performing various
acts of mercy traditionally described as humanitarian. In many
cases these private bodies work unquestioningly alongside U.S.
government agencies. Yet in Central America, the Horn of Africa,
and in many other places, private agencies and their employees
are increasingly forced to take sides, choosing whether to target
their humanitarian efforts with or against governmentally sponsored goals.

1

The dimension of humanitarianism addressed in this volume, humanitarian relief, may be broadly defined as the provision of assistance to victims of natural or political disasters. Its exponents, both in government and in nongovernmental bodies, have traditionally aspired to elevate the needs of the victims over limitations imposed by short-term political concerns. Yet humanitarianism in action—whether in efforts to assist displaced persons following World War II, airlifts of food to Biafra in the late 1960s, or famine relief to Ethiopia in the 1980s—has involved a combination of moral good and politically useful objectives. Far from representing a purely moralistic approach to the world, humanitarianism has been pragmatically incorporated into aspects of U.S. foreign policy.

From the beginning of modern humanitarian efforts in the late nineteenth century, it has been a constant struggle to inject principle into politics. While there have been marked American successes, beginning with aid to Cuban victims of the Spanish-American War and famine relief in the Soviet Union in the 1920s, the presumption of the complementarity of privately sponsored humanitarianism and government objectives in foreign policy has always been present. As long as we judge America to be a "moral nation," this complementarity makes sense. In the late 1940s and 1950s, for instance, the national assent to anticommunism in foreign policy supported the belief that aiding refugees from Eastern Europe was a humanitarian task the United States and its citizens should shoulder. Aiding these refugees provided both symbolic and instrumental gains for American foreign policy during the cold war. Consensus was much less evident when the refugee population consisted of Palestinians, Chileans fleeing Pinochet, Haitian boat people leaving the Duvalier regimes, or Salvadorans fleeing war and repression.

This book constitutes a study of humanitarianism as a significant component of American foreign policy. It examines current relations between nongovernmental organizations and the U.S. government in overseas operations and illustrates some of the difficulty of reconciling principles and politics in the administration of U.S. humanitarian policy. The topics covered in this book are among the most pressing foreign policy issues facing the United States in the 1980s and beyond. The authors include academics, journalists, human rights specialists and activists, former government officials, and leaders and representatives of voluntary agencies, nongovernmental organizations, and foundations.

The first section of the book concentrates on the moral and political philosophy of humanitarianism and its relationship to the conduct of U.S. foreign policy. Sidney H. Schanberg, the journalist whose wartime experiences in Cambodia in the 1970s were depicted in the film *The Killing Fields,* describes with simple eloquence the importance of humanitarian traditions in U.S. foreign policy. However, Schanberg's plea for foreign policy grounded in moral traditions raises fundamental questions of political philosophy and strategy. Henry Shue, an ethicist at Cornell, and Rogers M. Smith, a political scientist at Yale, take sharply divergent perspectives on how best to answer these questions.

Both Shue and Smith agree that nations, particularly the United States, define themselves by their ideals. Both find that an emphasis on national interests at the expense of broad ideals of humanitarianism is unacceptable. They disagree, however, on whether to base humanitarian action on communitarian, national, or universalist principles.

Shue describes humanitarian activity as work that "must be done." This is true, he argues, because the national interest of the United States cannot be defined without reference to moral principles. In his ordering of such principles, an absolute and fundamental commitment to justice is essential, and priority is given to cosmopolitan or universal principles over national aspirations and ideals. While Shue acknowledges that constraints and conflicts are inevitable in the pursuit of these ideals, their importance in the lives of individual victims of political or natural disasters is obvious. Further, Shue notes "the usefulness of a good reputation" that accrues to the United States through its involvement in such efforts. Through a strong commitment to humanitarian goals, the United States goes beyond being a "moral nation," and helps to establish universal standards of humanitarianism.

Smith, on the other hand, places more emphasis on morality rooted in communal and national aspirations and ideals rather than in cosmopolitan or universal ideals which Shue and others assume to be morally superior. Smith argues that the world is made up of individual nation-states which do not treat humanitarianism as moral truth above the fray of politics but as a political perspective which needs to take into account national actors with a diverse range of interests and beliefs. He believes that the United States would do better to begin with a sense of what America values, with its moral aims and purposes, and to see how these moral requirements could best be furthered in the world as we find it today. Smith distinguishes between the universal views held by humanitarian agencies and the national views of U.S. policymakers. Because of their different perspectives and values, U.S. government officials and private humanitarian agencies almost inevitably will clash. Perhaps the most striking difference between the two involves action that "U.S. officials see as buttressing political forces hostile to liberty." Thus, for example, permission to send private humanitarian assistance, including school supplies to schoolchildren in Cambodia, was denied by the U.S. State Department in the early 1980s because such aid constituted help to a government hostile to U.S. interests. Nevertheless, Smith argues that these contrasting perspectives can be "truly useful" and that the U.S. government and the private agencies can serve "to correct the characteristic blind spots of the other" and to engage in more "open-minded critical dialogue with each other."

In the second section of the book, two chapters examine the political and legal factors which must be addressed in looking at U.S. humanitarian policy today. David P. Forsythe, a political scientist at the University of Nebraska; and Peter Macalister-Smith, a jurist at the Max Planck Institute in Heidelberg, offer analyses of these two related topics. Forsythe looks at the evolution of American institutions, private and governmental, given over to international humanitarian action and places them in the context of an evolving international system for delivery of assistance. As his analysis indicates, while enormous progress has been made in the last forty years, institutional and political factors at times overwhelm the best efforts to sustain humanitarian standards. Macalister-Smith examines the evolution of international humanitarian law in the twentieth century. While offering a frank appraisal of the limits of humanitarian law, he remains cautiously optimistic that humanitarian principles in international law will continue to achieve incremental growth.

In the third section of the book, several authors examine refugees, the closely related topics of asylum and sanctuary in the United States, and the role of private humanitarian organizations in pressing human rights claims with U.S. and regional officials. Doris Meissner, former acting director of the Immigration and Naturalization Service, and Michael McConnell, an activist with the Chicago Religious Task Force on Central America, examine the issues of asylum and sanctuary for Central Americans who have sought refuge in the U.S. and explore how we might evaluate these issues in the context of U.S. and international law, morality, and church-state tensions. Few recent events in the humanitarian realm have erupted with such force on the American domestic scene as has the sanctuary movement. For many Americans, this issue more than any other has captured the confrontation between humanitarian ideals and politics.

Gil Loescher, a political scientist at Notre Dame and the co-editor of the book, addresses the issue of refugee policy in Central America, examining in detail the situation of refugees in Mexico, Honduras, and Costa Rica and the various actors, their interests, and the ways in which they are affected by geopolitics, ideology, and ethnic politics. He analyzes the attitude of the United States and its impact on refugee policy, the role of the United Nations High Commissioner for Refugees, and the problems faced by voluntary agencies in their struggle to preserve humanitarian "space" for their activities. A closely related chapter by Lowell W. Livezey of the Woodrow Wilson School of Public and International Affairs at Princeton examines the role of nongovernmental human-rights organizations and the conduct of American foreign policy in Central America in the 1980s. Livezey discerns a growing rift between those organizations that emphasize the political and cultural rights associated with American views of freedom and those that press for more expansive views of human rights that focus on the "tangible welfare" of individuals and groups in need. This latter group views the convergence of governmental and private ends in humanitarian assistance as increasingly unlikely.

In the Horn of Africa, famine and refugee problems have intertwined in recent years to create one of the most complex scenes of human need anywhere in the world. Each of the chapters in the final section of the book address the actual mechanics of how assistance is organized. As Henry Shue points out in his earlier chapter, Lawrence A. Pezzullo and Jason W. Clay offer strongly contrasting views of the Ethiopian famine. Starting with different premises, they reach different conclusions. Pezzullo, formerly a career State Department officer and now executive director of Catholic Relief Services, accepts the view that the famine was largely natural, and that accommodations to the Ethiopian regime, however distasteful, were necessary in order to provide any assistance at all. Clay, an anthropologist at Cultural Survival, a Cambridge, Massachusetts, research and advocacy organization, believes that private humanitarians, in their rush to capitalize on public sympathy for hungry Ethiopians, failed to understand the overwhelmingly political nature of the famine, the uses made of food supplies, and the meaning of the forced resettlement of untold thousands in the midst of Ethiopia's civil war.

Frederick C. Cuny, a disaster relief specialist who heads the Dallas-based consulting firm INTERTECT, points to many of the hidden political dimensions at work in famine relief operations. Sadly, many of these same forces seem to be repeating themselves in the Horn of Africa in early 1988 as this introduction is being written. Finally, Bruce Nichols, co-editor of the book and director of studies at the Carnegie Council on Ethics and International Affairs, turns to a unique operation designed to surreptitiously move 25,000 Ethiopian Jews, or Falasha, to Israel. When the private sector efforts of Americans and some Israeli officials broke down in eastern Sudan in 1985, the U.S. government was obliged to provide millions of dollars in covert aid to move endangered refugees and resettle them in Israel. The Falasha operation, like many other U.S. refugee relief and resettlement activities, points directly to the importance of prior foreign policy commitments and communal (versus international) norms in setting humanitarian policy.

I. THE HUMANITARIAN ETHIC
IN U.S. FOREIGN POLICY

MEMORY IS THE ANSWER

Sydney H. Schanberg

My father was poor growing up and when his hard work brought him in middle age to a place where he was no longer poor, his memory of those difficult years informed his life in a manner that made him very good at helping others who were down on their luck. He took care of his family first but he didn't forget the others.

These thoughts have rushed upon me because he died a little over a week ago, and when a parent dies we grope for meaning. Moreover, in the jumbled, private days following his death, the outside world—murmuring for attention—was also discussing memory and morality.

Elie Wiesel, our teacher of the Holocaust, a child of the concentration camps, was telling the President: "This is why survivors, of whom you spoke, Mr. President, have tried to teach their contemporaries how to build on ruins, how to invent hope in a world that offers none, how to proclaim faith to a generation that has seen it shamed and mutilated. And I believe, we believe, that memory is the answer, perhaps the only answer."

Speaking of the concentration camps, Mr. Wiesel said: "Mr. President, I was there. I was there when American liberators arrived. And they gave us back our lives. And what I felt for them then nourishes me to the end of my days. . . . We are grateful to this country, the greatest democracy in the world, the freest nation in the world, the moral nation."

Sometimes Presidents and policy makers, caught and distracted by their geopolitical balancing acts, seem to lose the memory of the great strength that is derived from being a "moral nation."

Even as Elie Wiesel was trying to persuade this President that to visit a German military cemetery where SS soldiers, members of the Nazi elite guard, are buried is to forsake memory, another debate—over a more recent memory, the war in Indochina—was sharing the headlines.

In this debate too, many participants have failed to include the strength and authority that we can possess as a "moral nation." They choose instead to frame the lesson of Vietnam narrowly. They see hawks versus doves, they see the press and Congress in combat against the White House, they squint so close at these perceived combatants that our larger history is blurred and overlooked.

Because I reported from Indochina, I have heard often the complaint that the American press was more critical of Washington than we were of the Communist superpowers, that we "tore down" our own government. Some say this means we lack patriotism.

It is true that, by and large, the press in Indochina wrote stories critical of the American policy there. But it was not because reporters were unpatriotic. It was, rather, because reporters saw America slipping toward the habits of the totalitarian powers, whose activities we deem as less than moral.

What we did was to hold this country to a greater standard. Since our government says that it stands on higher moral ground than the Communist powers, that it is different, it must behave differently, not just say so. That is the standard by which the press measured its country.

The humanitarian tradition in the United States is not a myth, not the result of an advertising campaign. So when we leave the humanitarian factor out of our foreign policy, when we use a small country, such as Cambodia, for an imagined larger geopolitical purpose without stopping to consider the potential consequences to the Cambodian people, we debase that tradition. It does no patriotic service to overlook such failures; on the contrary, it robs us of the strength of a moral nation.

We are right to expect more of our government than we expect of dictatorships. Thus, we are not terribly surprised when Moscow rolls its tanks into the capital of a small neighbor; but we are rightly anguished when our policies falter and we begin to imitate our totalitarian adversaries.

It is not logical to justify a misguided policy by saying that the Russians are immoral. A democracy, by its nature, must bear the burden of being judged differently. In a literal sense it is not fair, it is a liability, it makes us less efficient than totalitarian states—but in the end it is a fundamental strength.

This is not to suggest that we must be militarily weaker or in any way defenseless, just that we must try, as Elie Wiesel implored the President, "to do something else, to find another way."

MORALITY, POLITICS, AND HUMANITARIAN ASSISTANCE

Henry Shue

Clear thinking can be a profoundly political act, as we have learned from social thinkers as different as George Orwell and Albert Camus. Humanitarian elements and political elements are often inextricably mixed in fact, but we should still try to call them each by their right names.

THREE ASPECTS OF MORALITY

Upon the first superficial glance the problem appears to be that there is a conflict between two independent and incompatible concerns: national interest and humanitarianism. Upon a second superficial look the solution seems to be that although national interest and humanitarianism are sometimes incompatible and conflicting, they are also sometimes compatible, at least, or even mutually supportive. This construal of the problem and this suggestion of a solution, which accepts the original construal of the problem, fail to be enlightening because they rest content with what used to be called a simple dichotomy and is nowadays often called "binary thinking." On the one side is the national interest, clear and distinct and isolable, and on the other stands humanitarianism, also clear and distinct and quite a different matter in concept from the national interest. The crucial step, I want to suggest, is not to see that two quite separate and simple matters do in fact sometimes happen to coincide, but to see that neither the national interest nor humanitarianism is simple—each is complex—and part of the complexity of each is constituted by intricate interweavings with the other member of the pair. The main factor is not that the two occasionally happen to coincide in fact, but that the two can be to a considerable extent interrelated in concept. I take it as my project to highlight some of these conceptual relationships without becoming hopelessly entangled in them.

One of the complexities is that "humanitarianism" is no one thing. The same label is sometimes unthinkingly applied to each of several quite different activities. To become even slightly more precise we need a still fairly crude distinction among three areas of morality; we can then ask when what is properly called "humanitarianism" falls into one rather than the other two of these three activities. I shall call the three aspects of morality that I want to distinguish "constraints," "mandates," and "ideals," which are in part my own shorthand labels, not any standard categories. Constraints specify acts that must not be done. Mandates specify acts that must be done. An ideal specifies acts that must be done if one is committed to that particular ideal. One question that can usefully be asked about any case of so-called humanitarianism is: what is being satisfied, a constraint, a mandate, or an ideal?

What is more interesting, however, is that constraints, mandates, and ideals are not simply aspects of morality that determine a little more specifically what type of "humanitarianism" is being performed. Constraints, mandates, and ideals are each unavoidably involved as well in the specification of what the national interest is. Constraints, mandates, and ideals may affect the national interest in a fairly straightforward, if somewhat external, way. The relationship of the three to the national interest also can be more intimate and, I think, fascinating. We can look first at external relations and then at intimate relations between the national interest and aspects of morality. This will all help us to explain the respect in which humanitarianism is discretionary, or freely given, as it is often thought to be.

MANDATES FOR THE NATIONAL INTEREST

There are some things one does not do. Not many, perhaps, but some. And if the "one" is a government, it doesn't matter—

some things are still not to be done. To put the point a little more carefully, then: some constraints apply even to governments pursuing national interests, or, national interests are legitimate only if they can be pursued within fundamental moral constraints. Since abiding by the constraints upon pursuit of the national interest would fall short of humanitarianism, we need here note only that observance of the basic constraints is an essential precondition for going on to do anything genuinely humanitarian. This note is negative, but no less important for that. To concede that there were a national interest that might be pursued without restraint would be to legitimate the unleashing of the whirlwind of the unbridled State.

Similarly, there are some things one must do. Some mandates apply even to governments pursuing national interests; national interests are legitimate only if their pursuit is compatible with fulfillment of basic mandates. Here we come closer to part of what is usually meant by "humanitarianism." Some of what is normally called "humanitarianism" seems discretionary, and some seems compulsory. At least some of the compulsory part can be viewed as required by the fundamental moral mandates that are applicable to everyone, such as the requirement of elementary justice. Relevant international cases are involved and controversial, so I shall begin with a more homely and clearer case to make the basic point.

Suppose a friend and I cooperate in building something that we then sell for $1,000. In fact, our contributions to the project were equal: we each bought about the same amount of materials, we each worked about the same number of hours and equally hard, each of us contributed important ideas. I declare, however, that this was basically my project and that for "helping me" my friend deserves $250, but the other $750 is mine. She protests but to no avail, and I keep three times as much as she gets. Later I hear that her apartment has caught fire, and many of her belongings have burned up. I rush over, saying: "That's a shame—I would like to help," and donate $250 toward new things. She, however, if she knows she deserved another $250 for her equal contribution to our joint project, is less likely to think this is humanitarian assistance than to think, "Well, at least the scoundrel paid me the rest of what he owed me." The moral of the story, of course, is that one cannot—conceptually cannot—

give in charity what one actually owes in justice. It is incorrect to describe as "freely donated" what was already owed and therefore already belonged to the recipient.

International cases, naturally, are far more complex and controversial in several respects than this homely case, and I scratch the surface of one actual case in the latter half of this chapter.[1] Judgments about international justice may rest on any one or more of several very different foundations: theories about distributive justice, theories about compensatory justice, theories of human rights that include basic economic rights, theories about the ownership of natural resources, and theories about the mutual obligations of allies. It is often denied that there are any positive international duties of natural justice, as distinguished from voluntarily incurred obligations, as, for example, has recently been done eloquently but unconvincingly by Michael Walzer in *Spheres of Justice*.[2] It can, however, be shown that in a world with more than one society it is intelligible to think of domestic justice only if it is intelligible to think of international justice.[3]

Very briefly, principles of domestic justice concern the distribution within the society of what belongs within that society, but it is impossible to know what belongs within a society without having principles for distributing wealth and income among societies. One possible "standard" is that every society is entitled to keep whatever it has now, but that consideration is, then, being put forward to play the role of a principle of international justice and needs as much justification as any other proposed standard. One can be a skeptic about international justice only at the price of being a skeptic about domestic justice, since one has no basis, without principles for the international case, of determining what falls within the domain of any domestic principles. Most theorists who claim to be skeptics about international justice, including Walzer, are in fact close to adopting without argument the dubious principle that possession is ten-tenths of justice at the international level.

If, then, we are to know the application of principles of domestic justice, we must know principles of international justice to assign wealth, income, and resources among nations. I shall not attempt to say anything here about what the appropriate principles are. Whatever their content is specifically, they provide the grounds for both constraints and mandates. The constraint of avoiding the violation of justice is fundamental. The pursuit of national interest may not do injustice.

A mandate of justice is a required transfer of funds or resources, a transfer that has to be made in order to satisfy justice. This transfer might well be called in the media or by politicians "humanitarian assistance," but we are now in a position to draw one distinction between the "humanitarianism" that seems compulsory and the "humanitarianism" that seems discretionary. One kind of compulsory transfer of funds or resources is a transfer required by justice; because it is required by justice it is mandatory. It is the subject of a mandate and cannot—conceptually cannot—correctly be treated as a gift or as in any respect discretionary. It may be popularly called "humanitarian assistance" because it involves, say, food rather than weapons and ammunition. I briefly consider later, in connection with "contra" financing, how important it is what is given. For now it is important to see that this form of "humanitarian assistance" would not be beyond the call of duty—it would be precisely the fulfillment of a duty of justice. Those who would be humanitarians must first have done their duties.

It is well known that the United States falls far down the list ranking nations according to the percentage of their GNP budgeted for "development assistance" and that we provide only a fraction of one percent of our GNP. Further, much of this assistance has little or nothing to do with development: huge proportions go as general budgetary support for the governments of Israel and Egypt, and among the next largest recipients are Pakistan and Turkey, whose authoritarian governments are considered valuable to the defense of the "free world." For reasons given elsewhere, I would certainly doubt whether we are doing enough to be doing our duty.[4]

National Ideals and National Interest

Besides constraints and mandates, which apply generally, we have our own ideals, standards that we choose to try to live up to even though we may not, strictly speaking, have to. Most nations define themselves in part in terms of their ideals, and this is nowhere true to a greater extent than in the USA. Ask an American what is distinctive about America, and he or she will almost certainly start talking about ideals, like freedom. Other nations may fight wars for territory, markets, raw materials, or restoration of a balance of power, but the American self-perception is that we are always fighting for "freedom."

To the extent that we are simply deceiving ourselves into thinking that we are the one exceptional nation that does not have ordinary motives and concerns, this is bad—it builds foreign policy on self-congratulatory fantasy and convinces those who observe what we do, as well as what we say, that we are hypocritical and moralistic. However, irrespective of whether we do so to a greater extent than ordinary mortals, we have genuine and noble ideals. We do not believe only that we should observe, for example, the constraint against slaughtering the innocent— we have a positive vision of a world of peace that draws on deep beliefs about brotherhood rooted in our religious heritage. And we do not believe only that we should fulfill the minimum mandates of justice—Americans genuinely want to see a world that is more than merely just. And we do believe in an ideal of freedom even while we are a bit chaotic about deciding what it means.

These are called ideals because they do, at least in some cases, pull us beyond what not only the national interest but even moral constraints and moral mandates require of us. Consider, for example, the Reagan administration's indefensible policy of refusing even temporary haven ("extended voluntary departure") to Salvadorans fleeing the death squads or the war zones of that unfortunate ally of ours. A strong case could be made, I think, that because of U.S. complicity in the failure of the Duarte government to give sufficiently high priority to the elimination of death squads, we owe any intended victims who happen to escape their clutches legally secure temporary haven, at the least, as compensation.[5] An independently strong argument to the same conclusion can be built from the failure of the United States to restrain persistent outrages against Salvadoran refugees by its Honduran proteges, such as the armed assault by the Honduran COBRAS, "an elite counterinsurgency force," on the women, children, and old men in the Colomoncagua refugee camp on August 29, 1985.[6]

Suppose, however, that these arguments would, for some reason, not hold and that, therefore, we are not actually morally bound by complicity in their fate to grant temporary haven to Salvadorans who make their way here to throw themselves on our mercy. This is where ideals come into it. What, indeed, about mercy? Only justice is required, strictly speaking, but we could choose to be merciful. Many Americans want to live in a merciful society that admits some refugees whom it is not morally bound to admit. Consider too the moral costs of the executive branch's attempt to destroy the religious sanctuary movement on behalf of the Salvadoran refugees: U.S. government agents infiltrating religious groups and secretly taping private conversations. Such spying on religious groups sounds more like the work of the Polish secret police. The U.S. Justice Department should not sneak around the churches like the Polish authorities, even if the surveillance is constitutional (which I doubt). I have higher ideals than that for America and so, I imagine, do most Americans.[7]

Although ideals sometimes lift us beyond what national interest (or the morality of constraints and mandates) requires, they need not always draw us in different directions. We may find what could be termed contingent convergence, that is, sometimes it simply turns out conveniently to be the case that the pursuit of an ideal is in our interest. To use another example from immigration policy, our treatment of undocumented aliens, which has often approached the criminalization of the intense desire to work on the part of poor foreigners, has been both a scandal because of the subhuman working conditions to which many in this underground labor force are subjected and a threat to social order. Congress finally in 1986 stopped evading the tough decisions needed for the reform of immigration law and at long last began to formulate some coherent, if by no means flawless, policy. We do ourselves a favor and fulfill one of our ideals by adopting humane arrangements for immigration. Even when our national ideals and our national interest are shaped independently, they may in fact be mutually supportive or even converge. One powerful mechanism for the creation of this contingent convergence effect is the usefulness of a good reputation: it is in one's interest to be believed to keep one's word, including one's words about ideals, and the simplest way to strengthen that belief is to make it true.

INTIMATE RELATIONS

We have noted three aspects of morality—three kinds of moral principles—and looked at the relations of each with national interest, although extremely briefly in the case of constraints, fulfillment of which does not qualify as humanitarianism. The kind of relation we have noticed in every case might be described as external. Constraints stand outside the national interest and impose limits upon it; mandates come from outside and attach additional requirements; ideals stand outside national interest and pull beyond it, even if in some circumstances there is a contingent convergence. More fundamental, and certainly more interesting, are what might be called the intimate relations that each of the three aspects of morality may have with the national interest. This type of relation, without this label, was noted by William T. R. Fox, longtime director of the War and Peace Institute at Columbia, in a 1949 debate in which he refuted Hans Morgenthau's "realism" in its crib:

> According to Professor Morgenthau . . . national interest turns out to be another name for national security, and this in turn is revealed to mean the maintenance of the state's territorial integrity *and* its basic institutions. Now which institutions are basic? Can this question be answered except in the language of moral principle? . . . The camel's nose of moral principle is already under the tent when one admits that it is territorial integrity *plus* basic institutions which must "in the national interest" be protected. (emphasis in original)[8]

While Morgenthau was certainly wrong to suggest that national interest turns out to be another name for national security—national security is central to national interest but does not exhaust it—Fox is more importantly correct to see that the national interest cannot be defined or specified without reference to "moral principle," which, I submit, includes constraints, mandates, and ideals. It is not simply that, for some reason or other, one's conception of national interest ought to, but might not, reflect one's position toward principles. It is the much deeper point that one cannot formulate one's understanding of the national interest without deciding which of the nation's institutions matter most—in Fox's term, are basic—and one cannot decide what genuinely matters, or is most basic, except by reference to principles of morality (constraints, mandates, and ideals).

This "reference to principles" in the formulation of national interest occurs in various ways. At one extreme, if a nation's ideals play a major part in its self-definition and self-perception, as they do for many Americans, then the protection and promotion of the national interest will include the protection and promotion of the ideals in question. Part of the reason that the United States has a reputation for what gets called "moralism" in foreign policy is that many Americans actually do believe in, for example, the ideal of democracy and want to see democracy promoted abroad. My point here is not that this is either good or bad, but that promoting democracy may not constitute going beyond the national interest—it is part of the national interest of a nation fundamentally interested in the promotion of democracy.

Survival is not the only national interest, nor is "national security" if it is construed narrowly to mean not much more than survival. *The national interest is survival as a certain kind of nation in a certain kind of world.* The "kind of nation" and "kind of world" are not the icing added to the cake—they are the recipe for the cake. The national purpose is to survive as what you are, or as some principled variant of what you are. That is, it is not that a nation should want never to change, but that if it cares about its own survival—not just the survival of something or other—it wants change to occur in such a way that the new self is true to the old self; in such a way that the change is guided at each point by principles that are at least acceptable to the old self that is changing. The fawn may turn into a stag, but not into a butterfly. Change must contain enough continuity to constitute identity, or what began to change has not in fact survived but been replaced by something else.

At the other extreme, a nation can be utterly non-idealistic in that rather than being interested in the promotion of certain forms of government (like democracy), it concerns itself primarily with power advantages and economic advantages. It must nevertheless decide what are "its basic institutions"—what it is important to it to preserve. In doing so it will be expressing its moral principles: which constraints, if any, it will abide by; what mandates, if any, it will fulfill; which ideals, if any, it will honor.

One possible choice—unfortunately, one frequent choice—is the unbridled pursuit of power and wealth. The conception of national interest adopted may honor no constraints, no mandates, and no ideals. This is the limiting case in which there are no intimate relations between national interest and moral principle. No moral principles of any kind are incorporated into the understanding of national interest, and there are, therefore, only external relations between that national interest and moral principle. Such a conception of the national interest still has, if you like, a reference to principle: it simply is a negative reference—it denies principle. Some conceptions of national interest are structured largely or partly around principles of at least one of the three kinds; other conceptions are unprincipled. Some are between the extremes. None can be located fully without reference, positive or negative, to principle. On the necessity of taking a position, explicitly or implicitly, on questions of principle even in the mere *description* of the national interest, Fox was right and Morgenthau was wrong. One cannot even say what the national interest *is* without saying what must survive if that nation is to survive.[9]

FOUR TESTS FOR HUMANITARIAN ASSISTANCE

I would like now to look extremely briefly at a problem about the political and the humanitarian in Central America and then less briefly but still inadequately at a similar problem about the Horn of Africa. We are now in a position to assemble four points about what humanitarian assistance is, and is not, and what the relation is between granting humanitarian assistance and pursuing a national interest. Point one concerns the relation between humanitarianism and national interest. Is it a test for truly humanitarian assistance that it is contrary to national interest and can be granted only by sacrificing national interest? The answer is no. Then what is the relation between humanitarianism and national interest? This question has no answer in the abstract.

The answer in the case of a particular nation depends upon that nation's conception of its interest: how principled that nation's conception of its interest is and, especially, to what extent its self-conception is structured around humanitarian ideals. If part of what makes that nation the specific nation it is, is an active commitment to ideals of humanitarianism, humanitarian acts are not only not contrary to its specific interest but are partial expressions of that interest. If a nation is devoted only to the enhancement of its own military, political, and economic power, humanitarian assistance will at best seem irrelevant or pointless and may indeed conflict with single-minded acquisition and accumulation. Whether being humanitarian conflicts with our interest depends, in the end, on who we are. We might sum this up by saying: humanitarianism comes easier if one believes it is important.

Points two, three, and four can be made quickly by referring, in turn, to three terms in the definition of humanitarianism provided in the background essay for this volume by Bruce Nichols, which says: "Humanitarianism may be broadly defined as the provision of assistance to victims of political or natural disasters."[10] A word, in order, about the disaster, the assistance, and the victims. Points two and three together are: the disaster must not be one's own, and the assistance must be.

Point two: the disaster must not be of one's own making. This is where constraints are relevant. If there is indeed a disaster, but one is the cause of it, or has deep complicity in it because one has inflicted harm in violation of a fundamental moral constraint, then any assistance one provides is more accurately thought of as compensation for the harm done rather than humanitarian assistance. If the United States had sent assistance to the families of the nearly one hundred civilian victims of its April 14, 1986, night raid on Tripoli, for example, this would have been compensation for having bombed people in their beds, not humanitarianism.[11] It would be good to provide such compensation, and one might think of it as compulsory humanitarianism—compulsory because owed as compensation. Insofar as humanitarianism suggests generosity and giving that is discretionary, however, assistance that is owed fails the test of being discretionary.

Point three: the assistance must be one's to give. The point is once again that what is required is not freely given. This time the relevant consideration is mandates, not constraints. If some transfer of wealth or resources ought in justice already to have been made, it is of course right to make it. The making of the transfer is, however, not humanitarianism, insofar as humanitarianism suggests what is freely given. If I owe a colleague $250 for work done, my turning $250 over to her is no gift.

Point four is simply that humanitarian assistance must go to victims, to people who have suffered disasters. It seems almost silly to include this obvious point, and it would be gratuitous if we did not live amidst Orwellian doublespeak resulting from an obsession by a small but powerful clique with maintaining an invasion that the American people reject. By far the most notorious misuse of the term "humanitarian assistance" in recent American politics has been the so-called "humanitarian assistance" to the men in Honduras and Costa Rica who have been supposed to be invading Nicaragua, the "contras." One of the most shameful episodes of mendacity in recent American politics has been the sleazy attempt to peddle logistical support for an invasion force as "humanitarian assistance." In Washington the fighting in Nicaragua is classified as "low intensity warfare." It is low intensity only if one is not there, and it ought to be called "low visibility warfare," because the secret forms of support were originally designed to keep the war off the evening news. The lesson learned in Vietnam by some was: don't have dead U.S. boys on the evening news, and the solution is to let the dead boys be Central Americans, whose deaths are not newsworthy here. So elements in the U.S. executive hired a mercenary army, most of whom are young peasant boys who do not know what they are being paid to risk their lives for.

But the funds for the contras were to be spent for food, clothing, medicine, and transportation. These are nonlethal items—does that not make it "humanitarian assistance"? The answer is no. The food, clothing, and so forth are not humanitarian assistance because they are not going to the victims of a disaster. They are logistical support for an army in the field. The question is not *what* one gives—it is *to whom* one gives it. If the disaster that some people somewhere were suffering was that their village was being invaded by man-eating tigers, humanitarian assistance might consist of high-powered rifles or even machine guns. However, if an army in the field cannot afford both guns and food, giving it food is providing military assistance. If the soldiers had been defeated and were in a POW camp, underfed, then food would be humanitarian assistance. The question is: is the food preventing a victim of poverty from starving, or is it enabling an invasion force to move forward?

Nothing that I have said here depends upon whether one approves or disapproves of supporting the contras. All that I have said is that if one believes that the United States should hire enough Central American peasants to defeat the Nicaraguan army and overthrow the Nicaraguan government, one should say so forthrightly, and the matter could be settled according to democratic procedures. This country, however, has a worthy humanitarian tradition, and the cloak of humanitarianism may not be stolen to hide other kinds of activities, or the tradition will be sullied and shamed. If we are to have an honest debate about humanitarianism, we have to call things by their right names. Contrary to Churchill's comment, truth rarely needs a bodyguard of lies, though governments often do.[12]

FAMINE UNDER THE DERGUE

Because the national interest is survival as a certain kind of nation in a certain kind of world, many judgments that are ordinarily considered to be political cannot be made correctly without also deciding about matters ordinarily thought to be humanitarian, or so I have argued above. Now I want to illustrate how judgments that would normally be taken to be humanitarian cannot responsibly be made without also deciding about political questions. I venture into even the periphery of such a fearsomely tangled question as what ought to have been done in response to the famine in Ethiopia in 1984–1986 because two of the other chapters in this volume—each on its own and in its own very different way and, especially, the pair in all their conflicts with and contradictions of each other—constitute a splendid if anguishing study of politics and humanitarianism (and, probably, their tragic entanglement). Each of these two chapters conveys to this reader deep conviction and broad knowledge. Where they differ—and they differ on absolutely crucial points—my concern is much less with indicating who I think is correct, although I am sometimes forced to judge, than with exploring this second way that the humanitarian and the political are intertwined.

Diagnosis

Lawrence A. Pezzullo and Jason W. Clay provide flatly contradictory accounts of why millions were at risk of starving and at least hundred of thousands did starve earlier this decade in northern Africa. Pezzullo portrays the famine as a natural catastrophe, exacerbated by political decisions. Clay portrays it as a man-made, political catastrophe, exacerbated by natural events.

Here is Pezzullo's account:

> While world awareness of conditions in Ethiopia began in late 1984, the reality of the famine extends back to 1982. In that year, crops failed in the northern provinces of Eritrea and Tigray for lack of adequate rains, and the food situation became ever more acute. The drought extended into 1983, ravaging harvests and spreading hunger through more and more regions of the country.[13]

And here is Clay's:

> [G]overnment taxes and contributions from 1978 to the present (even from famine victims in the period 1984 to 1986) stripped peasant producers of the cushion (both grain and animals) that they needed to survive anticipated years of bad harvests. . . . Production was further reduced, both in famine areas and in surplus-producing areas, because farmers were required to perform unpaid days of labor on local militia and government officials' lands and on plots from which produce went to the government. . . . Government policies, both agricultural and military, played a major role in creating the famine. Even the "natural causes" of the famine advanced by the government had greater impact as a result of government policies. . . . drought did not *cause* the conditions that resulted in the famine, rather it exacerbated them—it was the final straw.[14]

In addition to noting the overzealous extraction of wealth from peasants who were as a result left no longer capable of providing for their own subsistence as they previously had, Clay summarizes evidence showing that throughout the famine the government mercilessly pursued a policy of forcible resettlement of northerners to the southwest, sometimes using trucks donated to move food for moving people instead and using donated food as "bait" to entice the hungry into centers at which the army could "capture"—the term used by the victims interviewed after escaping into Sudan—and truck them away. Clay:

> In some camps the Ethiopian government did not allow children to receive food from Western agencies until their parents agreed to be resettled. MSF [Médecins sans Frontières—"Doctors without Borders"] eventually left Ethiopia after an estimated 6,000 children died in a camp where they had adequate materials for assistance but were not allowed to distribute them because, according to government officials, a sufficient number of adults had not agreed to be resettled.[15]

Some of Clay's most important general conclusions about the Dergue's coerced movements of hundreds of thousands of poor peasants are:

> —Resettlement was, by and large, not voluntary.
> —Families were separated, in many cases deliberately.
> —Death rates were high in resettlement holding camps and sites, far higher, it appears, than in the feeding centers and famine-affected areas of the north.
> —Resettlement became an important, perhaps the single most important, cause of mortality in Ethiopia in 1985.[16]

Large numbers of children were, according to Clay, taken from their parents to be sent to "orphanages," where they were reeducated in the language and religion approved by the regime rather than the language and religion of their parents. A number of Western humanitarian organizations supply the food for these "orphanages."[17]

Clay has actually raised two analytically separable issues: the role of the regime in causing famine not directly related to resettlement and the extent of the starvation caused by resettlement itself. On the first issue, on the basis of what I know in general about famine, much of it learned from Amartya Sen's lucid *Poverty and Famines*, and what I know in particular about the Ethiopian Dergue, the military dictatorship that has seemed dedicated to inventing some brutality toward peasants overlooked by both Stalin and Haile Selassie, I am strongly inclined to accept Clay's heavily documented conclusion that this latest Ethiopian famine, like its predecessor in 1972–1974 under the emperor, was primarily inflicted by government.[18]

What Stalin did to the Russian peasantry, including man-made famine, was absolutely unforgivable and, one might have thought, unforgettable. It is stranger than fiction that Lt. Col. Mengistu Haile Miriam should a half century later have blundered into demonstrating yet again how much havoc can be wreaked upon national food supplies and how much misery and death can be inflicted upon individual peasants by the unrelenting pursuit of a misguided forcible collectivization of agriculture. Nevertheless, on his second thesis about resettlement-caused famine Clay seems to me again to have assembled disturbing evidence, although I am in no position to judge it independently.

Further, Pezzullo's brief and oblique references to the facts about resettlement do little to quiet one's concern:

> The situation in Eritrea and Tigray and the Ethiopian government's resettlement program, however, provoked conflicts within the community of private agencies involved in one way or another with the relief effort. In each case, some groups, while asserting a humanitarian status, have been advocates for political positions critical of the Ethiopian regime's policies. The general charge has been that the government has used the famine and the relief effort to pursue its war aims against the resistance groups or to forcibly relocate large numbers of people.[19]

I take Pezzullo to be admitting tacitly that the charge that the Dergue used the famine to conduct resettlement (and prosecute its military objectives) is true, but accusing those who focus attention upon such facts of interjecting political advocacy of a kind incompatible with humanitarian activity.[20] It cannot be the case, however, that those "critical of the Ethiopian regime's policies" are being *improperly* political and those supportive of the regime are *not* so simply because they are, respectively, critical and supportive. That could be the case only if in general being supportive of government policies, whatever and wherever they are, is humanitarian and being critical is, in a similarly universal fashion, improperly political.

One of Clay's charges against the Ethiopian dictatorship is that it used relief supplies as "bait" in order to "capture" peasants for a process of forcible relocation in which children were often separated from their parents and—not surprisingly if that is true—often died. Whether such claims are true cannot be irrelevant to the question of whether the humanitarian, or even the

decent, thing to do in the circumstances was to continue to
furnish the "bait." If Clay is correct, relief supplies delivered
during 1985 may have contributed to a number of deaths larger
than the number of lives they saved, because the supplies un-
derwrote a resettlement process which killed people who would
not otherwise have been likely to have died.

I want to re-emphasize that I do not know enough to make
an independent judgment whether this is true. But although this
is indeed a partly political question because it requires assessment of government policies, it is surely not an improperly political question to be raised by humanitarian groups supplying
the food. Humanitarians at least as much as anyone else must be
vigilant to see that their efforts produce the results they intend
and, at the very least, do not do more harm than they do good or,
perhaps, do not do more than a minimum amount of harm,
however much good they do. We shall return to examine a little
more fully the relation of the humanitarian and the political in
this case. First, we need for background to see part of the shape
of the arguments over the question of what should have been
done in Ethiopia.

Remedy

Suppose a humanitarian agency supplying food to an "orphanage" suspects that many of the children were not orphans at
all but have been forcibly separated from their parents for reeducation because they belong to a religious and/or ethnic group
to which the regime is hostile. Should the agency immediately
stop supplying food to the "orphanage" lest it be complicitous in
the regime's vicious policy? Surely not—letting the children
starve after they have already been taken from their parents
would simply add killing to all the other crimes already committed against the children. What, then? Clay's strongest recommendation is that the agency should both insist on discovering as
much information as possible about what is going on and communicate that information honestly to donors and to anyone else
in a position to pressure the regime. What does "insist" mean
under as brutal and tight a dictatorship as the Ethiopian Dergue?
Threaten to withhold food? Perhaps. Withhold it? No.

Suppose, then, one is supplying not an orphanage containing children already torn away from their parents but a feeding center in a famine area, and one suspects that parents are being coerced into "volunteering" for resettlement by the government's withholding food from their children until they do. Again, as Clay maintains, one ought at least to insist on finding out as much as possible about what is being done by the government with one's food and communicate that information clearly to people who actually care about the children, including people who were willing to donate money for the food. Suppose one's fears are confirmed—then what? Consider the case, quoted above, of Doctors without Borders witnessing 6,000 children starve in the presence of food because their parents had not complied with the government's demand that they agree to be trucked across the country. Was Doctors without Borders right, then, to leave the country? These are horrible dilemmas, of the "Sophie's-choice" genre which no one ought ever to face and few would face if they were not imposed by cruel dictatorships.

Some would counsel: "do no harm." If in order to save lives, one must contribute to killing, one ought not to do it, they would say, even if the number of lives saved substantially exceeds the number of lives taken. Much discussed among philosophers has been the general consensus that it would be wrong to kill one healthy person in order to use her organs for transplants to save the lives of several other people (her heart to one, one kidney to a second, the other kidney to a third, and so forth). Saving some people in a feeding center in a manner that makes it likely that other people will die in resettlement centers, on this view, is fundamentally, although through a more complicated process than the simplistic execution-for-organs case, helping to save some lives by helping to kill some other people.

This judgment may appear to be implied by the existence of constraints: "there are some things one does not do," I said earlier. Contributing to arbitrary deaths might appear to be one of these things, even if one were doing it in the course of saving (more) other lives. However, there are mandates too: "there are some things one must do," I also said. Saving now-helpless children—however they became helpless—from starvation might appear to be one of those things. The counsel of "do no harm" assumes that constraints always override mandates, if the two are equally fundamental. That I did not say, nor do I think any such priority can be established at that level of abstraction. What I mean by calling this a case of the "Sophie's-choice" genre is that this appears to be one of those awful circumstances in which one must either do what must not be done or fail to do what must be done. One will get one's hands dirty *either* way: one is responsible for the deaths one could have prevented if one had not withdrawn—if one had not violated the mandate to assist the desperately helpless—or one is responsible for the deaths to which one contributes if one stays—if one violates the constraint against cooperating with arbitrary killing.

Pezzullo, however, is firm on behalf of the moral judgment that to be humanitarian meant to stay:

> Advocacy groups have every right to hold and advance political positions and often play an important role in the debates that surround emergency responses, but that role is essentially different from that of humanitarian aid agencies. The latter must focus on those in need impartially, whatever the cause of their need, commensurate with the resources and access that they can command. The goal is to alleviate suffering to the maximum extent possible among victims of emergencies. If we at CRS [Catholic Relief Services] were to pull out of Ethiopia to make a political point, the over two million people we are feeding would bear the very human costs of such a gesture. Thus, while we have privately and publicly sought access to the [militarily] disputed areas and urged that no program of resettlement be undertaken that is not entirely voluntary and adequately prepared, we have seen our humanitarian role as one of extending our access to those in need wherever they are, rather than becoming political partisans.[21]

This important passage calls for a number of comments. First, it once again tacitly concedes that poorly prepared, forcible resettlement is being carried out, although it of course does not necessarily grant that the magnitude of this political disaster is as described by Clay.

Second, it engages in a little persuasive labeling: those who "advance political positions" by, for example, criticizing forcible resettlement are "advocacy groups" and "political partisans," *not* humanitarian agencies. "To make a political point" is scornfully contrasted with feeding two million people. As I have already indicated, I would not deny that those who criticize a government policy are in one sense raising a political issue. The question, however, is whether raising political questions directly relevant to the success or failure of humanitarian intentions either is being improperly political or is incompatible with acting in a humanitarian fashion. The suggested division of labor under which humanitarian agencies simply hand out food and do not ask questions strikes me as a very bad idea, incompatible with responsible humanitarianism, which must be concerned with consequences as well as good intentions. It seems to me clearly to be a mistake to dismiss those like Clay who raise these questions as "advocates" and "partisans" and to attempt, in effect, to read them out of the community of humanitarians. If some humanitarian agencies have covered up information about ways in which the government made their efforts counterproductive, as Clay charges, that is important to know for humanitarian, not partisan, purposes.

Causes

Most important, however, is what Pezzullo says about causes and does not say about effects. These take us back to the ineradicable political aspects of the humanitarian. About causes he says that one "must focus on those in need impartially, whatever the cause of their need. . . ." I take the underlying thought to be that victims of man-made famines may be just as desperately in need as victims of natural famines. The causation of a famine is irrelevant to *whether* the victims have a compelling claim to assistance. With some minor exceptions that does not matter here, this seems right to me.

The causation is, however, highly relevant to *who* ought to provide the assistance. It is almost always easier to make a case that it would be good if something were to be done, namely if the starving were to be fed, than it is to establish that someone or some institution in particular is the one who ought to do it. Why me? Why is it a problem *for Americans,* in the person of either governmental or nongovernmental agencies, that people somewhere on another continent are starving, especially if the famine is primarily caused by their own benighted government (which has generally made rather clear its hostility to many things American)? Pezzullo is quite right that there was a remarkable—perhaps literally "unprecedented"—outpouring of donations by

Americans in response to the showing of the BBC film footage of
the camp at Korem by NBC during the evening news on October
23, 1984 (and by the British in response to the BBC's own showing), and the subsequent uproar in all the mass media.[22] Yet this
may have been one more stampede of the TV-faithful produced
by the powerful medium on which they are hooked. Was this
huge reaction sensible or sentimental? Was it truly generous or a
belated rush to deal with a problem that unjustified neglect had
allowed to mushroom out of hand? Was it in part misguided and
counterproductive, too much too late?

Without fully tackling all these questions we can use the
framework set out earlier to sketch a few initial responses on
some of them. I would assume that any national government
that *allows* widespread malnutrition (or homelessness) is failing
to fulfill one of the basic mandates of government. If governments are to be good for anything, they ought to arrange for
people to be able to satisfy their basic needs. One must eventually argue further about the extent to which this should be done
through market systems or central planning, privately or cooperatively, and so forth, but it is up to national governments in the
world as it is now organized to make some workable arrangements of one kind or another. A government that permits any of
its people to starve is to that extent a failure.

A government that *causes* large numbers of its people to
starve by persisting for years in forcing upon them alien and
cockeyed policies that are clearly wrecking the agricultural system and destroying the ability of families to feed themselves is
violating a constraint that applies not only to governments but to
every agent who can affect people's ability to provide their own
subsistence. Clearly, the Ethiopian government was itself primarily and doubly responsible to deal with the famine.

Equally clearly, I gather, the Dergue failed either to alleviate
the famine or to stop making it worse. Does responsibility fall
next, then, upon Americans and Europeans, who are the ones
who in fact responded? I would think not, although obviously
one needs a general account of grounds of responsibility in order
to answer questions like this convincingly. Those next in line, I
would think, would be the rich and powerful supporters of the
Dergue, whose complicity in maintaining the Dergue in control
of the country by supplying it with military assistance gave them

a special responsibility to compensate for and correct the harm done by the Dergue with their material and political support, namely the Soviet Union and those of its allies directly involved in Ethiopia. The USSR is a rich nation, fully able to pay for massive assistance and probably best able to have pressured the Dergue to abandon its most Stalinist policies. Like the Ethiopian government itself, the Soviet government had special responsibilities to the victims because of prior direct involvement in their situation. Making this judgment about moral responsibility also involves acknowledging political connections.

The Soviet response too fell far, far short of fulfilling its responsibilities. Here there is a fork in the philosophical road, and the next judgment that one makes depends upon whether one continues to look at mandates or turns to ideals. We can only glance at each. As I indicated earlier when introducing the loose general category of "mandate," different theories of justice, of economic rights, of human equality, and of other related matters issue in different mandates—there are few mandates common to the most plausible accounts of each of these matters. Yet, the mandate that the well-off members of the best-off nations ought to assist the desperately helpless members of the worst-off nations might come close to being an item of consensus, and it is very close to Pezzullo's principle that humanitarians "must focus on those in need impartially, whatever the cause of their need, commensurate with the resources and access that they can command." Those with special responsibilities because of their own past involvement ought to act first, but if they do not, some such general requirement can be thought from several points of view to come into force. If a mandate like this applies, the assistance given is not voluntary or discretionary—it is morally required. One can, of course, be thoroughly happy to give what one believes one has no moral choice but to give. One might choose either a governmental or a nongovernmental agency to fulfill such a mandate.

On the other hand, one might—either instead of or in addition to some mandate like this—have an ideal specifically for one's nation that, especially if it is as rich and powerful as the United States still is, it should provide humanitarian relief to victims like the children of Ethiopia even if no mandate, special or general, applies. One might simply choose not to stand idly by while fellow human beings starved, whether one was bound to help them or not. One might not choose to see America survive as a heartless nation in a heartless world, but as a generous and merciful nation in a world in which no one is just left to die because those for whom he or she was a special responsibility failed to perform. If one had such an ideal for the nation, one would want at least some of the relief work carried out officially by the national government. It would be important that some of the bags of food could legitimately be stamped "Gift of the American People." All this assumes, naturally, that the assistance and relief efforts would have the good effects intended. Yet humanitarian intentions have no more guarantee than any others of achieving the consequences at which they aim. Political context can be crucial.

Effects

Pezzullo appears simply to assume that the effects of the distribution of the tons of food are virtually all good. If, however, the same dictatorship that was the main cause of the original famine was manipulating the humanitarian assistance in such a manner as to cause even more deaths, it matters. Whatever the correct final judgment turns out to be, it is not obvious whether, or when, agencies were right to stay and continue distributing food. The political question must be answered in order to answer the humanitarian question. Of Clay's two theses, the thesis that the famine was primarily caused by the government is far less relevant to this than the thesis that by the time massive amounts of aid began to enter Ethiopia, the resettlement for which the aid was the "bait" was killing more people than the original famine. The most disturbing questions are: was the dictatorship able to twist well-intentioned assistance into terrible actual consequences, given their oppressive power and wildly misguided ideas? And were these actual consequences so bad that it would have been better for the agencies to have stopped distributing food and left the country? This is a hard case.

First, numbers. Suppose that Clay is correct that significant numbers of impoverished Ethiopian peasants would never have approached feeding stations—many of the feeding stations themselves might never have existed—if the humanitarian agencies had not been there to distribute food. Thus some of the peasants "captured" for resettlement and later allowed to starve in the inadequately prepared resettlement centers would not have died in those resettlement centers without the activities of the humanitarian agencies. The vital issue, of course, is what would have happened otherwise. This is a hypothetical question, unfortunately, but then it is often possible to decide whether what one has done was right only by comparing it to the alternatives, the other actions one might (hypothetically) have taken in the same circumstances.

Let us assume that it was the case for many peasants that they were "captured" for resettlement only because the humanitarian agencies were operating the feeding stations. Is it also true that these peasants starved only because they were in resettlement centers? This we do not know—some of the same, or other, peasants or their children might have starved earlier out in the countryside if there had been no feeding center operated by the humanitarian agencies.

Clay's finding that in 1985 more people were dying because of resettlement than were dying from the original famine is, then, not decisive by itself, even if accepted. The same feeding centers that may have been partly responsible for the later deaths in resettlement centers were presumably also responsible for preventing deaths that otherwise would have occurred from the original famine. It would not be decisive to establish that more people in fact died during resettlement than in fact died from the famine. What one would very much like to know as well is: how does the number of people who died in resettlement only because food was available as "bait" compare to the number of people who would have died from the original famine if the humanitarian agencies had pulled out (or had never come)?

How many would otherwise have died is some function of the number who were at risk. Pezzullo, presumably accepting Ethiopian government figures, reports that "as many as eight million people were at risk of starvation."[23] Clay argues that government estimates of the numbers of people at risk from famine were greatly exaggerated. One of the Dergue's methods for doing this was to claim that a mythical census had earlier been conducted and that the population had been discovered to be about 10 million greater than thought by anyone else, including, for example, the World Bank (42 to 45 million instead of 32 to 35 million).[24] Clay thus concludes that the number who died during resettlement only because food was available as bait is larger than many humanitarian agencies want to admit and the number who would have died from the original famine if the agencies had never come or had left when they saw their food being used as bait is smaller than they like to admit. He does not claim, as I understand him, to know the relative sizes of these numbers, although he clearly does not consider it out of the question that the aid contributed to the loss of more lives than it saved.

All that he firmly suggests that the humanitarian agencies should have done differently was to have been more insistent on fuller access to information (and to have been more open with information gained):

> I am not suggesting that assistance should have been withheld from famine victims until assessments of the problems were undertaken. Rather, I am suggesting that agencies should have negotiated these conditions with the government so that as they began to provide relief assistance, they could also have begun the necessary work to understand the nature and the scope of the problem they hoped to alleviate. Even if such conditions could not have been negotiated with the Ethiopian government, each agency, as its understanding of the causes of the famine increased, could have modified its programs accordingly.[25]

These seem to me to be remarkably modest conclusions for Clay to have drawn from his alarming premises, some of which are quite well supported by his evidence. In addition, Clay seems quite judicious in taking a forward-looking attitude that seeks, not guilt for the past, but guidance for the future—and looks for it in a better understanding of the dynamics of the situation faced by humanitarian agencies under the Dergue. The pursuit of information that can guide in the future will be especially apt if he should prove correct that resettlement (and "villagization," which I have not discussed) will cause new famines among those resettled as well as among the actual inhabitants of the "uninhabited" areas in which the northerners are deposited. We may soon have to decide yet again what is the humanitarian response to a famine under the Dergue.

Good intentions and correct principles are no substitute for accurate information about the context in which one is acting. Where the crucial features of the context for humanitarian action are political, the relevant facts and judgments may be heavily political as well. Still, we must try to call things by their right names. No one ever said that would be easy.[26]

Notes

This paper was written in part while I was supported by a grant from the Division on International Affairs of the Ford Foundation to the Center for Philosophy and Public Policy of the University of Maryland at College Park, and I remain grateful for that support. The paper has benefited from the comments of a lively audience at Notre Dame, of Rogers M. Smith, and of the co-editors. Naturally I alone am responsible for the views finally expressed.

1. I explore some of the additional complications specific to international cases in Henry Shue, "Mediating Duties," *Ethics* 98, no. 4 (July 1988).

2. Michael Walzer, *Spheres of Justice: A Defense of Pluralism and Equality* (New York: Basic Books, 1983).

3. I have made the argument that follows in the text in summary form more fully in Henry Shue, "The Burdens of Justice," *Journal of Philosophy* 80, no. 10 (October 1983): 600–608.

4. See Henry Shue, *Basic Rights: Subsistence, Affluence, and U.S. Foreign Policy* (Princeton, N.J.: Princeton University Press, 1980).

5. Doris Meissner appears willing to settle for what she calls "*de facto* safe haven," which would mean that these refugees might be safe provided they live shadowy enough lives and no one in the government decides really to go after them—they would continue to have no legal guarantee against being thrown out. See Doris Meissner, "Central American Refugees: Political Asylum, Sanctuary, and Humanitarian Policy," this volume. Meissner also declares, without providing any basis, that "probably less than 25 percent" of the Salvadorans claiming to be refugees actually are (p. 140).

6. See Gil Loescher, "Humanitarianism and Politics in Central America," this volume, pp. 167-68.

7. Doris Meissner accuses proponents of public sanctuary of being guilty of "the same crime they charged the government with committing": pursuing a political objective in the name of the Refugee Act (this volume, p. 134). The government's "crime," to use Meissner's word, in

Central American policy is not politicization, however, but militarization. In using resources to infiltrate churches with undercover agents to
catch people attempting to protect Salvadorans against arbitrarily being
dumped back into El Salvador, instead of using the resources to process
those claiming asylum as required by U.S. law, the U.S. government
was internalizing its militarization. The brave and dedicated practition-
ers of "sanctuary" hardly deserve to be tarred with the same brush as
the federal church spies. The latter half of this chapter is devoted to the
issue of what counts as improper politics and what counts as intelligent
humanitarianism.

As this book goes into press, evidence is emerging that the use of
police-state tactics by the Reagan administration against innocent citizens who disagree with its Latin American policy was much more
widespread than previously known. See Philip Shenon, "F.B.I. Papers
Show Wide Surveillance of Reagan Critics," *New York Times*, January
28, 1988, pp. A1 and A18.

8. William T. R. Fox, "The Reconciliation of the Desirable and the
Possible," *American Scholar* 18, no. 2 (Spring 1949): 212-16; quotations
from 213 and 214.

9. Besides Fox's brief classic, two other essays (quite different from
each other) stimulated me to think about the importance of national
identity: Alan Geyer, "The Redemption of Prudence: An Ethical Analysis of National Self-interest" (1973), mimeo, especially pp. 9-13; and
Jerome Segal, "What Is Development?" (October 1986), Working Paper
DN-1 (College Park, Md.: Center for Philosophy and Public Policy,
1986), especially pp. 23-29.

10. Bruce Nichols, "The 'Moral Nation': Humanitarianism and
U.S. Foreign Policy in the 1980s," Carnegie Council on Ethics and
International Affairs (March 1986), photocopy, p. 1.

11. For the number of casualties—little mentioned in the United
States—see the *Economist* (London), April 19–25, 1986; also see the
Times (London), April 16, 1986, p. 1.

12. In defense of an American disinformation campaign intended
to cause Colonel Qaddafi to panic, Secretary of State Schultz resurrect-
ed Churchill's declaration: "In time of war, the truth is so precious, it
must be attended by a bodyguard of lies." See Bernard Gwertzman,
"Schultz Justifies Scaring Qaddafi by Use of Press," *New York Times*,
October 3, 1986, pp. A1 and A6; quotation from p. A6.

13. Lawrence A. Pezzullo, "Catholic Relief Services in Ethiopia: A
Case Study," this volume, p. 218.

14. Jason W. Clay, "Ethiopian Famine and the Relief Agencies,"
this volume, pp. 247-48.

15. Ibid., p. 264.

16. Ibid., p. 262.

17. Ibid., p. 251.

18. For an account of the dynamics of famine that explains which groups within a nation starve, see Amartya Sen, *Poverty and Famines: An Essay on Entitlement and Deprivation* (Oxford and New York: Oxford University Press, 1981), passim; specifically on the earlier famine under Emperor Haile Selassie, see ch. 7. A valuably relevant study of Ethiopia under both the emperor and the early Dergue, written prior to the latest famine, is John M. Cohen, "Foreign Involvement in Land Tenure Reform: The Case of Ethiopia," in *International Dimensions of Land Reform,* ed. John D. Montgomery (Boulder, Colo.: Westview Press, 1984), pp. 169-219.

19. Pezzullo, p. 225.

20. Doris Meissner similarly, and not very plausibly, accuses the movement for public sanctuary—in making use of appearances by refugees telling their stories to the media to mobilize opposition to U.S. policy—of "a fundamental departure from humanitarian objectives into politics." See Doris Meissner, this volume, p. 134.

21. Pezzullo, pp. 225-26.

22. Ibid., p. 218.

23. Ibid.

24. Clay, pp. 246-47.

25. Ibid., p. 245.

26. Almost certainly the single greatest accomplishment of this paper is to have provoked the eloquent and rich response by Rogers M. Smith, which is the next paper in this volume. For anyone attempting to sort out our respective views it may help for me to note that Rogers Smith did not have available the second half of my paper, which could be written only after I saw chapters written still later, when he wrote his response. However little I may actually have succeeded in either half of my paper, or in previous writing, in dealing with concrete cases, I could not agree more with Smith's plea for the detailed working out of the "more specific understandings" that must implicitly give meaning to abstractly stated principles.

On the other hand, in spite of my admiration for his fine paper I still disagree profoundly with some of its fundamental assumptions. Most important, his splendidly specific threefold structure of national moral goals is generated, as he of course well understands, by combining two theses I reject: priority for compatriots and priority for liberty. (In denying *priority* for liberties I do not deny that liberties are *among* the most important subjects of rights, but I do deny that no other interests are equally as important to protect as liberties are.) Since our differences are too deep for any brief response here, I can for now only refer interested readers to the work cited in note 4 above: on whether compatriots take priority (over all other people), ch. 6; on whether liberty takes priority (over all other interests), chs. 1 and 5. I have taken up the difficult issue of the role of compensation in the *Ethics* essay cited in the first note above.

MORALITY, HUMANITARIANISM, AND FOREIGN POLICY: A PURPOSIVE VIEW

Rogers M. Smith

What should be the relationship between humanitarianism and American foreign policy, and between humanitarian agencies and the agencies of the United States government? These questions are embedded in the perennial debate over the proper relationship between morality and the national interest. In that debate, many stances can be discerned, but two cast the longest shadows.

The orthodoxy in government, perhaps in academia, surely remains some version of the disenchanted "realism" advanced in the postwar years by George Kennan, Hans Morgenthau, and others. Realism soberly admonishes us not to make too much of morality in international dealings. It often sanctions the harnessing of humanitarian ideals and agencies to other, more hard-hearted governmental objectives. Especially since the mid-1970s, many academic writers have therefore rejected such "realism" as cynical selfishness. They have instead called on us to strive to heed morality, and humanitarian organizations and advocates, in international affairs. Most of these writers have identified "morality" with cosmopolitan perspectives derived from the idealism of Immanuel Kant and sometimes from universalistic religious outlooks, as Henry Shue did, for example, in his noted book *Basic Rights,* and as he continues to do in his contribution to this collection.[1]

While these two positions, the "realist" and the cosmopolitan "neo-Kantian," come down on different sides, in many respects they depict the relationship of morality to national interests similarly. Morality is held to express the grand aspiration to

41

do right by all humanity. Although it may sometimes be taken as
an element of national policies, it is at heart distinct from, and in
tension with, purely national interests. Those interests are not
thought of as chiefly moral, but as "pragmatic" or "political." By
these terms writers usually mean that national interests center on
preserving if not enhancing the wealth and power of a nation's
government and people. Hence both camps agree: morality is
fundamentally something apart from national interests, so that
however often the two may coincide in practice, sooner or later
morality must be subordinated to national claims, or vice-versa.

Neither side, let me stress, maintains this distinction absolutely. "Realists" often contend that avoiding excessive moralism
in foreign policy leads to *more* moral results. Neo-Kantian moralists often stress, as Shue does, that certain moral considerations
are part of the very definition of, at least, American national
interests. Both are points on which I will build, especially the
latter, for I believe that writers like Shue have done a service in
arguing persistently for the relevance of morality to American
foreign policy and international affairs. But the neo-Kantian moralists have not fully captured the genuine wisdom about practical
possibilities contained in realism.

Consequently, in this essay I will argue for an understanding of the relationship of morality to national interests, and of the
proper substance of American national morality, that differs from
each of these dominant camps. Instead of taking our bearings
from the somberly amoral worldview of *realpolitik* or cosmopolitan idealism, I will suggest we adopt a more consequentialist
view of liberal morality, traceable to one dimension of John
Locke's pragmatic, yet morally directed, political philosophy.

In brief, this view goes beyond the neo-Kantians' critique of
realism by arguing that certain moral principles are not merely
intertwined with American national interests. They constitute the
very core of those interests. Indeed, they give moral standing to
imperatives to provide for national welfare and defense so long
as the nation does not permanently abandon the precepts that
give its existence moral value. Those precepts are not best understood, however, as embodying transcendentally based universal
principles of social justice. Rather, they express the nation's re-
flectively chosen moral goals—to respect human liberties
throughout the world and to advance them, initially and espe-

cially, at home. This view encompasses the concerns for actual consequences, and the recognition of certain national claims, which form the strengths of the realist perspective, without sanctioning the dismissiveness toward morality realism can foster. And while it does not overcome the real differences in private and public perspectives on humanitarianism and national claims, it does clarify those differences and their moral appropriateness in ways that may make healthy dialogue and cooperation between governmental and private agencies more feasible.

WHY NOT COSMOPOLITAN MORALISM?

The position I defend clearly endorses recent attacks on realism's disavowal of moral considerations.[2] Why then challenge the moral perspective of those critiques? After all, contemporary international moralists like Henry Shue and Charles Beitz do articulate some widely shared moral intuitions. Most of the time, most of us do speak of morality as superior to national self-interest, as something universal and enduring, applicable to and for all human beings. That is why Shue has such force when he writes in this volume that there are some things one simply "does not do" and "some things one must do," and when he asserts that "clear thinking" can demonstrate what truly is humanitarian aid and what is actually only military assistance, or at best compensation owed for past injustices. Amidst the obscuring smog of political rhetoric, such crisp assertions can come as a breath of fresh air.

Yet even though these sorts of arguments can accomplish much good, they strike me as misleading in several ways that culminate in a failure to discern why humanitarianism can properly mean connected but distinct things to governmental and private agencies. First, they suggest an unjustified certainty about the requirements of morality that can prevent us from acknowledging the frailties of our views and exploring others. These are serious handicaps in striving for moral agreement, or even open and honest discourse, among different governments or among governments and private agencies.

Second, these writers also tend to equate morality with principles of right, particularly principles of distributive and compensatory justice, held to be morally prior to conceptions of purposes, of the good and the good life. That approach leads them to label as "nonmoral" purposeful strivings which, I believe, actually constitute the core of many moral traditions, including some central to the United States.[3]

Finally, their treatment of morality as principles of justice standing above national senses of purpose prevents these writers from seeing why a nation may legitimately presume that the preservation of its collective existence and interests generally constitutes a valid moral imperative, a presumption private humanitarians quite properly need not make. This failure means that these analysts do not provide great insight into either the moral disputes governments and private humanitarians inevitably have or their likely areas of agreement.

Let us begin with the rather assured certainty conveyed by statements like those of Henry Shue just quoted. While they express our deep commitment to our moral intuitions, to which we must indeed give great weight, such assertions fail to remind us that we also recognize these intuitions as *our* intuitions—as convictions shared by persons shaped by particular moral and cultural traditions. It is a notorious fact that persons shaped by different traditions sometimes display intuitions that, at least arguably, are different as well. That fact does not mean we must view our moral notions purely as accidents of our cultural identities, with no transcendental or natural foundation. They may well be more than culturally "relativistic," and many of us hope and believe they are. But we cannot claim certain knowledge that they are, while we do know many of their particular roots.

Hence I believe that in making moral arguments we ought always to look past our moral intuitions to the substantive claims and arguments on which the traditions that convey them to us rest, an exercise which often clarifies those intuitions and sometimes reveals their vulnerabilities. We should admit, to ourselves and others, that our positions can be traced to controversial Kantian claims about the status of rational beings, or Lockean assertions of natural rights, or Christian claims of the Holy Spirit within us, or other such views. We ought not to speak as if we know that moral principles are things external to us, plainly identifiable by "clear thinking," dictating what we simply must or must not do without need of any further argument. Such language can prevent us from reaching better understandings of ourselves while making us unduly intolerant of others.

Yet despite their frequent, sensible qualifications, contemporary international moralists do repeatedly speak in ways that imply apodictic certainty, while discouraging these sorts of moral explorations. In *Basic Rights*, for example, Henry Shue identifies a "moral minimum" that "every person, every government, and every corporation" must somehow "be made to do," a minimum which includes "socially guaranteed" subsistence rights. He also lays out what basic rights indicate "must be done" in U.S. foreign policy.[4] And in his contribution to this volume, he similarly strives to show that we can sharply distinguish between humanitarian charity and compensatory justice. He offers as evidence a story about a hypothetical confiscation of an excessive share of the proceeds from a jointly constructed building. Shue thereby builds to a point also stressed by Charles Beitz, that there are "global redistributive obligations founded on justice" which render some foreign aid not a discretionary matter of charity but a morally inviolable duty.[5]

Those conclusions are obviously relevant to the topic at hand, so we must look carefully at how they are reached. It is striking how these international moralists, who speak of our obligations with great confidence, fail to probe very deeply the arguments for, and even more importantly against, the intuitions they uphold. Shue's tale of illicit confiscation, for instance, includes no hint of why his hypothetical person claimed a larger share than appears just. Yet ordinarily people give reasons for such actions. They may be transparently thin rationalizations, but until we hear them, we cannot be sure. It may appear appropriate, in defining a paradigmatic case of injustice, to simplify things by presenting an action as having no proffered justification whatsoever. But this is a simplification that deprives the example of any ability to illuminate how we should explore and somehow resolve competing definitions of morality. That task is central and inescapable in all real world distributive cases. Instead, the example may lull us into believing that we can properly evade this labor by simply asserting what we "know" to be just and then dismissing other views.

In *Basic Rights*, Shue does offer a number of useful arguments for his various positions. Even so, the "moral minimum" of rights he defines there appears to rest especially on a belief that "degrading" inequalities, those that are damaging to persons' self-respect, are "morally unacceptable." Shue indicates that this principle is for him the "moral rock bottom," for which he cannot provide "another level" of argument.[6]

Certainly this intuition against degrading inequalities has appeal, but again it is misleading to suggest we can stop with it. How do we decide which inequalities are degrading and which are appropriate? Different moral traditions would answer those questions very differently. The public awards given to a nation's poet laureate, and not to its leading pornographers, may damage the latter's self-respect; yet is this immoral? Many social conservatives see denials of equal rights to homosexuals as appropriate, and their conferral as degrading and unjust; are they right? Revolutionary Marxists have regarded the political inequalities, economic confiscations, and forced collectivization of productive labor involved in leadership by a vanguard party as necessary. Others have experienced them as humiliating and inhuman. The point is that Shue's "rock bottom" moral principle must actually gain most of its practical content from more concrete moral traditions that give arguments as to what constitutes human worth, what degrades it, and why. But as in his hypothetical story here, in *Basic Rights* Shue proceeds from the intuition stated in bare form, implicitly relying on more specific understandings without baring their historic and philosophic premises—and weaknesses—or analyzing opposing outlooks.[7]

And when morality speaks through the pens of most recent international moralists, it speaks almost exclusively of distributive justice. That is overtly the focus of the relevant books by Beitz and Shue. In his paper here Shue adds a more elaborate framework of constraints, which tell us what we cannot do, mandates, which tell us what we must do, and ideals, which tell us what to do if we happen to be committed to them. That framework does not, however, alter his basic identification of universal morality with justice alone. As Shue indicates, "principles of international justice" provide "the grounds for both constraints and mandates." Thus he really presents us only with a contrast between "just principles" and "ideals," such as the promotion of freedom, the ideal Shue attributes to the United States. And Shue treats his principles of justice, expressed in constraints and mandates, as *more authoritative* than "our own ideals." Just principles "apply generally," while ideals are only "standards that we choose to try to live up to even though we may not, strictly speaking, have to." Thus justice remains the only "rock bottom," universally binding dimension of morality.

This assignment of priority to justice over ideals, over moral aims and purposes, is characteristic if not definitive of current neo-Kantian moral outlooks, but it seems fundamentally misguided. Although I cannot defend either claim rigorously here, I believe it both misdescribes our reasons for subscribing to moral principles, and it leads us into remedial inquiries that we cannot hope to answer satisfactorily. If we ask ourselves why we believe we should have constraints and mandates, why we want justice, why we find certain inequalities degrading, I think our answers will inevitably involve arguments about why human life is worthy, that is to say, why it is morally good. For it is the qualities that give worth to human life that make its degradation morally wrong, and its advancement via just constraints and mandates, right. Hence our sense of the right will not be found to be analytically prior to a sense of the human good. It will rather be dependent upon some such sense. Of course, notions of the qualities that make for human worth are controversial; that is why neo-Kantians prefer not to talk about them. In the long run, however, we cannot avoid those controversies by keeping our assumptions about what they are implicit and professing to be neutral on the question.[8]

If these points are correct, then it will usually be clearest to argue directly in terms of our moral goals and purposes, indicating why we think they sustain and advance human qualities we value, and what they imply for justice. Moral requirements would then be presented as flowing directly from our pursuit of our sense of appropriate human ends; they would not appear as outside and above our aims and interest, but rather as integral to their realization. It is true that this teleological mode of reasoning always raises fears of Machiavellianism, in which the end justifies the means. I nonetheless will dare to contend that we need not be so disturbed by this prospect, because when we aim at substantively good ends we find they are always to some degree corroded by evil means and rarely justify them.

One might respond that real governments often aim at bad

ends, and we need autonomous principles of justice to constrain
them. If just principles inevitably rest on a sense of the good,
however, then when we invoke those constraints we really are
only weighing some goods against others. And the approach of
defining morality ultimately in terms of justice presents other
difficulties. In a world shaped by innumerable past and present
injustices, it inevitably points us to the task of achieving rectifica-
tion or compensation for past harms. In particular, it may seem
that affluent nations such as the United States can quickly be
assigned the extensive redistributive obligations Shue and Beitz
both stress. Yet while Americans are all undoubtedly beneficiaries of many historic and current injustices, most benefit only
indirectly, and largely unconsciously; and most can be accurately
portrayed as victims of injustice as well.

If we recognize all these injustices and then try to "correct"
for them, we must first ask what counts as a "remedy" or as
"compensation." Should we try to restore the world to what it
was before these myriad ongoing evils occurred—a task that
points us back before the dawn of historic time—or should we
make it what it would be if these injustices had not occurred—a
counterfactual speculation of truly breathtaking immensity? I
suggest that these questions of compensatory justice in our highly imperfect world are in fact so complex that such principles are
simply not the best place to start moral reasoning, even if it is
analytically possible to do so. It is more prudent to begin with a
sense of what we value, with our moral aims and purposes, and
to see how they can best be furthered in the world as we find it.
Again, if those purposes are genuinely good, they will include
significant concern for others, motivated in part by an awareness
of our own wrongdoings.

A Purposive View of Liberal Morality

What would it mean to consider principles applicable to
foreign affairs as elements of the particular moral traditions that
bear them to us, and to focus on the purposes, the senses of the
good, those traditions articulate? These questions can only really
be answered in terms of specific substantive moral outlooks.
Here I will focus on an understanding of liberalism that I believe

forms the most persuasive element in the United States' traditions; for I agree with Henry Shue that most Americans see their
basic national ideal as the preservation and advancement of human freedom as they conceive of it. That goal must therefore
anchor their government's view of the principles of international
relations and of its relationship to private humanitarianism.

As I have argued elsewhere, I believe the Lockean philosophic traditions that formed so large a part of early liberalism
express this sense of freedom as a political purpose, a purpose
derived from a still-plausible portrait of humanity's fundamental
condition and needs.[9] We can make progress toward relief of the
human estate and the realization of human dignity only if we
personally and collectively devise ways of life that are not destructive, for all or some, of meaningful capacities to compre-
hend our circumstances, to choose, and to realize in practice the
most beneficial courses available to us. This is the great constraint of liberal morality that provides most of the content for
liberal justice. A purposive view of morality, however, tells us
more than what is just. It indicates that we can achieve genuine
moral accomplishments by adopting personal pursuits and social
systems that genuinely empower people to lead the lives they
find most fulfilling, consistent with the constraint just stated.

How to do so is, of course, enormously difficult. For example, distributive policies aimed at supplying ample resources to
all and efforts to provide real access to diverse vocations can run
counter to fostering a productive economy—a painful tension
that neo-Kantian calls for international redistribution persistently slight. Moves toward more international institutions can ignore genuine sentiments of meaningful national membership;
yet simply to accept the existing array of national communities is
to countenance extensive inequality and subjugation.

I think our task is not so much to explore hypothetical
"ideal" worlds as to consider how we can best promote freedom
in this world as we find it, with the limited capacities we possess.
This world, for better or worse, is predominantly structured as a
set of diverse nation-states, relatively large-scale and centralized
political systems that govern populations who, because of language, ethnicity, religion, culture, ideology, propaganda, or some
other factor, feel themselves to be a distinct people. While these
feelings and political structures often advance policies of sense-

less hostility toward outsiders, they also help constitute the vital aspirations of millions, which must be taken seriously in moral and political reflections. These competing considerations will frequently render it advisable, for the present at least, to advance liberty through existing forms of collective life, by making contemporary politics more liberal.

That is certainly the most obvious course in the United States, which is already significantly dedicated to liberal principles and realizes them in part. The government of the United States often presents itself as a regime that aspires to respect and promote freedom above all, and as one that embodies in its institutional structure and ongoing activities a collective life that its citizens value as a crucial social realization of freedom.

This self-presentation, so easily dismissed by all who perceive the regime's very real shortcomings, is nonetheless essential for understanding the relationship of liberal moral perspectives to American foreign policy and to private humanitarianism. The liberalism that is so vigorous in America's political traditions is, of course, often criticized or praised precisely because it belongs to the family of universalistic moral outlooks that are concerned ultimately with individual human rights. It is therefore thought to have no real capacity to indicate the value of membership in a political community or to prompt strong feelings of civic allegiance. Consequently, when Americans ostentatiously display such civic attachments and sentiments, it is thought that these loyalties stem from "nonmoral" or "premoral" primordial sentiments; or else they disguise self-interested judgments of the nation's utility in enhancing Americans' individual wealth and power.[10]

To the contrary, I believe many Americans agree with their government that their national membership is morally valuable because it furthers their aspirations for human freedom in several significantly different ways. The government is or should be an instrument of individual freedom, by opposing repressive social institutions and behavior at home, by adopting policies that enhance individual resources and opportunities, and by aiding human freedom elsewhere when truly suitable opportunities to do so arise.

And many Americans also believe that the collective political life of the United States citizenry should itself be a social embodiment and realization of freedom. Their national life is meant, at any rate, to represent a reasonable approximation of political, economic, and social self-governance among persons who are bonded together by their agreement that American arrangements for these purposes are generally suitable and satisfying (though virtually all favor modifications and improvements).

Of course one can dispute whether existing arrangements in the U.S. are in the least satisfactory as a vision of free communal life, particularly given the costs they impose on many persons here and abroad. Many American political struggles center on what actions will really advance freedom, at home and abroad. At times, moreover, Americans may conclude that prevailing arrangements are becoming so hostile to liberty that the nation's existence will lose its moral justification unless those arrangements are altered. That, arguably, is the conclusion Abraham Lincoln reached when he chose to accept civil war and possible national destruction rather than to embrace slavery as a permanent part of American national life.

It is nonetheless perfectly appropriate, I believe, for United States policymakers to presume routinely that American national interests, including concerns for the nation's economic welfare and military defense, have moral standing in terms of liberal commitments to freedom. Indeed, the most plausible interpretation officials can make of their authorization is that the national life they govern forms a crucial dimension of the lived freedom Americans have chosen to establish and experience. While America's governors and citizens alike must recurringly ask themselves whether their national institutions and policies truly are conducive to liberty as they understand it, effective public decision makers can only rarely rethink first principles. Hence they must usually take this liberal value of American national life as a presupposition in their work.

Private humanitarians, on the other hand, ordinarily should not be expected to make such benign presumptions in favor of American national interests. They are situated to speak for different, though linked, moral outlooks. As Bruce Nichols points out,[11] existing domestic humanitarian agencies have generally originated in Protestant, Catholic, or Jewish religious traditions. All tend to offer more universal and supranational views of morality than governmental bodies do, though each is significantly different. Protestant and Catholic perspectives express the Christian concern for the ultimate welfare of all human beings, regarded as moral equals—though Protestants are more wary than Catholics of working with states in the pursuit of this concern. Jewish charitable agencies, while often allied with the global efforts of Christian groups, also feel it appropriate to give special attention to needy Jews.

The key point here is that, despite these contrasts, none of these private humanitarian actors have any reason to assume, as U.S. policymakers do, that the interests of American national life are especially crucial to the cause of aiding people to lead freer and more fulfilling lives, in America and around the world. The usual focus of private humanitarians is, appropriately, on the immediate needs of victims of some political or national catastrophe. Private agencies may well decide that aspirations to be part of a particular political community, and to have that community preserved, are basic to the moral and material welfare of some of those they assist. But they need not presume this is so, nor that it is especially so in the case of Americans and their nation. And they need not because, with the exception of Jewish agencies and the state of Israel, they do not see themselves as authorized by any particular peoples to realize a certain social form of freedom for those peoples. Their consequent refusal to treat the collective lives of most nations, including the United States, as *prima facie* moral ends is the fundamental difference between the moral perspectives of private humanitarians and that of the United States government (along with many other governments as well).

THE DIALECTIC OF LIBERAL NATIONAL INTERESTS AND PRIVATE HUMANITARIANISM

Who is more nearly right in this contrast of moral perspectives? There are times when, as political actors, we must take sides on these questions; but I have no definitive moral proofs to offer, and I do not wish here to defend further my particular judgments. In any case these differences in moral outlooks would surely persist, relatively unaffected. Hence I will try instead to specify what this basic difference means for how U.S. government officials and private agencies tend to view the relationship of humanitarianism to moral obligations. That account can help illuminate predictable areas of disagreement over foreign policy and humanitarian aid and to highlight avenues for improved mutual understanding, dialogue, and cooperation where public and private purposes coincide.

From the fundamental difference in the presumptions they make about the moral status of the American polity, there flow quite different structures to the moral obligations U.S. governmental and private humanitarian agencies believe they possess. It may be useful to summarize those structures in the simplest possible form. If Americans believe their nationhood rests on their shared commitments to liberty, as I believe they should, then the basic structure of their government's obligatory moral goals is threefold, with the goals arranged in order of moral priority.

First, the United States must strive to avoid violating the fundamental liberties of all human beings, citizens and noncitizens alike, at home and abroad. This requirement entails some conception of what constitute fundamental human liberties, and this is of course a controversial question. But Americans who take their principles seriously must nonetheless strive to answer that question as honestly as possible, in light of available moral knowledge and experience, and then to abide by their answers. That means they can infringe the basic liberties of others only when their own basic liberties are at stake—a sadly common occurrence, yet not so common as governments sometimes assert.

Second, governmental agencies should attempt especially to establish policies and institutions that enhance the secure possession and enjoyment of such liberties for Americans. Since the first objective has moral priority, this enhancement cannot properly be sought through violations of what Americans acknowledge to be basic human liberties. But within the bounds of that constraint, American officials can properly place the interests Americans share ahead of the claims of others. The citizenry's common national membership is, after all, understood to rest precisely on mutual commitments to assist compatriots in the collective endeavor of providing for what they judge to be shared lives of freedom.

Even so, on this view the commitment to freedom for all

remains a defining element of America's national aims. Hence
the final objective must be for the United States to strive similarly to promote liberty for nonnationals, insofar as it can do so
consistently with the prior two goals. This is an objective that
will sound reassuringly internationalist to some and dangerously
interventionist to others. I believe its (very real) potential dangers
can be diminished if Americans remind themselves that while
they believe their commitments to liberty are morally correct,
and while they have every reason to defend those commitments
against those who claim authority to override them, they still
must recognize that their beliefs are at best matters of practical
wisdom, not certain knowledge. Hence it is appropriate for the
United States to try to persuade states and peoples with different
moral traditions of the propriety of liberal values; to enhance the
opportunities of others when it can do so in noncoercive ways;
and even for the U.S. to prevent clear violations of the liberties of
others when it can do so without great risk to its own citizens or
innocent parties. But the limits of our moral knowledge mean
that it is proper for the United States to approach other nations
in a spirit of tolerance and willingness to compromise on some
differences, instead of attempting to impose forcibly the values it
finds compelling on those to whom they are as yet alien.

This three-part system of national moral obligations obviously leaves much unsettled, yet it does take stands on some
controversial questions, including whether compatriots have special claims.[12] Hence it is not vacuous. The structure of moral
obligations for private humanitarians I offer is simpler yet, being
twofold. Humanitarian agencies find it equally appropriate, we
may assume, to take the ban on violating any person's basic
liberties as a first priority. Then they strive to help meet the basic
needs of the most helpless and endangered persons they can
reach (with Jewish groups, again, feeling a special responsibility
for Jews in distress). In some instances, those needs may be met
best by helping people to remain in or return to their homeland,
where natural disasters, for example, might otherwise compel
them to leave. In other instances, the most beneficial aid may be
transport away from dire conditions to a nation that can provide
safe harbor. But as suggested above, private humanitarians will
not otherwise attach any special value to helping persons maintain the life of any particular polity. Indeed, they may well be-

lieve that the existing world system, dominated by nation-states, ought to be ultimately transcended so that human needs can be better met by different institutions.[13]

These differences in national and private moral perspectives inevitably issue in different senses of what is genuinely humanitarian. United States officials cannot be expected to view as truly humanitarian any policy which threatens fundamental interests of the national life that Americans regard as a morally valuable form of communal freedom. Instead, denigrations of Americans' nation-centered interests will seem morally wrong. Furthermore, governmental decision makers are likely to regard as genuinely humanitarian any policy that truly enhances basic liberties for nonnationals, furthering their third, less mandatory moral objective. This fact partly explains their temptation to label even military actions aimed at "liberation" as functionally "humanitarian."

As Henry Shue observes, sometimes that label may seem appropriate; he gives the example of supplying guns or, presumably, gunners to a village threatened by tigers. Yet describing even nonmilitary aid to wars of liberation as "humanitarian assistance" obviously threatens to turn the third moral goal of American policy into a rationale for imperialism. Given this risk, given the cautions about America's right to impose its values on others noted above, and given the real violations of basic liberties that inevitably occur when a government supplies weapons, soldiers, or logistical support for battles waged against human beings, it seems clearly preferable for American policymakers generally to limit their uses of the term "humanitarian." It could most plausibly be confined to nonmilitary assistance aimed at meeting material hardships of noncombatants (including those rendered *hors de combat* by injury). Yet equally clearly, there will be contexts when this usage strikes not only U.S. officials but many outside observers as unduly confined—morally grey areas, where the most humanitarian deed possible seems to be to risk involvement in combat in order to help supply the basic needs of the oppressed. So perhaps we should acknowledge that clear thinking will not always quickly resolve these grey areas into black and white. Careful probing of competing moral claims and the empirical possibilities for success in various courses of action are necessary for adequate judgments.

Furthermore, the structure of their moral obligations helps

indicate why U.S. officials will often be very reluctant to hold that "compensation," not "humanitarian aid," is in question when they offer aid to persons harmed in the course of protecting what they take to be morally appropriate American national interests. And again I think this issue will often be legitimately cloudy: the priority U.S. governors must accord to protecting American lives and liberties can drive them to measures that may almost unavoidably harm others. There will be real disputes over whether these measures were truly called for or not.[14] Hence once more I think moral and empirical exploration of what are recognized to be grey areas is needed.

This is one of the areas, moreover, where often the best results will not be reached by endlessly wrangling over the precise nature of American compensatory obligations. American policymakers are usually more receptive to arguments that focus on how they can best proceed in fulfilling their goals, including American commitments to advancing human capacities for free lives, than to contentions premised on their alleged immoralities. And their focus may be valid enough, if officials recognize that American involvements in others' hardships, however defensible, normally constitute good reasons for giving the needs of those persons higher priority on the national agenda.

The more straightforward structure of moral obligations for private humanitarians renders their choices somewhat less complex. Again, they can usually define humanitarian assistance simply as the provision of nonmilitary aid that helps meet the immediate needs of natural or political disaster victims, without considering how their actions affect the long-term capacities or inclinations of governments to provide individual and communal freedom for aid recipients. Sometimes, however, those considerations will seem unavoidable. When resources are scarce and the American government is providing adequate aid to one side of a military conflict, humanitarian agencies may decide they should devote their energies to helping the other side. But this will inevitably be labeled partisan, "political" assistance, and in fact it may prove important to the viability of the political movement in question. Even providing refugees with transportation may shape the political character of the regimes thus emptied of dissidents, and of those landed with many new immigrants, in ways that affect the capacity and willingness of the regimes to provide for the basic needs and liberties of those they govern.

In short, when private humanitarians take actions that U.S. officials see as buttressing political forces hostile to liberty, and even more when they appear to aid movements that threaten American national interests, such assistance will inevitably be depicted officially as not genuinely humanitarian, perhaps even as unlawful. Yet if private humanitarians were simply to adopt the U.S. government's presumption in favor of the moral validity of American interests, they would betray in principle, and at times in practice, their deepest commitments to the welfare of all human beings. This no government can realistically expect them to do; and given the vulnerabilities of all governments' moral claims, I believe no government can morally expect them to do so, either.

Thus there will inevitably be conflicts between private humanitarians and governments in general, and the U.S. government in particular, over what constitute genuine moral obligations and genuine humanitarianism. Sometimes these differences form tragic obstacles to the attainment of objectives that may be deemed worthy from almost any moral point of view. Yet in two ways I think this picture of the views of the U.S. government and private agencies toward humanitarianism gives some grounds for optimism.

First, the disagreements these contrasting perspectives ineluctably generate can often be not destructive but truly useful. Each side has the potential to correct the characteristic blind spots of the other. On this account, the U.S. government is, after all, committed to respecting basic liberties for all as a first priority and also to promoting them when possible. Yet its belief in the moral significance of American national interests can lead it to neglect to honor adequately basic liberties of outsiders and to slight real opportunities for their advancement. Since private humanitarians strive to attend equally to the needs of all, they can be valuable critics of the U.S. government's excessive parochialism, calling it to conform to its own best principles.

At the same time, private humanitarians ought in theory to acknowledge that forms of communal life can often be essential interests of those they assist. Yet their concern for the immediate material needs of individuals may lead them to give little weight to these concerns, even though viable polities are necessary for the provision of basic resources and opportunities in the long run. U.S. policymakers can frequently be counted on to provide reminders of this reality of the contemporary human condition, so extensively ordered into nation-states and other particular communities. I think, moreover, that if both sides appreciated the inherent differences in their moral perspectives just sketched, and if they also bore in mind the arguments against moral absolutism I have reviewed, they might be better equipped to engage in perceptive and open-minded critical dialogue with each other. Such dialogue would enable them to realize these mutual corrective functions more effectively.

Secondly, and finally, we should recall while this canvassing of the moral attitudes of U.S. policymakers and private humanitarians has highlighted real differences, there are considerable areas of moral agreement as well. The most plausible definitions of basic liberties all recognize that they are not really provided through abstract legal or political rights alone. They require the achievement of actual conditions that give people meaningful opportunities.[15] Those conditions plainly must include capacities to meet persons' basic material needs. The priority that Americans as a people accord to respecting fundamental liberties and to advancing them not only for themselves but for others thus involves a significant commitment to helping the needy, at home first but also abroad. Many Americans, moreover, understand that commitment as stemming in part from the religious beliefs for which private humanitarians often speak. Hence if this portrait of public and private moral outlooks is at all close to the mark, we should expect there to be many areas where governmental and private representatives can agree wholeheartedly on what humanitarian objectives entail. Their discovery of these common purposes, as well as their constructive mutual criticism, can form an ongoing dialectic of liberal national interests and private humanitarianism that benefits both sides.

And if the other elements of the analysis offered here also have merit, then increased attention to the substance of these partly differing moral perspectives, especially to their basic moral goals, and to what those goals imply for progress in the world as we find it, may help to identify areas of agreement more effectively than an insistence on the absolute rectitude of a particular moral view, or an emphasis on the strict apportionment of responsibility for past inequities. The basic contrasts between governmental and private outlooks would, to be sure, be affirmed, not overcome, by adopting the understanding of liberal morality and humanitarianism reviewed here. Even so, that understanding might in practice foster better communication and cooperation in the realization of what almost all of us would regard as morally worthwhile and humanly beneficial public and private endeavors.

NOTES

1. All such writers have been heavily influenced by the neo-Kantian liberalism of John Rawls's *A Theory of Justice* (1971), though many find him too conservative in drawing out the international implications of a commitment to justice. See Charles Beitz, *Political Theory and International Relations* (Princeton: Princeton University Press, 1979); Henry Shue, *Basic Rights: Subsistence, Affluence, and U.S. Foreign Policy* (Princeton: Princeton University Press, 1980); Brian Barry, "Humanity and Justice in Global Perspective," and D. A. J. Richards, "International Distributive Justice," in J. R. Pennock and J. W. Chapman, eds., *Ethics, Economics and the Law* (New York: New York University Press, 1982); and T. W. Pogge, "Liberalism and Global Justice: Hoffman and Nardin on Morality and International Affairs," *Philosophy and Public Affairs* 15 (1986): 67-81.

2. Beitz, *Political Theory and International Relations*, pp. 11-66.

3. Charles Beitz, "Cosmopolitan Ideals and National Sentiment," *Journal of Philosophy* 80 (1983): 591-600.

4. Shue, *Basic Rights*, pp. ix, 23, 26, 155.

5. Beitz, *Political Theory and International Relations*, pp. 172-73.

6. Shue, *Basic Rights*, pp. 119-20, 123.

7. Charles Beitz does the same thing in another way, using a global application of John Rawls's famous "original position" to discover the redistributive obligations Beitz believes justice imposes. But Rawls's hypothetical choice situation, draped by an extensive "veil of ignorance," gains its moral power only from the degree to which its structure conforms to moral intuitions we would accept in "reflective equilibrium," that is, through a process of testing our intuitions against rival moral beliefs in light of known experience. Rawls himself has provided only a slice of the comparisons of different moral perspectives reflective equilibrium requires, contrasting utilitarianism to his own view fairly

extensively. Even if that partial survey is sufficient for Rawls's purpose, the definition of domestic principles of justice, a wider canvassing certainly seems necessary if we wish to adjudicate among claims of justice advanced by widely disparate peoples and cultures. Yet Beitz engages in no such further exploration of contrasting moral perspectives. After ably critiquing realism, he essentially takes the intuitions expressed in Rawls's depiction of the original position for granted. Again, the net effect is to lead us away from analyzing the concrete particular outlooks our moral intuitions rely on, and toward proclamations of international moral obligations that stand outside and above human societies, dictating sternly to all (in ways few are likely to hear).

8. For similar contentions see W. Galston, "Defending Liberalism," *American Political Science Review* 76 (1982): 624-26, and I. Shapiro, *The Evolution of Rights in Liberal Theory* (Cambridge: Cambridge University Press, 1986), pp. 286-87.

9. Rogers M. Smith, *Liberalism and American Constitutional Law* (Cambridge: Harvard University Press, 1985), pp. 198-259.

10. Shue, *Basic Rights*, pp. 104-9, 139-49; Beitz, *Political Theory and International Relations*, pp. 161–69; "Cosmopolitan Ideals and National Sentiment," p. 599.

11. Bruce Nichols, "Rubberband Humanitarianism," *Ethics and International Affairs* 1 (1987): 191-210.

12. Shue and Beitz each wish to reject such claims, but Shue acknowledges that his discussion shows at most that claims for compatriots are "unproven," not that they are rebutted (*Basic Rights*, pp. 139, 150). Beitz believes he has effectively challenged priority for compatriots, but he does so in part by simply labeling as "nonmoral" not only feelings of national loyalty, but even national devotion to some sense of the good, to "perfectionist" goals ("Cosmopolitan Ideals," pp. 599–600). This usage, which would deprive Plato and Aristotle, among others, of "moral" perspectives, seems indefensible. Thus I think the case against priority for compatriots remains at best "unproven" as well.

13. Pogge, "Liberalism and Global Justice," pp. 68-75.

14. The arguments in these two paragraphs should not be read as defenses of any particular American governmental actions. They are rather efforts to provide more complete pictures of the considerations involved in many circumstances. A fair weighing of these considerations would, I believe, still generate sharp criticisms of many American policies, such as the labeling of nonmilitary aid to the contras as "humanitarian."

15. Shue, for example, properly stresses this point in *Basic Rights*, pp. 15-16.

II. HUMANITARIANISM: POLITICAL CONSTRAINTS AND LEGAL PROTECTIONS

HUMANITARIAN ASSISTANCE IN U.S. FOREIGN POLICY, 1947–1987

David P. Forsythe

> Of the seeming and real innovations which the modern age has introduced into the practice of foreign policy, none has proved more baffling to both understanding and action than foreign aid.—George Liska, *The New Statecraft*, 1960.

> There was a rock concert held to take care of the starving in Ethiopia. There was another rock concert held to raise money to take care of the (American) farmers who were going bankrupt because they were producing too much food. That doesn't make any sense at all.—Senator Mark Andrews (R., N.D.), Hearings, U.S. Senate, 1986.

INTRODUCTION

From certain points of view U.S. humanitarian assistance does not exist. One might be entitled to draw this conclusion from a random sample of literature. If one picked up a textbook on international relations, one on U.S. foreign policy, a traditional book on foreign aid, and a more recent, well-received book on economic diplomacy, one would search in vain for some mention of humanitarian assistance, disaster relief, or emergency assistance.[1]

Two philosophical approaches, of varying nature, lead to the same conclusion. According to the realist philosophy of Hans Morgenthau, since all foreign policy is a struggle for power to protect the self-interests of states, foreign aid of all types is just another dimension of this struggle. "What distinguishes foreign aid from those other branches of foreign policy are the means through which foreign aid endeavors to achieve its purpose. Its ends are no different from those of other branches. In other words, from the perspective of foreign aid as an instrument of foreign policy, foreign aid is but the continuation of diplomacy by other means."[2] From this philosophical perspective George Liska is able to quickly dismiss humanitarian assistance with the pithy comment that "Aid suggests love; but few will doubt that in conditions of insecurity the more compelling motive is self-interest based on interdependence."[3]

In a more humane version of this realist philosophy, Rogers Smith in this volume offers the argument that what is called humanitarian assistance can be encompassed within the conception of the national interest. When the U.S. offers humanitarian assistance, he suggests, it is really working to promote U.S. interests. That is, U.S. interests are broad enough to entail charitable works. What is humanitarian becomes expediential; what is done for others becomes what is done for self-interest.[4]

In the abstract Smith's solution is satisfactory. If one starts with the realist assumption that what is moral in foreign policy is that which is done to advance the nation's interests, and if the nation's interests are conceived broadly enough to encompass not only physical and economic security (power and wealth) but also its commitment to human dignity both for itself and others, then what is said to be moral (with humanitarianism as a subset) in foreign policy is equated with self-interest. By definition, there is no difference between moral and expediential acts; the former become part and parcel of the latter. This was a core point of classical realism; Smith has extended the scope of national interest to eliminate, at least philosophically, a conflict between self-interest defined in terms of power and wealth and moral action directed toward individuals abroad.

One should admit at the outset of this critique that at times the classic realist argument about the morality of national interest is persuasive. For example, I accept the proposition that the United States was morally justified to align itself with Stalin to defeat the Nazis, the latter presenting a clear and present danger to the morally superior Western democracies. American foreign assistance of every sort to the Soviet Union was justifiable in context, not only expedientially but also morally. It was unfortunate that many Soviet nationals suffered under Stalin, but it was not immoral for the United States to focus on its own defense rather than on individuals under Stalin during the war. In such a context it is defensible to kill in a war for the defense of basic U.S. values and interests.

The problem with this approach is not to be found in the realm of abstract argumentation, but rather in the empirical record of the U.S. government. It is not so easy to justify the U.S. overthrow, say, of the government of Guatemala in 1954, which had offended what was then United Fruit, and the U.S. support for subsequent murderous military regimes in Guatemala, in the abstract name of the free world. In this context an expediential argument made in defense of U.S. power and American wealth does not fit so easily with moral concerns. One can project this same critique to much of U.S. foreign policy to the non-European world.

Thus what seems a satisfactory merger of moral and expediential concerns in the abstract begins to unravel in the real world given the perceptions that have existed in Washington since 1947. Since the dominant view in Washington (certainly during the Reagan administration) is that the United States faces a clear and present danger to its existence from Soviet-led communism, the margin for introducing a genuine humanitarian assistance program has been very small indeed. What happened to individuals abroad was of less importance than the larger national competition with communism. Philosophers like Reinhold Niebuhr and statesmen like Henry Kissinger argued and acted on the basis that national group morality allowed the exploitation of foreign nationals. The danger to the United States was seen to be so imminent that support for repression and oppression abroad became magically moral.

What one author wrote in 1964 remains valid today: "The (U.S.) foreign aid program is formulated and promoted in an administrative and political setting that is not very amenable to humanitarian considerations."[5] At least from the perspective of this author, the last forty years has seen the U.S. government overstate its own virtue while understating the virtue of its adversaries. Other authors see most nations in most eras as engaging in the same misperceptions, at least until traumatic events force a more accurate view.[6] To the extent that most states in the nation-state system of international relations feel insecure, most aspects of foreign policy will be expediential rather than humanitarian. These policies will be rationalized as moral in terms of classical realism, with Smith's neo-realism struggling to find acceptance.

A second philosophical approach, represented by Henry Shue in this volume, sees other metaphysical norms as causing conventional humanitarian assistance to disappear. In his view, if the United States provides economic assistance for the benefit of others, but in a context in which the United States morally owes that assistance to the less fortunate because of past events, then such aid is not humanitarian or charitable because it is owed under principles of justice. What is owed because of past colonialism or imperialism or hegemonic exploitation cannot be considered humanitarian when provided. Justice supersedes charity.[7]

The problem with this approach again is to be found not in metaphysical argumentation but in observable reality. What is just payment for past wrongs may be more clear in the theorist's mind than in the statesman's eye. Those with something to offer are more likely to provide it if it is promoted as humanitarian rather than as justly owed. Since the United States was supposedly acting all along for the greater good of democracy and the free world, Shue's formulations become mostly irrelevant in Washington. A classic example is the U.S. rejection of a New International Economic Order; no U.S. administration, not even Carter's, believed there was a moral obligation based on justice to restructure international economics for the benefit of the poorer nations.

These sorts of arguments aside, U.S. policymakers and administrators do distinguish humanitarian assistance from other types of foreign aid. The former is said to be motivated by an effort to make a short-term impact on individuals regardless of national, party, or other political identification. Unlike other types of foreign aid, it is supposedly provided without concern for how it might redound to the power and wealth of the donor. The primary motivation is said to be short-term aid to alleviate civilian suffering, whatever the side effects of a strategic or economic nature. It is sometimes called disaster relief, famine relief, emergency relief, refugee relief, or war relief.

Despite problems of exact definition and precise boundaries, there is in the real world something called humanitarian assistance whose existence is largely captured in the following terms. The provision of material and medical assistance is directed to

> emergency situations in which there is an urgent need for international assistance to relieve human suffering. In such situations normal patterns of social and economic interaction may be disrupted, or the impact of a specific event may simply exceed the local capacity for response within the limits of available resources. This view of disaster encompasses a wide range of empirical situations and suggests that the common urgency of human needs in all such events should be seen as the decisive criterion for their identification.[8]

Seen this way, U.S. humanitarian assistance has amounted over the years since 1947 to about 1 to 2 percent of total U.S. foreign assistance, or to about 20 or 25 percent of total U.S. economic assistance. Exact figures are hard to come by. What is humanitarian relief, and what is developmental assistance partly designed to produce permanent food security and disaster preparedness? Only the former is called humanitarian. What is economic assistance, and what is a payoff to a political ally through Economic Support Funds (formerly Security Supporting Assistance)? In addition to direct U.S. contributions to refugee relief through the UN High Commissioner for Refugees and to war relief through the International Red Cross, how many food commodities has the United States transferred from the Food for Peace Program and the Commodity Credit Corporation for those two particular humanitarian causes, in addition to food relief programs more generally? Full answers to such complicated questions cannot be provided in this brief essay, or perhaps not at all.

It is clear, however, that in the American public there has been considerable support for U.S. humanitarian assistance as defined. Polls show a strain of "cosmopolitan internationalism" supportive of humanitarian relief, among other programs like developmental assistance.[9] One study refers to a "missionary spirit" among parts of American society, supportive of efforts to do good for others.[10] The Carlucci Commission Report of 1983, designed to provide an overview of the status and needs of U.S. foreign assistance, reminded us that humanitarian assistance was built on national values.[11] Even circles of opinion critical of U.S. foreign assistance in general acknowledge the short-term benefits of most disaster relief.[12]

This is not to say, however, that public support for humanitarian assistance has not been crosscut by other, somewhat contradictory views. As summarized by a 1967 study:

> Aid is favorably received insofar as it appears to project American values or practices abroad, furthers humanitarian aims, avoids deep involvement in the affairs of other nations, and assists cold-war allies. The public and Congress view aid with disfavor to the degree that it offers assistance to nations not allied with the United States, appears to be expensive, and results in deep involvement in overseas problems.[13]

It would appear that this statement still holds true.

If a U.S. humanitarian assistance program can be roughly defined by the primary intention to help suffering civilians in the short term regardless of considerations of U.S. power and economic gain, and if this general program is broken down into categories of general disaster and food relief, refugee relief, and war relief, we do rule out U.S. expediential interests as a primary consideration. (They may be present in a secondary or tertiary way, via Rogers Smith's interpretation or otherwise.) But such a conception does not rule out politics.

As I have argued elsewhere,[14] and as a more recent study reminds us, "all humanitarian action has a political content because it takes place within a political context."[15] Even supposedly natural disasters, whether sudden or slow-developing, may be greatly affected by governmental acts of omission or commission. Said an official of the U.S. Agency for International Development (AID) in congressional testimony, "Let me just briefly confirm what you probably already know. Droughts do not necessarily produce famines. More often, famines result from the venality of governments and ineptitude of their social, economic, and political policies."[16] Humanitarian assistance is a political subject in the sense that it deals with the struggle to implement national and international public policy for the immediate benefit of those intensely in need. It competes in a political process with strategic, economic, and factional politics.

Against this background, this essay has modest objectives.

It seeks to give some historical flavor, then to analyze certain patterns and problems in general food relief as the core component of disaster relief, refugee relief, and war relief. Special attention will be given to the important role of private voluntary organizations (PVOs) or nongovernmental organizations (NGOs). An overall objective, besides delineating more clearly the realm of humanitarian assistance, is to show its importance at different times to different persons.

HISTORY

Until 1947 American humanitarian assistance abroad was largely a function of the private sector, with only sporadic forays into this domain by the U.S. government because of war or other "abnormal" calamity. Or, the humanitarian role of the U.S. government was "an ad hoc, limited duration response. . . ."[17] In the early nineteenth century the U.S. Congress was somehow moved to provide funds for a natural disaster in Venezuela. The same occurred in the early twentieth century concerning Martinique and Italy. After the U.S. provided war relief during World War I, it progressively retreated into its former passivity. In the debate in the 1920s and 1930s over the fledgling International Relief Union, the United States never became a party. Insofar as there was a definite view on such matters in Washington prior to World War II, it was that emergency relief should be the domain of the International Red Cross and thus lodged in the (mostly) private sector.

War relief, however, was an exception. Yet even in wartime there was as late as 1914 considerable reluctance in Washington to take on the job as a proper governmental function. During the First World War, American relief to civilians can best be described as quasi-public. Herbert Hoover, wearing at one time the hat of private citizen, at another the hat of government official, headed the Commission for Belgian Relief. Perhaps it is not too much of a simplification to describe this commission as governmental coordination of private charity. In any event sizable war relief was distributed to the civilians of Belgium and other U.S. allies, mainly Britain and Italy (but not to civilians on the other side).

After the Great War Hoover remained in charge of a continuing relief program to Europe, the American Relief Administration, which displayed more of a public character, although a number of PVOs were involved. Much of this effort eventually was directed to the ongoing civil war in Russia. Again, this war relief was not entirely impartial, for much of it was sent to the White Russians but not the Red. Its impact on that situation was considerable, and a sizable number of lives were saved.[18]

By the time of the Second World War, and especially from 1941, the Roosevelt administration was fully committed to providing civilian relief to the allied side, even if it meant skirting U.S. laws designed to continue isolationism. That administration used the Lend-Lease arrangement with Great Britain and others to provide more than six billion dollars worth of agricultural commodities.[19] There was sizable civilian relief provided by U.S. military forces during the war. Immediately thereafter, the United States played the leading role in the creation of the UN Relief and Rehabilitation Administration (UNRRA) and provided 73 percent of the $2.9 billion that was channeled to civilian war relief, largely in Europe.[20]

As for refugee relief, again the starting point for analysis of the U.S. government role is to note historical deference to private agencies. It became clear after the First World War, however, that the volume of those dislocated by the war was simply too great for the PVOs to handle. Considerable activity on this subject thus took place within the framework of the League of Nations in the 1920s and 1930s, but since the United States was not formally involved there is no need to go into its analysis here. Despite the fact that an American headed one of the League's agencies dealing with refugees (defined not just in relation to flight from persecution but flight from war as well), the U.S. government did not play a major role in League endeavors.[21]

In the late 1930s the Roosevelt administration did move progressively into refugee issues, trying to coordinate governmental policies outside the moribund League, and continuing to seek in the 1940s some solution to the large and perplexing refugee questions stemming from Fascist and other repression (as long as the solutions did not entail U.S. acceptance of large numbers of Jewish and other refugees). Limited U.S. policymaking did not lead to massive funding for refugees, and private groups remained essential to the humanitarian work that occurred.[22]

In retrospect it is clear that the U.S. government moved haltingly in the twentieth century to develop a policy of humanitarian assistance, driven largely by wartime needs which dwarfed the capabilities of the private sector. Those who believe the United States has usurped a primary or dominant role for non-governmental organizations in humanitarian relief would do well to re-examine the events traced here in cursory form.[23] In many instances it was the NGOs themselves that approached public authorities, as on refugee matters during the League period, asking them to move into an issue area which had become too problematical for the private sector to handle well. Ironically, the public sector was to discover, post-1947, that it seemed to need the PVOs as much as they needed it.

DISASTER AND FOOD RELIEF

The heart of the U.S. humanitarian assistance program has been food relief. This is true whether one is talking about acute or chronic emergencies, so-called natural or man-made disasters (all disasters are man-made in the sense of resulting from the lack of prevention and preparedness measures through public or private actors), or peacetime or wartime needs (and refugees can arise out of either). If one is going to respond to the needs of individuals in emergencies, one has to provide them adequate nutrition, whatever else might follow.

The difficulties of precise analysis are immediately evident when one looks at the first major bilateral assistance program undertaken by the United States in 1947-48. What became known as the Marshall Plan, or economic assistance to European nations, was a combination of humanitarian assistance, developmental assistance, and containment of the power of Communist forces. It was to counteract short-term food shortages, provide the economic foundation for the reconstruction of at least Western Europe, and contain the power of the Soviet Union, both by undercutting the appeals of Communist political parties and forcing the Soviets to integrate their economy with that of the West on terms acceptable to the United States.[24] A major commitment by the United States, amounting to some 2.5 percent of its GNP, it was followed by separate commitments to food relief in both Yugoslavia and India. (Interestingly, the United States and other Western nations had not responded to famine in India in the 1940s when tens of thousands had died; cold war competition could produce humanitarian results.)

These separate policies, at least partly humanitarian in nature, began to be made less ad hoc and more systematic in 1953–54, with the adoption by Congress of Public Law 480, the Food for Peace Program. If it be granted that the major interest behind this legislation lay in the economic need to dispose of the American agricultural surplus in a way that maintained high market prices, and in the desire to produce more markets abroad for agricultural products, nevertheless a sizable part of P.L. 480 was for emergency food relief abroad. If some 75 percent of agricultural commodities have been provided under Title I authorizing concessionary sales, and if about 5 percent have been provided under Title III authorizing the bartering of food products to promote agricultural self-sufficiency abroad, that leaves some 20 percent of commodities under Title II as grants. It is reasonable to say as a summary that most of Title II authorizations, and some of Title I, have gone for humanitarian food relief. As of 1984, the P.L. 480 program had delivered some 653 billion pounds of food valued at more than $32 billion.[25]

Later, in both 1966 and 1974, Congress made significant amendments to P.L. 480 which had the effect of increasing the moral as compared to the expediential aspects of the program. Congress specified that much of the program was to go for humanitarian relief and developmental assistance, and that only stated amounts could be oriented toward political allies. That was a congressional reaction to what might be termed the (strategic) politicization of the Food for Peace Program by U.S. administrations; Food for Peace had become, from one perspective, Food for War because of its orientation to the likes of South Vietnam, South Korea, Pakistan, Israel, and other political allies.[26]

Even as it became clear that American agricultural surpluses were evaporating, Congress insured that under P.L. 480 and the Commodity Credit Corporation (CCC) food supplies would be available for humanitarian purposes. For example, the 1985 Food Security Act authorized the release of wheat from U.S. reserves "to provide urgent humanitarian relief in any developing country suffering a major disaster when the wheat could not otherwise be made available in a timely manner."[27]

Sometime between 1947 and 1953, and lasting at least until the 1970s if not to the present, the United States defined for itself the role of guarantor of world food security—to the extent that it exists. Progressively the economic, expediential interests in this role were reduced, although never eliminated completely, and the moral interests increased (including humanitarian). The political interests, defined in strategic terms, were also limited by Congress. The Food for Peace program was the substantive heart of the role, but two additional factors need to be noted in a cursory essay such as this.

In 1964 within AID there was created the Office of Disaster Relief. This was intended to be the focal point for U.S. efforts in natural disasters, and represented a further effort to rationalize and systematize not only food relief in acute or chronic emergencies but other types of humanitarian assistance as well. There continues to be debate over how much this office should focus on relief as compared to preparedness and prevention measures. Funded in the 1980s at an annual level of $25 million, a congressional study urged the doubling of its budget.[28] Others preferred to continue with a system in which the office could draw on developmental assistance to respond to natural disasters.

In 1963 the United Nations created the World Food Program. This was part of a chaotic UN attempt to systematize food relief as well as the broader concept of food security on a multilateral basis. The resulting jungle of agencies and plans can hardly be called a coherent and efficient system.[29] Nevertheless, the World Food Program has become an important conduit for U.S. food assistance in emergencies. Over the years the United States has provided somewhere between 25 and 50 percent of the resources of that program.[30] About 15 percent of this goes for emergencies, not development.[31] Unlike the League period, the United States has been a major actor concerning emergency food relief, although it, like other states, has not been keen on resurrecting the idea of guaranteed food and other humanitarian relief via international law.[32]

Despite P.L. 480 (and the CCC), AID's Disaster Relief Office, and the UN World Food Program, it cannot be said that either food relief or other more general disaster relief flows from a systematic, streamlined process. That both bilateral and multilateral humanitarian assistance (the two cannot be so easily separated in the real world) are plagued by problems is seen in the fact that both the U.S. and the UN had to create ad hoc agencies to manage humanitarian relief in the Horn of Africa and in Southeast Asia in the 1980s. The existing agencies were not adequate for the task, especially the UN Disaster Relief Organization (UNDRO), which has never lived up to original expectations.[33] Adding to the complications is the problem of how to coordinate the many PVOs which are active in food and disaster relief, and I will return to this subject later in this essay.

Yet for all the problems, one should emphasize that the U.S. government has accepted that humanitarian assistance abroad in general is a proper function of public authority, and the United States remains the most important of all governments involved in this undertaking (although that importance has declined drastically since the 1950s). Even the Reagan administration, the most nationalistic and unilateralist administration since 1947, never followed the line of the Heritage Foundation in arguing that the U.S. governmental role in humanitarian assistance should be reduced. It never accepted the argument that the U.S. government had no moral obligation to non-nationals, and it provided emergency relief to the peoples of Communist Ethiopia, Mozambique, and Cambodia.

TABLE 1

U.S. Foreign Disaster Assistance

Yr	ND	Co	T USG Asst	PL 480	Am PVO Ct	Intl Comm	Self-Help
80	32	27	$ 139,024,932	$57,814,655	$ 1,533,448	$ 35,810,102	$ 11,847,900
81	22	19	70,419,224	12,100,000	23,890,844	211,844,949	6,022,007,896
82	35	29	90,774,943	29,000,100	27,258,957	237,092,847	147,901,880
83	43	34	178,577,480	87,333,943	2,452,734	203,946,587	119,800,332
84	41	33	169,368,143	102,891,700	5,999,463	238,707,189	198,095,040
85	38	33	800,910,234	674,159,700	80,634,275	961,557,220	87,906,439
Tl	211		1,349,074,956	963,300,098	141,769,721	1,888,958,894	6,581,559,487
Av	35	29	224,845,826	160,550,016	23,628,286	314,826,482	1,096,926,581

Abbreviations:
Yr = fiscal year
ND = new disasters
Co = countries
T USG Asst = total USG assistance

PL 480 = Public Law 480 contribution
Am PVO Ct = American PVO contribution
Intl Comm = international community
Tl = total
Av = average

From 1964 to 1984 the U.S. provided aid in 772 disasters in 128 countries with fatalities beyond two million and with other effects on more than 750 million persons, costing the U.S. $2.4

billion; table 1 gives a brief overview of the cost of disaster assistance during the first half of the 1980s, as reported by the United States.[34] One can see that U.S. financing frequently exceeded that of the rest of the international community. One can also see that in particular years when the disaster involved famine, the P.L. 480 program was indeed crucial to humanitarian assistance. One can also see that the financial contribution of PVOs in certain years was not insubstantial, although this may not be their most important type of contribution.

WAR RELIEF

The real world does not always oblige those searching for neat categories. It is not always possible to distinguish war relief from other types of humanitarian assistance. In 1971, for example, there was armed conflict on the Indian subcontinent out of which the state of Bangladesh was created. In the midst of that situation a typhoon compounded the human suffering. In the 1980s in Ethiopia, a multifaceted internal armed conflict coexisted with general famine resulting from both political and natural causes. At least one can distinguish war relief theoretically from peacetime disaster relief.

One of the distinguishing characteristics of war relief is that the international delivery system is special. On the basis of some 125 years of tradition, somewhat codified now in international law, the International Red Cross movement has a special status. The Geneva Conventions of 12 August 1949, pertaining to victims of war, supplemented by two additional Protocols of 1977, provide special humanitarian status for Red Cross agencies in international and noninternational armed conflict. Perhaps even more importantly, it has become customary for the International Committee of the Red Cross (ICRC) to play a leadership role in humanitarian matters arising out of armed conflict.[35]

The ICRC is, technically speaking, a Swiss private association. It was the first Red Cross agency and is now internationalized in three ways: its humanitarian work is international; it is not only recognized but given rights in international public law; and it is part of the International Red Cross Movement which is ostensibly an international, nongovernmental organization. In fact, the situation is more complicated legally and politically. Legally, states parties to international humanitarian law vote in the Red Cross Conference which sets general, but nonbinding, policy guidelines for the movement; also, National Red Cross Societies are usually created by state action and have officers appointed by governmental officials. Politically, most National Red Cross Societies function in close cooperation with their governments; in some cases these National Societies are for all intents and purposes part of the government or party-state system.

Operationally, when there is war, international or internal, the ICRC tries, among other things, to coordinate humanitarian relief to civilians in need in the name of the Red Cross movement. It draws on the resources of not only the National Societies but also their federation, the League of Red Cross Societies. It appeals to public authorities, national and multilateral, for contributions and various other types of support. The exact role of the ICRC in any given situation of armed conflict may depend on the politics of the situation.[36]

In Afghanistan after the Soviet invasion, ICRC personnel were admitted, then excluded for a number of years, then readmitted and allowed to begin to exercise their traditional humanitarian activities. In Cambodia after the Vietnamese invasion, the ICRC was afforded only very limited rights within the country, in conjunction with the UN, and was compelled by circumstances to direct most of its work to the Thai-Cambodia border area (where it focused on war refugee relief). If one goes back to the civil war in Nigeria (1967-70), the ICRC shared war relief activities with an ad hoc coalition called Joint Church Aid (JCA); the ICRC finally had to suspend relief operations for political and security reasons, and its head of delegation was declared persona non grata by the federal government in Lagos.

These examples suffice to indicate that while international law and practice confirm a special position for the ICRC and the rest of the Red Cross movement in war relief, actual relief operations may vary considerably in a given situation. Other PVO actors such as JCA may resist coordination under the Red Cross label. Governments may provide their own, independent relief for political purposes, or, while ostensibly acting through the Red Cross framework, may direct "their" Red Cross personnel to maintain a certain independence. Several UN agencies such as

UNICEF, the UNHCR, the World Food Program, etc., may also be active in war situations and may have an unclear relationship to the putatively private Red Cross network. Particularly where armed conflict is combined with so-called natural disaster, no one agency may clearly be in charge of humanitarian assistance.

TABLE 2

U.S. Contributions to ICRC 1980–86
(in Swiss Francs)

	U.S. Contributions to Regular Budget	Total Regular Budget	U.S. % of Total	U.S. Rank
1986	8,302,500	62,493,840	13	2
1985	4,630,625	36,743,820	12	2
1984	4,881,250	37,422,480	13	2
1983	4,256,250	33,516,950	13	2
1982	3,037,500	31,966,830	10	2
1981	2,231,875	23,738,980	9	2
	690,000*	2,959,360		
1980	1,821,000	21,997,405	8	2
		1,275,420*		

	U.S. Contributions to Special Budget	Total Special Budget	U.S. % of Total	U.S. Rank
1986	57,214,299	151,008,858	37	1
1985	72,570,976	185,400,985	39	1
1984	62,069,333	167,218,668	37	1
1983	42,696,480	124,640,038	34	1
1982	38,266,850	91,789,078	42	1
1981	29,298,040	71,978,955	40	1
1980	17,528,097	58,749,540	30	1

	Total U.S. Contributions	Total All States	U.S. % of Total	Rank
1986	65,516,799	213,640,718	31	1
1985	77,201,601	224,236,230	34	1
1984	71,311,366	211,413,481	34	1
1983	50,627,730	166,233,508	30	1
1982	44,206,850	130,865,017	34	1
1981	35,386,415	104,762,259	34	1
1980	19,416,790	82,577,032	24	1

*Money pledged but not yet paid excluded

The United States is one of the major supporters of the ICRC and larger Red Cross movement, both financially and diplomatically. Table 2 shows first of all that the ICRC operates with two budgets. A regular budget covers the basic, usually administrative expenses of the organization. When sizable and emergency situations arise, the ICRC makes public appeals for special contributions leading to a special budget. There is thus a total budget, which does not include "contributions in kind," often agricultural commodities. The U.S. is second only to the Swiss government in states supporting the regular budget. Excluding multilateral aid from the European community, it is far and away the largest state contributor to the special and total budgets.

The ICRC also draws support from National Red Cross Societies and other private sources (not shown in table 2), although governmental contributions (including the EEC) in 1986 amounted to 73 percent of the total budget (not including contributions in kind). Thus the ICRC is able to provide material and medical assistance in situations of armed conflict thanks largely to voluntary state funding (about 75 percent of the total) and only slightly because of private contributions.

From the total contributions the ICRC acts not just to provide war relief or assistance, but also to seek the protection of prisoners of war through largely diplomatic means. The distinction between protection and assistance is not clear theoretically or practically. Moreover, the ICRC also utilizes part of its budget for its work with persons outside of armed conflict who are detained "by reason of events," i.e., political prisoners.[37] And there are a few other expenses not associated directly with armed conflict. According to ICRC calculations, in 1986 about 55 percent of its total budget was expended on medical and material assistance, as compared to such other categories as humanitarian protection, administrative expenses, etc. But some of this humanitarian assistance went to political detainees and their families. Thus it is not possible to say, on the basis of published figures, just how much the United States contributes strictly to war relief coordinated by the ICRC, but it is a substantial amount of the ICRC total.

The subject of war relief is complicated, and it would be easy to draw erroneous inferences from the discussion thus far. There is no indication that large U.S. contributions (and relatively sizable ones from the American Red Cross) dominate the ICRC or determine its policy choices. The ICRC is not likely to ignore the United States, but it is probably closer to the Swiss government than the U.S. diplomatically and mostly independent of both operationally. Large U.S. contributions do not signify that humanitarian considerations are always dominant in U.S. policymaking.

Finally, it has been said of the Swiss authorities, but even more so of the U.S. ones, that if they didn't sell so many arms in tense situations and didn't pursue so many policies which exacerbated political tensions, the ICRC would not need to be so active in armed conflict and make so many appeals for humanitarian assistance. This essay does not address these larger issues but merely notes that the U.S. has a relatively large program of humanitarian assistance in war situations, largely coordinated by the ICRC on behalf of the International Red Cross.

REFUGEE RELIEF

The reader by now would expect to find that refugee relief is not totally distinguishable from disaster or wartime relief. That this is indeed true is confirmed by both law and practice. According to the 1951 Refugee Convention and 1967 Protocol, a refugee is one who has crossed an international boundary and broken the normal bond with the government of his or her habitual residence, because of a well-founded fear of persecution.[38] Thus, technically speaking, one who flees armed conflict or a natural disaster is not a refugee—only one who flees across a boundary to escape persecution, whether political, social, or religious.

African regional law on refugees, however, as well as certain UN General Assembly resolutions, mandate that public authorities are to protect and assist persons fleeing not just persecution but also war or warlike situations. The practice of the lead UN agency in this issue-area, the office of the United Nations High Commissioner for Refugees (UNHCR), is to respond to those who appear to be refugees while delaying technical judgments about individual persecution versus other reasons for internal displacement or international flight.[39] Thus contemporary practice goes beyond the UN legal definition of a refugee, making clear that the UNHCR should deal with persons fleeing war or other general disruption of public order, as well as those fleeing individual persecution. Seen thusly, refugee relief can overlap considerably with peacetime and wartime relief.

In this cursory discussion focusing on humanitarian assistance, several important dimensions of refugee affairs will necessarily be omitted. One of the most important of these for the United States in recent years has been the question of admission of refugees to the United States, especially when it is the country of first asylum. This discussion is drawn out much more directly in the chapters by Doris Meissner and Michael McConnell.

If one looks at "generosity" understood as state contributions to the UNHCR, and neglects "openness" understood as acceptance of refugees within one's borders, there arises a distortion in analysis of state policy.[40] It is by now a well-known fact that the United States progressively in the late 1970s and into the 1980s adopted restrictive policies pertaining to openness, especially concerning those claiming to be refugees from Central America and the Caribbean and seeking asylum in the United States. At the same time that the United States, along with other traditionally open states for refugees, was moving toward a more closed-door policy, it was continuing to contribute in a relatively significant way to international refugee programs in Africa and Asia. Therefore the larger picture leads to a complex analysis of U.S. policy toward refugee affairs, but this essay remains focused only on assistance abroad.

One of the characteristics which allows one to distinguish, more or less, refugee relief from other types of humanitarian assistance is once again a special delivery system. According to what might be called the UN refugee regime, meaning the rules and agencies for managing refugee issues, the UNHCR is typically the lead coordinating agency for international refugee assistance (and protection). There are two major exceptions. Western governments created a special agency to handle refugee migration in Europe after the Second World War: the International Committee on European Migration. After the 1948 war for Palestine, the UN created the UN Relief and Works Agency (UNRWA) to provide for those who found themselves outside the state of Israel and who were unwilling or unable to return to their previous homes within that new state. The United States supported both of these agencies over the years, and it remains the largest contributor to UNRWA's budget whether because of humanitarian or other motives.[41]

The UNHCR tries not to be an operational agency for refugee relief but rather tries to coordinate the activities of public and private agencies. In this role the UNHCR has secured major U.S. support, at least since the Hungarian crisis of 1956. At that time the United States realized that the UNHCR could play a useful role in helping those in flight from communism. Since then the U.S. has become a major actor in international refugee affairs: it became the largest contributor to the UNHCR, became a party to the 1967 Protocol, and adopted a statute in 1980 patterned on the Protocol. The effect of the last two legal actions was to theoretically broaden the U.S. conception of a refugee from flight from communism to flight from persecution of whatever nature.

Starting in the 1970s with persecution and armed conflict on the Indian subcontinent, expenditures for humanitarian assistance through the UNHCR mushroomed. Its expenditures had been generally constant at well below $50 million per annum. By the late 1970s its expenditures were in excess of $300 million, by the 1980s in excess of $450 million. As one refugee situation was terminated another erupted, and several parts of the world—the Horn of Africa, for example—seemed to give rise to refugees perennially. The UNHCR began to engage in deficit spending in order to cope with a seemingly permanent refugee crisis, and a certain amount of compassion fatigue set in on the part of the industrialized democracies who were the main donors to refugee relief.

Despite the fact that critics in the executive and legislative branches raised serious questions about the UNHCR's performance during this period of expansion,[42] the United States continued to be the largest contributor to the UNHCR. Even if one looked not at total dollar amounts but at contributions as a percentage of GNP, the United States still had to be considered a relatively generous contributor.[43] Usually its annual contribution was around 35 to 40 percent of UNHCR's total budget, peaking in 1972 at 62 percent and dropping to 12 percent in 1967. In the mid-1980s the United States supported the UNHCR in its special conferences and other efforts directed at refugee problems in Africa, contributing a great part of the monies and commodities in that African program. By 1987 the Reagan administration was trying, mostly unsuccessfully, to hold U.S. contributions to about 25 to 30 percent in requesting that slightly over 60 percent (almost $200 million) of all U.S. federal money for refugee and migration affairs at home and abroad be directed to humanitarian assistance abroad.[44] Special transfers of funds from development assistance, if not supplemental money bills, usually raised those spending levels in response to unplanned emergency situations.

It was common for U.S. officials to picture the United States as "the acknowledged world leader" in dealing with refugee affairs from a humanitarian point of view, but in addition to humanitarian matters the United States was also concerned with the economic growth and sociopolitical stability of allies like Thailand, Malaysia, and Nimiery's Sudan who were impacted by an influx of refugees.[45] Progressively into the 1980s questions were raised about whether the United States was exercising so much influence over the UNHCR that the agency was becoming more concerned about pleasing its major donors than pressing those and other governments to afford better protection and assistance to refugees.[46] Refugees were inherently a political force, both in symbolizing rejection of a ruling regime and in affecting politics and public order in the host state. In that context some U.S. refugee relief served strategic as well as humanitarian ends, as could be seen in special U.S. targeting of refugees from Afghanistan and Cambodia-Vietnam.

The Private Agencies

The analysis presented thus far might lead one to conclude that PVOs had been excluded from international humanitarian assistance as it has evolved in this century. Nothing could be further from the truth. There are three roles for PVOs which are important and widely acknowledged.

First, PVOs naturally collect important information—about impending emergencies, culturally acceptable assistance, the infrastructure of efficient relief. Second, they play an educational or lobbying role on the basis of this knowledge. It has been said, for example, that the absence of effective PVO lobbying in the mid-1970s contributed to shortfalls in humanitarian food relief, and that improved lobbying in the next couple of years helped to restore the food relief system.[47] It is clear that PVOs interact with U.S. officials in devising procedures for humanitarian assistance,[48] whether this is called lobbying or not. Third, PVOs help to administer humanitarian assistance and are relied on extensively by AID, the ICRC, the UNHCR, and other agencies such as the World Food Program and UNICEF.

Humanitarian or charitable PVOs possess a number of positive characteristics, in the opinion of many, which allow them to play these three roles well.[49] They are numerous and thus make a sizable impact on an emergency situation. There are some 500 PVOs based in the U.S. alone which administer some type of economic aid abroad. Funds expended abroad by these PVOs are probably in the neighborhood of $1 billion per annum in 1988. The budget of CARE alone was around $300 million, Catholic Relief Services $370 million. About 15 percent of AID's budget is administered through PVOs. Some 60 percent of P.L. 480 Title II food grants are moved through PVOs.[50]

Most PVOs are free from any taint of strategic, factional, or partisan politics. As Rogers Smith has explained, there is no logical reason to assume that a private organization oriented to humanitarian concerns would have any interest in, or obligation to, U.S. strategic or economic goals. This makes them acceptable channels both by recipient parties and by multilateral agencies. As far back as the 1940s and 1950s, despite McCarthyism and the cold war, the U.S. was able to use PVOs to "sanitize" U.S. humanitarian assistance to Communist Yugoslavia and Poland.

PVOs display, usually, a good deal of flexibility and creativity in their activities, not being encumbered by the bureaucracy and need for political consultation that characterizes governmental and multilateral institutions. These private organizations generally have good contacts at the grass-roots level in foreign countries, having people there year-round for religious or secular reasons, and thus are in a position to implement people-to-people programs.

These same characteristics may give rise to some problems. The sheer number of PVOs from the industrialized democracies makes coordination extremely difficult for those supposedly in charge, like the ICRC and the UNHCR, or for those responsible for efficient use of scarce resources, which includes the above agencies as well as those in the U.S. government. Also, while freedom from strategic and partisan politics may be a good thing, ignorance of humanitarian politics may not be so desirable. For example, it was said of Joint Church Aid that it did not understand how secessionist Biafra was using the issue of starving children to promote its political objectives during the Nigerian civil war and that JCA consequently became a political actor on the side of Biafra. (Of course something similar was said of ICRC as well.) While many PVO personnel do develop an excellent understanding of local politics because of being familiar with the grass-roots scene, there are some examples of political naivete which give rise to difficulties in humanitarian assistance.

As far as general disaster and food relief is concerned, PVOs are more important as conduits for U.S. and multilateral relief than as donors. According to one source, about 14 percent of total food relief goes via PVOs. As for war relief, it has been shown that the quasi-private International Red Cross movement has a special leadership role. While about 75 percent of the funding for this type of humanitarian assistance is from public sources, most of it is administered by private agencies in the form of the ICRC and various National Red Cross Societies— although intergovernmental agencies are also frequently involved in particular situations.

Comprehensive figures about how much refugee relief is channeled via PVOs is elusive. It is clear that, again, PVOs have played important administrative roles, and it is likely that public and private activity is so intertwined in many situations that a precise delineation is not possible. According to one source, the refugee situation on the Thai-Cambodian border in the late 1970s attracted sixty PVOs, sixty governments, and five intergovernmental organizations.[51]

CONCLUSIONS

Some observers would like to return to a system of international humanitarian assistance which is essentially private.[52] This view reflects an erroneous understanding of the situation.

The reason that governments and intergovernmental organizations became involved was that the PVOs acknowledged the lack of financial and commodity resources to handle the problems, and asked public authorities for aid. It is only governments, especially the U.S. government, which have access to money and commodities in sufficient quantity to respond to the sizable humanitarian problems arising principally out of the developing countries. Particularly from the standpoint of donations of all types, but also at times from the standpoint of logistical support, governments must necessarily play a central role in international humanitarian assistance.

The U.S. government is likely to remain directly involved in all phases of international humanitarian relief, whether it is disaster relief centered around food, war relief, or refugee relief. The lead agencies like the ICRC and the UNHCR depend on that support, as do the charitable PVOs themselves. There is strong support for an active humanitarian assistance program in Congress, with some elements trying to increase the level of funding despite general budgetary and economic problems.[53] With considerable public support, Congress has protected the moral and humanitarian aspects of the Food for Peace Program. There is increased competency in AID and its Office of Disaster Relief, although questions remain about the sufficiency of ties to intelligence sources, proper staffing, and clarity of priorities.

NGOs like the ICRC, as well as IGOs like the UNHCR and the World Food Program, remain important to the United States as lead agencies and focal points for action. Many charitable PVOs are still seen as acceptable, flexible, knowledgeable conduits for assistance. The task for the U.S. is to find the proper mix of public and private agencies that will provide the best and most rapid delivery of assistance to those civilians in exceptional need.

The United States has shown over the years that there can be an assistance policy that is primarily driven by humanitarian concerns, even if at times strategic and economic considerations of an expediential sort get mixed in.[54] Some of this is inevitable in an imperfect world. The use of multilateral agencies and PVOs can help restrain this sort of influence, so that, at least at the margins of its foreign assistance program, the United States can claim without controversy to be a moral nation. So much the better if this form of morality turns out to be expediential as well.

NOTES

1. Bruce Russett and Harvey Starr, *World Politics: The Menu for Choice*, 2d ed. (New York: Freeman, 1985); Cecil V. Crabb, Jr., *American Foreign Policy in the Nuclear Age*, 4th ed. (New York: Harper and Row, 1983); John D. Montgomery, *Foreign Aid in International Politics* (Englewood Cliffs, N.J.: Prentice-Hall, 1967); David Baldwin, *Economic Statecraft* (Princeton: Princeton University Press, 1985).

2. Quoted from the Foreword of George Liska, *The New Statecraft* (Chicago: University of Chicago Press, 1960), p. ix.

3. Ibid., p. 1.

4. Rogers Smith's paper, this volume.

5. Edward S. Mason, *Foreign Aid and Foreign Policy* (New York: Harper and Row, 1964), p. 27.

6. For a penetrating analysis of self-image and image of others in foreign affairs see John Stoessinger, *Nations in Darkness*, 3rd ed. (New York: Random House, 1981).

7. Shue's paper, this volume.

8. Peter Macalister-Smith, *International Humanitarian Assistance: Disaster Relief Actions in International Law and Organization* (Dordrecht: Martinus Nijhoff, 1985), p. 3.

9. Susan Welch, "American Public Opinion: Consensus, Cleavage, and Constraint," in David P. Forsythe, ed., *American Foreign Policy in an Uncertain World* (Lincoln: University of Nebraska Press, 1984), pp. 21-48.

10. Michael K. O'Leary, *The Politics of American Foreign Aid* (New York: Atherton, 1967), p. 13.

11. U.S. Department of State, Commission on Security and Economic Assistance, *A Report to the Secretary of State*, November 1983, 74 pp.

12. E.g., Frances Moore Lappe et al., *Aid as Obstacle: Twenty Questions about Our Foreign Aid and the Hungry* (San Francisco: Institute for Food and Development, 1980), ch. 16.

13. O'Leary, *Politics of American Foreign Aid*, p. 111.

14. David P. Forsythe, *Humanitarian Politics: The International Committee of the Red Cross* (Baltimore: Johns Hopkins Press, 1977).

15. Macalister-Smith, *International Humanitarian Assistance*, p. 72.

16. Julia Chang Bloch in *U.S. Food Aid Programs and World Hunger,* Hearings, Subcommittee on Foreign Agricultural Policy, Committee on Agriculture, U.S. Senate, 99th Cong., 2d Sess. (Washington: GPO, 1986), p. 13.

17. Mitchel B. Wallerstein, *Food for War—Food for Peace: United States Food Aid in a Global Context* (Cambridge, Mass.: MIT Press, 1980), p. 31.

18. Ibid., p. 28. According to this source Hoover was quite prepared to use food relief for political purposes.

19. Ibid., p. 4.

20. Ibid., p. 29; Macalister-Smith, *International Humanitarian Assistance,* p. 13.

21. Louise W. Holborn, *The International Refugee Organization* (Oxford: Oxford University Press, 1956), Introduction.

22. Ibid.

23. Doug Bandow, ed., *Critical Issues—U.S. Aid to the Developing World: A Free Market Agenda* (Washington: The Heritage Foundation, 1985), especially chs. 1 and 2.

24. For a new interpretation of the Marshall Plan see Michael J. Hogan, *The Marshall Plan: America, Britain, and the Reconstruction of Western Europe, 1947–1952,* (Cambridge: Cambridge University Press, 1987). Particularly good on the political calculations behind the marshall Plan is James A. Nathan and James K. Oliver, *United States Foreign Policy and World Order* (Boston: Little-Brown, 4th ed., forthcoming).

25. John Cathie, *The Political Economy of Food Aid* (New York: St. Martin's Press, 1982), p. 19. And AID, "Thirty Years of Progress: The Food for Peace Program," *AID Highlights* 1, no. 1 (Spring 1984): 1. See also James R. Walczak, "New Directions in United States Food Aid," *Denver Journal of International Law and Politics* 8, special issue (1979): 543-71.

26. Cathie, *Political Economy of Food Aid,* p. 22; see also Wallerstein, *Food for War—Food for Peace.*

27. Senate Agricultural Hearings, 1986, note 16 above, p. 9.

28. *Enhancing the Effectiveness of the U.S. Government's Foreign Disaster Assistance Program: A Policy Analysis and Review with Recommendations,* Report, Select Committee on Hunger, U.S. House of Representatives, September 1986 (Washington: GPO, 1986).

29. See especially Cathie, *Political Economy of Food Aid,* p. 40.

30. Wallerstein, *Food for War—Food for Peace,* p. 63.

31. Ibid., p. 95.

32. David P. Forsythe, "Diplomatic Approaches to the Political Problems of Relief," in Lynn H. Stephens and Stephen J. Green, *Disaster Assistance: Appraisal, Reform and New Approaches* (New York: New

York University Press, 1979), pp. 267-92; and Macalister-Smith, *International Humanitarian Assistance.* The real problem is not the attitude of the developed states but rather the strong nationalism and commitment to the formalities of national sovereignty on this issue by the developing states. The United States simply defers to this state of affairs. For an interesting argument in behalf of an international legal right to food and disaster relief, see Dinah Shelton, "The Duty to Assist Famine Victims," *Iowa Law Review* 70, no. 5 (July 1985): 1309-19.

33. In Stephens and Green, *Disaster Assistance,* ch. 2 by Thomas Stephens; more recently see Macalister-Smith, *International Humanitarian Assistance,* and Cathie, *Political Economy of Food Aid.*

34. AID, "Disaster Assistance: A Proud American Tradition," *AID Highlights* 2, no. 1 (Winter 1985): 1. The table is an interpretation from House Report, note 28 above, p. 7. For an update see "U.S. Foreign Disaster Assistance FY86," in *Foreign Assistance and Related Programs Appropriations for 1988,* Hearings, Subcommittee on Foreign Operations, Committee on Appropriations, House, 100th Cong., 1st Sess. (Washington: GPO, 1987), 1401-05.

35. Statements of fact in this section, not otherwise attributed, are drawn from Forsythe, *Humanitarian Politics.*

36. It should be emphasized that the ICRC has other activities in armed conflict besides coordinating relief, such as attempting to protect prisoners of war, civilian detainees, and others entitled to a humane quarantine—and tracing missing persons. There is also medical assistance.

37. See J. D. Armstrong, "The International Committee of the Red Cross and Political Prisoners," *International Organization* 39, no. 4 (Autumn 1985): 615-42, which draws heavily on Forsythe, *Humanitarian Politics;* and Jacques Moreillon, *Le Comite International de la Croix-Rouge et la protection des detenus politiques* (Lausanne: L'Age d'homme, 1973).

38. Standard legal interpretations are Guy S. Goodwin-Gill, *The Refugee in International Law* (Oxford: Clarendon Press, 1983); and Atle Grahl-Madsen, *The Status of Refugees in International Law,* 2 vols. (Leiden: Sijthoff, 1966, 1972).

39. For a new interpretation see David P. Forsythe, "The Political Economy of UN Refugee Programs," in Forsythe, ed., *The United Nations in the World Political Economy* (London: Macmillan Ltd., 1989), forthcoming.

40. For a good discussion of these points see Harto Hakovirta, *Third World Conflicts and Refugeeism* (Helsinki: Finnish Society of Sciences and Letters, 1986), pp. 123-27.

41. The United States did support the International Refugee Organization, but it refused to become a party to the 1951 Refugee Con-

vention and held itself apart from the UNHCR until 1956. For an overview of UNRWA over the years see David P. Forsythe, "The Palestine Question: Dealing with a Long-term Refugee Situation," *Annals of the American Academy of Political and Social Science,* special issue on refugees, May 1983, pp. 89-101.

42. Polite executive criticism, hinting at management problems, is contained in James N. Purcell,nJr., Director of the Bureau for Refugee Programs, "Refugees: The Need for Continuing Support," *Current Policy* No. 752, Washington: Department of State, October 1985. For a sample of congressional criticism see *Reports on Refugee Aid,* Reports, Staff Study Missions for the Committee on Foreign Affairs, House of Representatives, 97th Cong., 1st Sess. (Washington: GPO, 1981). For private criticism of both the UNHCR and U.S. policy see William Shawcross, *The Quality of Mercy: Cambodia, Holocaust and Modern Conscience* (New York: Simon and Schuster, 1984).

43. Hakovirta, *Third World Conflicts and Refugeeism.*

44. "Foreign Assistance and Related Programs Appropriations for 1988," Hearings, note 34 above, p. 130.

45. Both aspects are acknowledged in ibid.

46. Shawcross, *The Quality of Mercy,* argues that the UNHCR was reluctant to press the United States about its rejection of refugee claims arising out of Haiti and El Salvador because of U.S. contributions to the agency. But for an example of UNHCR legal involvement via an *amicus curiae* brief that successfully challenged U.S. policy concerning a refugee from Nicaragua, see the brief in question in the case of *INS v Cardoza-Fonseca,* decided by the U.S. Supreme Court, March 9, 1987. Court reasoning closely follows the UNHCR brief. In 1987 and 1988, press reports indicated growing PVO disenchantment with the new leadership of the UNHCR on the grounds that the agency was too deferential to donor governments and not attentive enough to refugee needs.

47. Wallerstein, *Food for War—Food for Peace,* pp. 48-51.

48. See Senate agricultural hearings, 1986, note 16 above, p. 12.

49. For an overview see Landrum R. Bolling, with Craig Smith, *Private Foreign Aid: U.S. Philanthropy for Relief and Development* (Boulder, Colo.: Westview Press, 1982). See also Merle Curti, *American Philanthropy Abroad: A History* (New Brunswick: Rutgers University Press, 1963).

50. The Hunger Project, *Ending Hunger: An Idea Whose Time Has Come* (New York: Praeger, 1985), p. 215. *Status of American Foreign Food Assistance Programs,* Hearing, Subcommittee on Agricultural Research, Committee on Agriculture, Senate, 100th Cong., 1st Sess. (Washington: GPO, 1987), 5.

51. Shawcross, *The Quality of Mercy,* p. 219.

52. The Heritage Foundation, as cited in note 23 above.

53. House report, 1986, note 28 above.

54. These expediential uses of disaster assistance are acknowledged and criticized in ibid.

HUMANITARIAN ACTION AND INTERNATIONAL LAW

Peter Macalister-Smith

INTRODUCTION

It seems reasonable to start out from the assumption that present humanitarian efforts are inadequate and could be improved. Despite some progress in the humanitarian field, it is apparent that the need for urgent humanitarian action continues to grow, as demonstrated by contemporary events in Africa, Latin America and elsewhere. At the same time, the methods and even the objectives of such action are increasingly called into question. The considerable experience of development aid, refugee assistance and disaster relief accumulated at the national and international levels over recent decades is helping to alleviate some suffering and poverty, but the basic causes of these problems have hardly been attacked. Moreover, the shortcomings of humanitarian action at times may contribute to creating even worse disasters than would otherwise occur.[1]

A very broad spectrum of humanitarian problems can be discerned. At one end could be situated some of the chronic problems of growth and progress which face both developed and developing regions alike, although in their severest forms these problems disproportionately affect the developing countries. At the other extreme are the so-called purely "natural" disasters apparently caused by natural phenomena such as earthquakes and droughts. Such disasters, which are increasing in frequency and severity, are misnamed because in reality they are usually the result of a mixture of causes, partly natural and partly man-made, nearly always including an important component which reflects people's relationship with their environment.

In addition, major industrial accidents and technological disasters resulting from the pursuit of ultrahazardous activities, such as the nuclear industry, must be included. Internal conflicts, wars, other military activities, refugee movements, and economic migrations complete the picture of human misery.

Although the action taken in specific cases has often been inadequate in relation to the needs which have had to be met, humanitarian principles themselves have received not only moral but also legal expression at both the national and international levels throughout the twentieth century, and indeed long before.[2] However, while in theory the potential ambit of humanitarian law can extend to all situations of human suffering and need, in fact the development of law applicable to humanitarian actions in peacetime remains largely a task still to be undertaken.

In armed conflict, the right of individuals to receive humane treatment, and the right of humanitarian organizations, in particular the Red Cross and Red Crescent movement, to carry out humanitarian actions, are legally established in the Geneva Conventions and their additional Protocols, albeit subject to many conditions. This alone cannot guarantee that humanitarian principles are upheld in conflict situations, or that suffering people are always adequately cared for, but at least such legal rights provide an important foundation enabling the Red Cross and Red Crescent movement to maintain its humanitarian presence in situations where the victims might otherwise be left without help.

In view of the considerable needs, it may seem paradoxical that there is at present no binding global international legal instrument devoted to humanitarian action outside the context of armed conflict. The short explanation lies in the fact that it proved to be in the interests of at least some states to attempt to regulate one aspect of warfare, namely, here, that affecting the welfare of their soldiers. The real or potential self-interest of states in carrying out humanitarian actions in peacetime, on the other hand, has not yet become sufficiently apparent to either governments or enough people. Only then can international regulation of humanitarian action be developed more systematically than at present.[3]

Historical forces have led to the establishment of the present highly diversified humanitarian system with its largely separate, mutually exclusive and even competing elements concerned *inter alia* with relief actions in war, refugees, children, food, health, and development generally, all lacking effective coordination. In these circumstances, what may be in the interests of the whole is often perceived to be against the interests of one component or another of the system. The result is that response and evolution are neither planned nor progressive but depend instead on the ongoing outcome of a more or less political struggle for survival and supremacy within the humanitarian movement itself.

Nevertheless, and although there is no room for undue optimism, the virtually certain continuing recurrence of major problems requiring humanitarian action suggests that those concerned with future policy in this area must give increased attention to the role of international law and organization which have so far proved to be among the factors working in favor of some real progress in the field.

Many of the problems now confronting international law and organization reflect the interdependence of the interests of states. Such problems, some of which were once considered to lie solely within domestic jurisdiction, include those of world population, finite resources, availability of food and energy, and the environment. The increasingly wide concerns of international law and organization are gradually being extended to matters related to the well-being not only of states, but also of individuals. However, international law, while concerned to varying degrees with the many and diverse relations of states, does not regulate these relations exclusively, comprehensively, or systematically. Broadly speaking, there is no firm separation between law and politics in international relations. Attempts to give international law a truly global form in all its aspects have not yet reached fruition, and it remains essentially a form of law between states and not above them.

Law is an instrument which supports policy. It carries purposes and objectives, often conservative and lagging behind social requirements, but also capable of playing a leading role in bringing about necessary change. The potential of all law, national and international, is to serve the interests of human beings, who are always its ultimate creators and addressees. As will be seen, the development of international humanitarian law has not matched the expansion of functional or operational humanitarian activities, and much less the human needs which remain to be met, and this has in turn hindered the work and the further development of the existing humanitarian organizations and structures. Herein, then, is a challenge for those involved with humanitarian matters, whether from the standpoint of politics, law, or administration.

HISTORICAL AND COMPARATIVE BACKGROUND

In armed conflict, efforts to limit the use of force and to mitigate its destructive consequences are probably as old as the history of mankind. Yet despite the fact that many early civilizations reveal evidence of the existence of humanitarian concepts, it is certain that the advance of humanitarian customs was generally slow. Only the secular movement of nineteenth century humanitarianism provided a new impetus towards the legal codification of humanitarian principles, leading to the adoption of the original Geneva Convention of 1864 and to the creation of the Red Cross and Red Crescent movement.[4] The 1864 convention gave legal protection to field ambulances, military hospitals, and their personnel, and it reflected a special priority accorded to humanitarian action in favor of the members of armed forces, based on practical considerations. The convention provided the foundation for the subsequent development of the humanitarian law of armed conflict, culminating in the 1949 Geneva Conventions and their additional Protocols of 1977.[5]

Probably the first large-scale international humanitarian operation was undertaken during World War I on behalf of the starving civilian populations of occupied Belgium and northern France, without a formal legal basis except for the exchange of certain notes of understanding between the parties concerned. In this undertaking, the Commission for Relief in Belgium (CRB), founded by Herbert Hoover in London in 1914 as a neutral relief agency, set lasting precedents for the conception and organization of later humanitarian assistance programs.[6] The commission's operational independence, backed by considerable American support and a network of assisting voluntary organizations, enabled it to develop a degree of international cooperation previously unknown in humanitarian matters, and which was only repeated in conception and scale during and after World War II in the operations of the United Nations Relief and Rehabilitation Administration (UNRRA).[7]

Turning to wholly peacetime relief actions, it is clear that the ideal of humanitarian service has been expressed in all regions of the world since antiquity in the form of samaritan work, usually organized in response to immediate needs. Nevertheless, with the exception of some early religious charitable orders which operated on a transnational basis, truly international cooperation in relief actions is largely a phenomenon of the twentieth century.

Taking a significant initiative at the end of World War I, the American National Red Cross proposed that financial resources be devoted to international public health work and to organizing international disaster relief, providing the motivation for the national Red Cross and Red Crescent Societies to create their federal organization, the League of Red Cross Societies, a few weeks before the signing of the Covenant of the League of Nations in 1919. Shortly thereafter, the disastrous famine in Russia in 1921 led to the establishment of several international relief commissions, mostly of a nongovernmental nature. The operations of the American Relief Administration to bring relief to the needy, especially children, are well known and were conducted partly on the basis of an unusual agreement concluded with the Soviet authorities, while in other situations many different types of humanitarian action were also undertaken by American organizations.[8]

The League of Nations, as the first governmental institution of the potentially universal type, offered a new opportunity for the development of humanitarian principles and action at the international level. The 1927 Convention establishing an International Relief Union was adopted and eventually ratified by some thirty states.[9] The convention did not expressly formulate a right to relief but sought to further the progress of international law in this field as well as to provide a basis for practical action in the field. The Union itself was ill-fated, however, being a premature institutionalization of international humanitarian concern, which by the outbreak of World War II had outlived its useful existence.

Humanitarian action on behalf of refugees also first became a matter for international organization in the aftermath of World

War I. Due to initiatives within the League of Nations, refugees gradually came to have greater benefits as a result of collective measures taken beyond the immediate interests of the states of origin and refuge. However, neither the Covenant of the League nor general practice established any binding obligations for the assumption of permanent responsibility for humanitarian action in the form of material assistance. Legal protection of refugees rather than assistance was nearly always the dominant theme until the creation of UNRRA, which was the first and major operating agency on behalf of refugees and displaced persons until it was replaced by the International Refugee Organization and subsequently by the Office of the United Nations High Commissioner for Refugees.[10]

Upon UNRRA's termination, the patterns were set for post-World War II humanitarian efforts. Aid from the United States was continued under the European Recovery Program, better known as the Marshall Plan.[11] In the multilateral sector, UNRRA's most direct successor was the United Nations Children's Fund, while projects in the field of agriculture and health became the responsibilities respectively of the Food and Agriculture Organization and the World Health Organization. The earlier underlying concept of sharing resources by gathering them on the basis of availability and distributing them in accordance with needs was abandoned in favor of a division of functions, leading to the emergence of a new piecemeal policy.

The states members of the United Nations were increasingly unwilling or unable to maintain their cooperative approach to humanitarian problems at such a high level as before. Nevertheless, the concept itself of achieving international cooperation in the solution of international humanitarian problems found a place in the statement of fundamental purposes of the United Nations, in Article 1 of the UN Charter.[12] The form and circumstances of humanitarian operations remained to be determined thereafter in practice.

SOURCES AND FOUNDATIONS OF HUMANITARIAN LAW

Beyond the context of armed conflict, there is no international body of treaty law relating exclusively to humanitarian action. The Geneva Conventions and their additional Protocols constitute a highly evolved and complex body of law relevant to humanitarian action, in which the strongest rights and duties concern victims of international conflict who are members of armed forces, both in conflict and as prisoners of war. Under the Conventions and Protocols, protection of and assistance to civilians is dealt with only in much weaker and more restricted terms. In noninternational conflicts there are few if any unqualified legal rights or duties in this field resulting from international law.

As to peacetime humanitarian actions, there is a paucity of relevant treaties. There are some bilateral treaties of direct interest, however, and many scattered provisions of relevance in other instruments. Such provisions are found, for example, in treaties relating to health and epidemics, to international transportation, and to the environment and pollution. The question of treaty law in this area is thus a matter requiring detailed investigation and presentation, which cannot be attempted here.[13] Moreover, an adequate treatment would involve not only analysis of the formal legal position in each case, but also of implementation of and compliance with the law, requiring a lengthy comparative survey.

Turning to customary international law, the usual view is that the creation of a customary rule requires two elements: first, the existence of a general practice of states; and second, the acceptance by states of the practice as law.[14] If this is correct, international humanitarian practice alone, however extensive, is not capable of leading by itself to the creation of customary humanitarian law. Since state practice includes collective acts, the activities of states through international organizations can be a factor in the development of international law, but the resolutions of the United Nations, for example, which concern humanitarian assistance do not claim to embody general or particular international law. Nevertheless, on the basis of the good number of existing UN resolutions which are seeking to establish policy in this field, it may be possible to further develop some principles—and eventually even legal principles—relating to humanitarian action.[15] At the same time it must be admitted that the uncertainty as to the general character of humanitarian practices and, above all, the influence of political factors in humanitarian action, work firmly against the crystallization of particular international legal rules in this area.

Some are of the opinion that international humanitarian action, rather than possessing any legal characteristics, is essentially a matter of comity, courtesy, or international good neighborliness. By definition, the rules of international comity lack a legal nature, although a broad conception of comity extends so far as to include basic notions of international solidarity and cooperation.[16] Thus, fundamental humanitarian considerations may form the basis for legal principles in international law without themselves having the status of law. On the other hand, since fundamental humanitarian interests are universal and common to everyone, they may in some circumstances take on a special higher status, even an international legal status of an inalienable nature. However, this is an area in which great difficulties are encountered in establishing the existence of such a legal principle of general humanitarian consideration.[17]

Respect for state sovereignty is a central principle of international law, also applicable to humanitarian action.[18] A government may request international assistance or it may choose to deal with humanitarian problems in its own way. Likewise, international law imposes no obligation on states to agree to requests for assistance or to make offers of contributions. At the same time, the duty of states to achieve international cooperation in solving international problems, explicitly including those of humanitarian nature, was laid down in Article 1 (3) of the UN Charter, and this duty probably has the character of a general principle of international law.[19] It should therefore take an important place as a basic factor in establishing global policy relating to humanitarian action. One manifestation of the principle of cooperation could be the recognition of a duty of samaritanism in international law.

Article 55 of the UN Charter, dealing with economic and social cooperation, sets out a basis for UN human rights activities, but no field referred to corresponds explicitly to the humanitarian problems included in Article 1(3). In other words, humanitarian problems were raised once only in the Charter, in general terms together with other problems, and were then ignored. Moreover, a clash may arise between Article 1(3) of the Charter and the provisions of Articles 2(4) and 2(7) insofar as humanitarian problems are matters within the domestic jurisdiction of states and thus protected from intervention both by states individually or collectively and by the UN itself.

Among the provisions of human rights instruments which take on special significance in the humanitarian context are the rights to life, health, food, and shelter, and to special care for children and the sick. First among all human rights is the right to life, but insufficient attention has been given to the fact that this most basic human right, together with others, is threatened both by the consequences of disasters and by the failures of humanitarian actions.[20] The relevance of basic human rights to humanitarian action is made more clear when rights to the minimum necessities of life are considered, including a right to food.

The issues of development, human rights, and humanitarian actions are closely associated with one another, especially in the context of world food security.[21] From this perspective, it seems that a coordinated system of humanitarian action may best be viewed as a concomitant of an appropriate international development strategy. However, the idea of need as a basis for entitlement has not yet been accepted by states in legal commitments to programs of action embodying the concept.

Finally, to give one pertinent example from treaty law, it is worth noting briefly that the principle of rescue or emergency humanitarian assistance has been established as a binding legal obligation in the special areas of maritime and astronautical safety, on the basis of a number of national and international instruments which are widely accepted around the world.[22] In developing this branch of international law relating to transportation accidents, states found it to be in their best interests to cooperate with regard to predictable emergencies involving a risk to human life in areas outside their territorial jurisdiction, in particular involving ships on the high seas. The provisions in question well illustrate the adoption of a universal moral humanitarian obligation into legal form through state practice and codification.

THE CONTEMPORARY HUMANITARIAN SYSTEM

National Responsibilities

The degree of responsibility for humanitarian action assumed at the national level by both the governmental authorities and the general population is frequently underestimated. In humanitarian emergencies the material and personal contributions made by the people of the affected region, including the efforts of the victims themselves, can be on a scale that is greater than that of any international assistance which may be provided. The sense of human solidarity generated by a disaster is strongest at the local and national levels and complements the duty of the public authorities to respond with measures within their ability and resources.

Probably no government would deny publicly that humanitarian action in case of need is a primary responsibility of the state concerned. The most basic legal constitutional concepts recognized by most countries, such as the maintenance of public order, the promotion of welfare, and the protection of fundamental rights of an economic, social, and political nature, are all relevant in situations where humanitarian action is required. Thus, the national government in a disaster-affected country can be said to have a duty to respond with humanitarian assistance or other necessary measures, even though in practice the authorities may not have adequate means to take action, or may be unwilling or unable for political reasons to do so. In addition, the functions of prevention, preparedness, and pre-disaster planning, often based on legal or quasi-legal administrative foundations, are also primary responsibilities of the public authorities at the national level.

Some functions in humanitarian operations can be performed only by the national public authorities, except in the most exceptional circumstances. Such functions include notification of an impending disaster to a threatened population, formulating and broadcasting other official announcements, and supervising relief tasks. Even assessment of needs, distribution of assistance, monitoring of operations, and evaluation are primary responsibilities of national authorities under normal circumstances.

In this regard, the UN General Assembly resolution which established the Office of the United Nations Disaster Relief Coordinator (UNDRO), contained a number of subparagraphs addressed to potential recipient states including recommendations relating to measures to be taken at the national level.[23] More recent resolutions have reaffirmed the primary responsibilities of national authorities. However, unfortunately, the worst disasters in which humanitarian action is required rarely if ever occur in circumstances where national authorities are able to respond adequately and effectively.

Bilateral Action

The most important international contributions to humanitarian operations are frequently made bilaterally. In such situations the direct provision of assistance by one state to another is an area where humanitarian and political considerations are closely interwoven. Humanitarian assistance is not usually given in the expectation of reciprocal treatment in the future, and it is frequently provided to countries with few resources and great problems of economic and social development. On occasion, humanitarian actions are also undertaken across ideological frontiers. Contributions are often accompanied by an expression of sentiments of humanitarian obligation, albeit of a nonbinding nature.

The existence of established bilateral relations provides a common basis for the extension of assistance in time of need, and some states undoubtedly consider that bilateral donation provides the most effective way of delivering their contributions, avoiding delays inherent in the procedures of intermediary organizations. Another advantage is that donor states may be able to maintain the individual identity of their contributions. However, the potential benefits of bilateral actions must be offset against the inevitably increased problems of coordination of the overall international response.

The offer through diplomatic channels of a sum of money provides a simple method of bilateral action involving no association with humanitarian operations themselves. Alternatively, assistance may be supplied in kind and delivered to a port of entry or to the zone of operations. In some cases humanitarian actions may be undertaken in accordance with the terms of a bilateral agreement concluded with the recipient party. In the case of assistance provided on a government-to-government basis, such agreements frequently take the form of an exchange of letters at the ambassadorial level. A bilateral agreement may provide for relief to be supplied to the national or local public authorities or also to nongovernmental agencies.

Legal agreements of a general or specific nature concluded

in advance in order to establish contingency procedures and to facilitate future humanitarian operations are much more the exception than the rule. In many areas of policy, including the humanitarian, states have proved to be extremely reluctant to commit themselves in advance. However, some bilateral agreements between states have laid down provisions in considerable detail governing relief and planning in cases of disaster, especially in frontier areas,[24] with regard to nuclear safety and radiation accidents,[25] and concerning other types of environmental emergencies.[26] Although not widely known, these texts and the approaches on which they are based can serve as useful examples for further development.

Multilateral and Other Actors

The United Nations System

In the aftermath of World War II large-scale humanitarian actions were carried out for several years by intergovernmental organizations of an operational nature established principally by the Western Allies. Increasing support was also given to the humanitarian programs of the United Nations specialized agencies and subsidiary organs. The expansion of humanitarian activities through these bodies up to the present time has involved the majority of states, both as members and as donors or recipients of assistance.

Among the subsidiary organs created by the United Nations are several with primary responsibilities extending into the humanitarian field, including the Office of the United Nations High Commissioner for Refugees (UNHCR),[27] the United Nations Children's Fund (UNICEF),[28] the more specific operational agencies such as the United Nations Relief and Works Agency for Palestinian refugees in the Near East (UNRWA),[29] as well as the Office of the United Nations Disaster Relief Co-ordinator (UNDRO),[30] and a considerable variety of ad hoc bodies. The United Nations Development Programme (UNDP)[31] has also evolved various roles in connection with humanitarian action. As examples of specialized agencies with humanitarian tasks, the Food and Agriculture Organization (FAO)[32] and the World Health Organization (WHO)[33] may also be mentioned. The International Atomic Energy Agency (IAEA)[34] is also concerned with emergency assistance in the event of several types of accidents involving radiation. The United States is among the major financial donors to these bodies and in some cases provides the largest contribution of funds.

Within the United Nations itself, early resolutions relating to humanitarian problems at first followed much the same pattern for a number of years. Adopted upon the occurrence of specific disasters, they expressed sympathy with the afflicted state and they attempted to stimulate relief offers by putting forward an invitation to contribute assistance. The next period was characterized by the realization on the part of various member states and of the Secretariat that the United Nations, although possessing a fundamental potential humanitarian role, lacked adequate procedures for practical response. After gaining experience in a number of international relief operations, re-evaluation resulted in a belated movement to place the UN Secretariat more at the center of international humanitarian activities. However, the principal specialized agencies concerned had by then developed their own largely independent responses. In addition, only some member states favored a stronger role for the United Nations in this field.

The emergence of humanitarian problems where there was little or no effective UN response represented a further turning point into the present period of mass humanitarian emergencies.[35] The failure of attempts to equate international relief in natural disasters with relief in armed conflict situations, and the increasing role of the UN Secretary-General, including in relief coordination, are two features of this more recent period. The Secretary-General's good offices have continued to be invoked on many occasions of humanitarian need, and have received endorsement by the political organs.[36]

Up to the present, the consistently repeated themes which emerge in the relevant UN resolutions and reports are the following: the problems of coordination, both within and beyond the UN system; national responsibility, in particular for preparedness, which includes a link to international action; and the importance of comprehensive information-sharing. Attention is also being given to the potential contribution of modern forms of technology, especially in information gathering, monitoring, communication, logistics, and planning generally.

The Red Cross and Red Crescent Movement

The Red Cross and Red Crescent movement has a complex organizational structure, with various focal points and channels for its humanitarian activities. The movement comprises national Red Cross and Red Crescent Societies which are auxiliaries to the medical services of national armed forces, as well as the International Committee of the Red Cross, and the League of Red Cross and Red Crescent Societies. The movement's supreme deliberative body is the International Conference of the Red Cross and Red Crescent, which is composed of delegations of all the above-mentioned institutions and of states parties to the Geneva Conventions.[37] Although taking part in the Conference, states are not members of the movement, and there is no commitment of powers by governments. The largest financial contribution to the movement is made by Switzerland.

The statutes of the movement refer to the fundamental principles of the Red Cross and Red Crescent, first among which is the principle of humanity: that the movement endeavors to prevent and alleviate human suffering wherever it may be found. The other principles are those of impartiality, neutrality, independence, voluntary service, unity, and universality. States have recognized the fundamental principles as basic determinants of the movement's assistance actions for the benefit of victims of conflict by including mention of them in the Geneva Conventions and additional Protocols, and it cannot be denied that these principles deserve to be better known and more widely applied.

Two Conference resolutions adopted in 1969 attempt to provide a comprehensive strategy for international relief actions by the movement. The first resolution takes the form of a short declaration, entitled Principles for International Humanitarian Relief to the Civilian Population in Disaster Situations,[38] which is notable in that it concerns, equally, relief actions in armed conflict and so-called natural disaster situations. The second resolution approved a set of principles and rules for Red Cross disaster relief, which provides a detailed basis for regulating the relief actions of the movement in disaster situations.[39]

The Red Cross and Red Crescent work on a long-term basis for humanitarian ends, seeking to be acceptable to all types of governments. The capacity of the movement for extensive humanitarian action in areas without clear authority in a specific body of law indicates the extent of the fund of respect and goodwill which it has built up internationally and nationally, maintained by intimate and confidential links of diplomacy. The movement has acquired a status beyond its formal legal status which may enable it to act in humanitarian situations at least as effectively as any other permanent international organization.

The present period of evolution is of considerable importance for the Red Cross and Red Crescent. The law of armed conflict has flourished in a formal sense during the twentieth century, but its central principle of respect for the human person is threatened by the existence of weapons of mass destruction. The problem of mass suffering arising from injustices and inequalities in the world is also a severe test for the movement's principles and traditional forms of response. Thus, the task of both maintaining and further extending the basis for humanitarian action in future situations of great need is likely to remain among the principal concerns of the movement.

Other Organizations and Actors

The humanitarian policies and activities of the European Economic Community (EEC) are closely associated with the Community's development cooperation programs which involve many developing countries and various aid instrumentalities. EEC disaster relief is provided mainly in three ways: to states of the African, Caribbean, and Pacific (ACP) group under the emergency assistance provisions of the Lomé Conventions; to any beneficiary, under the provisions for cash payments in the Community budget; and in the form of special food aid. [40] Important contributions are supplied by the EEC to international governmental and nongovernmental organizations involved in humanitarian actions. In addition, the EEC may conclude special agreements providing for humanitarian assistance to associated and nonassociated states or other parties.

Whether EEC food aid should be dependent on the internal agricultural policy of the region, or whether it should form part of the EEC's external development aid policy remains an unresolved question. EEC member states are still unable to agree on the size and duration of community aid commitments and they do not all give the same priority to emergency assistance. Moreover, the associated ACP states generally consider the sums available to be insufficient. Thus, a full definition of EEC humanitarian policy is still emerging.

Within other regional intergovernmental organizations various developments have arisen from approaches to disaster relief and pre-disaster planning, including in the Council of Europe, the North Atlantic Treaty Organization, the Organization of American States and the Association of South East Asian Nations. Apart from these regional developments, other international organizations of a more specialized nature, particularly in the field of transport and transit of goods and persons, can play a role in the humanitarian system. For example, the Customs Cooperation Council, an intergovernmental organization established in 1950 and having worldwide activities and influence in customs matters, promoted the Kyoto Convention to simplify customs procedures which includes an annex adopted in Brussels in 1976 relating to urgent consignments, including relief materials.[41]

Mention could also be made of other organizations and actors on the international scene that play a role in the humanitarian system. The Holy See, for example, and the Sovereign Order of Malta both lack the conventional elements of a state but nevertheless have a certain international personality recognized in international law. In particular in the case of the Holy See, this personality is manifested in a wide variety of activities, including those in the humanitarian sphere at the legal and functional levels.

The Role of Nongovernmental Organizations

An important role in humanitarian action is played by a wide variety of national and international nongovernmental organizations (NGOs), albeit a role which cannot easily be characterized or precisely quantified. While particular mention deserves to be made of the activities of the specialized humanitarian NGOs, including many different religious and secular organizations, difficulties arise in fully acknowledging their contribution within the perspective of public international law. This is so because international law does not regulate the establishment of NGOs, nor provide a legal status for them. Thus, for example, there appear to be no agreements granting international NGOs a unified legal capacity throughout the territory of states in which they carry out their activities, and international humanitarian NGOs and their personnel do not usually benefit from any special privileges, facilities, or immunities under international law.

The UN Charter acknowledges the existence of NGOs as a group by providing a basis for regulating NGO participation in the work of the UN Economic and Social Council through the establishment of consultative relations.[42] The system of consultation is intended to permit the securing of information and advice from organizations with particular competencies. However, despite the development of cooperation between the United Nations and NGOs in humanitarian matters, the difference between truly effective participation and the present arrangements for consultation is still fundamental. Entities which are not states are still far from being in a position to contribute decisively to the shaping of international policy.

On the other hand, it is obvious that the assumption of certain responsibilities for humanitarian action by states in bilateral relations and through intergovernmental organizations has in no way undermined the importance of private and nongovernmental activity.[43] Development and humanitarian action pursued through governmental channels is likely to continue to be problematical and even counterproductive because of several inherent and fundamental factors which are high among the causes of problems of poverty, disaster vulnerability, famine and starvation. These problems have economic and political causes, and cannot be tackled only in narrow terms, for example by increasing production in the agricultural or other sectors. In particular, the influence of long-term political factors in perpetuating inequalities and injustice could be emphasized.

The issue concerning the state and its government cannot be

easily ignored, for in an essential form this issue reflects reality at all levels of social interaction: namely, that a policy which benefits the weak or the poor will only be accepted by the members of the dominant group if it also serves the latter's own interests in some way.

In this context, the first claim to recognition of an international status for NGOs and their work remains the pragmatic toleration and acceptance of their *de facto* existence. NGOs have no choice but to operate within the framework of state control, albeit loosely at times. What seems important, however, is simply that international humanitarian NGOs exist and carry out their activities, thereby reinforcing the significance of private and individual action in international relations.

COORDINATION OF HUMANITARIAN ASSISTANCE

Humanitarian action in armed conflict and other disasters can involve a great variety of institutions and participants all operating simultaneously, including national civil defense organizations, military units, Red Cross and Red Crescent Societies, international governmental organizations and nongovernmental organizations. Coordination, in particular of humanitarian assistance or operational relief actions, is therefore inevitably a complex and delicate matter. This is all the more so because the concept of coordination is relevant to both donor and recipient parties.

The political problems inherent in many situations where humanitarian action is required create additional difficulties. Indeed, even the basic task of transmitting information can raise not only questions of the limits of institutional independence, for example with respect to verification or assessment of needs, but also the possibility of differences with official sources, thereby further complicating the process of coordination.

The success of coordination can do much to remove the confusion which may accompany humanitarian operations, although to a certain extent some such confusion is by definition inherent in all situations where emergency actions are required. Since it is not questioned that the overall effectiveness of humanitarian operations can be improved by coordination designed to take into account the contribution of the many different organizations and forms of relief administration involved, an important problem of humanitarian action at the global level is to define and to achieve the most appropriate national and international coordination mechanisms.

During the 1960s and early 1970s various proposals were made to improve the coordination of relief actions.[44] In 1971 a comprehensive report of the UN Secretary-General envisaged the creation of a UN disaster office, while various emergency situations at this period demonstrated the need for permanently establishing an effective relief coordination mechanism.[45] General Assembly Resolution 2816 (XXVI), entitled "Assistance in cases of natural disaster and other disaster situations" and adopted in December 1971, established in Geneva the Office of the United Nations Disaster Relief Co-ordinator, who is appointed for a term of five years.

UNDRO was created to be the focal point in the United Nations system for disaster relief matters. Although UNDRO was enabled to receive and channel donations for relief operations, the office was not conceived as a relief agency but rather as a central service to governments and organizations engaged in disaster-related activities. The Co-ordinator was authorized to "mobilize, direct and co-ordinate"[46] the relief activities of the UN system in response to a request for disaster assistance from a stricken state. Numerous other functions were also laid down.

In practice, however, UNDRO was not able to mobilize, direct, or coordinate relief efforts in a systematic way. Many of the organizations concerned were simply not willing to be coordinated, even if such a function would have been possible with UNDRO's limited resources. In addition, a number of other problems remained open, including the meaning of the expression "other disaster situations" which occurs in UNDRO's mandate and was never clearly defined.

Two important studies published in 1980 and 1981, undertaken with a view to strengthening UN relief coordination, revealed continuing problems. An evaluation report on UNDRO emphasized the uncertainties over the intended responsibilities of the office and noted that UNDRO's function of mobilizing, directing, and coordinating UN relief activities had in practice been successfully resisted by most UN organizations concerned.[47] The second UN study concluded that the main progress achieved during the previous ten years consisted in the strengthening of the resources available to the individual agencies rather than in the creation of working coordination procedures.[48]

Within the context of coordination, legal means have been considered to adopt certain measures designed to expedite international relief.[49] However, these measures have not yet been adopted in a binding form. Such legal moves relating to coordination and humanitarian action may yet prove to be necessary steps in the process of the closer definition by states of the parameters within which the donation, acceptance, and coordination of humanitarian assistance will be undertaken in the future.

SOME CONCLUSIONS

Legal rights and duties with regard to humanitarian action already exist in certain restricted circumstances, in particular under the terms of existing international instruments applicable in armed conflict and in the important area of rescue at sea. However, extending such rights and duties to humanitarian action in the situations of greatest need is a difficult task which remains to be achieved. The problem for the development of humanitarian law is that it should be based on objective criteria of human need, but must also take account of the practical political requirements of donor and recipient states.

Although the pressure of urgent circumstances alone is often found to be the motivating force behind developments at the operational level, only comparatively slow change or progress may be expected with regard to the assumption by states of binding or general responsibilities. Thus, several of the important UN specialized agencies and subsidiary organs involved in humanitarian action have undergone considerable change over the course of time, but this has tended to come about mostly through interpretation and usage rather than through formal amendments. Functional responsibilities have not been transformed into legal duties.

The problem of international legal measures relating to humanitarian action appears to arise at several levels. One important level concerns technical arrangements to expedite assistance; the concern here is with measures which facilitate the efficient delivery of relief consignments, the movement and functioning of relief personnel, and arrangements in connection with communications. A further level of legal interest relates to the principles of humanitarian action, which are still neither universally nor uniformly recognized; nevertheless, developments in humanitarian activities undertaken by states bilaterally, by governmental and nongovernmental organizations and by private individuals all contribute to establishing standards of responsibility for disaster victims, and they provide some norms for the conduct and evaluation of humanitarian operations. A third task is to relate existing legal and operational approaches in the field of humanitarian action to contemporary understanding of the role and purposes of international law and thereby to indicate the scope for development of both humanitarian law and action. In essence, this means how to establish a broad field of humanitarian law relevant to all who may require international assistance.

There is considerable merit in the legal approach based on relatively detailed technical rules, because progress depends ultimately on the success of practical measures. At the same time, a framework of principles relating to humanitarian action would usefully supplement any technical measure, if such principles could be both reasonably comprehensive and widely acceptable. More broadly, it could be appropriate to re-examine the foundations for international humanitarian cooperation, in particular those contained in Article 1(3) of the UN Charter which are no longer adequate to meet the current need for humanitarian action. These foundations should be developed and reinforced so as to allow them to serve as a basis for legal, organizational, and functional progress, all interdependent prerequisites of an improved humanitarian order. The importance of firm foundations for humanitarian policy as well as guiding principles for action, and in addition the necessary technical measures, should all be emphasized more than ever in a period of greatly increased humanitarian needs.

In seeking progress in the humanitarian field, it has become clear that the attempt to extend and improve humanitarian actions themselves also involves—however slightly—an attempt to change the whole humanitarian order, or the context in which humanitarian problems and responses interact. At the same time it may be perceived that some fundamental constraints seem to operate, which hinder such change or prevent it from being too rapid.

Since at least the time of the League of Nations, international law and organization have manifested a greatly increased attention to the situation of the individual, and individuals have increasingly become the beneficiaries of international acts. However, these developments have not led to recognition of a commensurate transformation in the international legal position of the individual. States and the doctrine of state sovereignty remain cornerstones of international law, although in reality individuals are both the creators and ultimate addressees of all law, national and international. People continue to be subordinated to the power, and law, of the state. International law in turn continues to give primary emphasis to the interests of states rather than to individual human values.

The field of human rights highlights an underlying problem which to some extent is symptomatic of the whole international order. The problem stems from a fundamental contradiction in this field, namely, that human rights law and its accompanying mechanisms are the creations of states, yet have the supposed purpose of protecting the citizen from abuses perpetrated by those same entities. This contradiction or dichotomy between the interests of the state and those of people goes a long way toward explaining the gap which exists between law and practice in many different fields of international relations, especially where human welfare is concerned.

Accompanying this underlying problem it may be observed that many humanitarian actions, like most if not all governmental humanitarian organizations, are designed only to alleviate symptoms and not to tackle basic causes.

The practical response to humanitarian emergencies at the national and international levels is still of a fragmentary nature, and the global humanitarian system has only barely evolved beyond a mere series of ad hoc reactions. The United Nations was supposed to be a center for coordinating the specialized agencies and subsidiary organs, but most of them presently retain considerable autonomy. There is even much competition in humanitarian matters. Whatever future developments take place in the field of humanitarian action, it therefore seems certain that the need to improve the coordination mechanisms at the national and international levels will remain for the foreseeable future. Yet while the need for coordination within the international humanitarian system is generally accepted, it has proved extremely difficult in practice to define coordination more closely, and to agree on necessary measures. Probably no one would deny being in favor of coordination of humanitarian action in principle, but the real problems arise in practice in determining who shall coordinate and who shall be coordinated.

While it is only gradually becoming clear what steps are required or are likely to be acceptable to confront increasing humanitarian problems, at least it is fully apparent that increased international cooperation is necessary in order to extend and improve the effectiveness of humanitarian actions. Greatly increased international cooperation is also required in many other fields if serious economic and ecological problems are to be averted, not to mention the dangers of military conflict. The question therefore arises whether such cooperation can realistically be expected to materialize in the humanitarian sphere in the foreseeable future.

The best answer seems to be that global humanitarian problems should be perceived as a challenge which has the potential of drawing the world closer together rather than further dividing it. This answer leaves plenty of scope for the development of individual action, particularly by the private person and by nongovernmental organizations. On the other hand, the fact that the world is organized on the basis of exclusive states, upholders of the doctrine of sovereignty, suggests that changes—if any—in the international humanitarian order are still most likely to come about primarily through state actions.

Even in traditional international law, resting heavily on the foundation of reciprocity, elements of common interest already blend with those of self-interest, albeit only to a slight degree. Herein lies a kernel for development, however, for self-interest can ultimately be seen to lie first of all in protecting common interests. Thus, the search should continue to find new bases for cooperation, while seeking to maximize the potential of humanitarian policy to serve this end.

Perhaps the following idea deserves to be more generally

recognized and expressed: *taking new steps in cooperative interna-*
tional action to tackle humanitarian problems can in turn engender
wider international effects of a beneficial nature.

There is much room for further progress based on awareness that the development of international humanitarian law,
organization, and action is a reciprocating and self-reinforcing
process which seeks to fulfill the purpose of bringing definite
humanitarian benefits to individual people. The aim must be to
seek for ways to ensure that the principle of humanity prevails—
in a time of greatly increased needs but also of greatly increased
means for responding. With this in mind, the present challenge is
to draw practical lessons from the many existing texts and approaches, which are still insufficiently systematic, and to apply
those lessons so as to achieve a closer working relationship between functional and legal aspects of humanitarian policy.

NOTES

Abbreviations used: *EPIL=Encyclopedia of Public International Law,* R.
Bernhardt, ed. (Amsterdam: North-Holland, 1981-); ILM=International
Legal Materials (Washington: American Society of International Law);
LNTS=League of Nations Treaty Series; RdC=Recueil des Cours, Collect-
ed Courses of the Hague Academy of International Law; *TIAS=Treaties*
and Other International Acts Series (Washington: Department of State);
UNTS=United Nations Treaty Series.

1. For a more detailed treatment of the matters dealt with in this
paper, and for further references, see P. Macalister-Smith, *International*
Humanitarian Assistance (Dordrecht, Boston, Lancaster: Martinus Nijhoff Publishers; Geneva: Henry Dunant Institute, 1985). See also note
3 below.

2. In his treaties on international law, E. de Vattel wrote: "if a
nation is visited with famine, all those who have provisions enough
and to spare should come to its assistance, though not to the extent of
self-impoverishment. . . . Whatever the nature of the disaster that
overtakes a nation, the same help is due to it," *The Law of Nations* (Le
droit des Gens), 1758, II, 1, 5.

3. Cf. B. Morse, "Practice, Norms and Reform of International
Humanitarian Rescue Operations," *RdC,* vol. 157 (1977-IV): 125 et seq.;
J. W. Samuels, "The Relevance of International Law to the Prevention

and Mitigation of Natural Disaster," in S. Green and L. H. Stevens, eds., *Disaster Assistance* (New York: New York University Press, 1979), pp. 245 et seq.; and M. Bothe, "Relief Actions," *EPIL*, Installment 4 (1982): 173 et seq.

4. Geneva Convention for the Amelioration of the Conditions of the Wounded in Armies in the Field, 22 August 1864; text in *Consolidated Treaty Series* (C. Parry, ed.), vol. 129; 361 et. seq.

5. For the texts of the four Geneva Conventions of 12 August 1949, see *UNTS*, vol. 75 (1950): 1 et seq.; as of January 1988, there were 165 states parties. For the texts of the two additional Protocols of 1977, see *ILM*, vol. 16 (1977): 1391 et seq.; as of January 1988 there were 71 states parties to Protocol I, and 64 to Protocol II.

6. See G. I. Gay, *The Commission for Relief in Belgium, Statistical Review of Relief Operations* (Stanford: Stanford University Press, 1925); G. I. Gay and H. H. Fisher, *Public Relations of the Commission for Relief in Belgium, Documents*, 2 vols. (Stanford: Stanford University Press, 1929); and B. M. Weissman, *Herbert Hoover and Famine Relief to Soviet Russia: 1921-23* (Stanford: Hoover Institution Press, 1974).

7. See Agreement for the United Nations Relief and Rehabilitation Administration, Washington, 9 November 1943; text in G. Woodbridge, *UNRRA, The History of the United Nations Relief and Rehabilitation Administration*, 3 vols. (New York: Columbia University Press, 1950), 3: 23 et. seq.

8. See, e.g., J. L. Barton, *Near East Relief, 1915-30* (New York: Macmillan, 1930); and H. Kraus, *International Relief in Action, 1914-1943* (Scottdale, Pa.: Herald Press, 1944).

9. Convention of 12 July 1927, text in *LNTS*, vol. 135 (1932): 247 et seq. The convention only entered into force in December 1932, whereupon the Union came into belated and shortlived existence. See P. Macalister-Smith, "The International Relief Union," *The Legal History Review* 54 (1986): 363-74.

10. See below, note 27.

11. See the Economic Cooperation Act of 3 April 1948 (Public Law 472, 80th Congress, 2d Sess.) enacted as Title I of the Foreign Assistance Act of 1948, which established the Economic Cooperation Administration in Washington to administer the plan.

12. Art. 1 states in part: "The Purposes of the United Nations are: . . . (3.) To achieve international cooperation in solving international problems of an economic, social, cultural, or humanitarian character. . . ."

13. For references, see P. Macalister-Smith, *International Humanitarian Assistance*, 1, e.g., pp. 124-126; and see below notes 22, 24, 25, and 26.

14. Art. 38(1)(b) of the Statute of the International Court of Justice refers to "international custom, as evidence of a general principle accepted as law."

15. E.g., UN General Assembly Res. 2816 (XXVI), 4 December 1971; Res. 36/225, 17 December 1981; Res. 37/144, 17 December 1982.

16. See P. Macalister-Smith, "Comity," *EPIL,* Installment 7 (1984): 41-44.

17. The judgment of the International Court of Justice in the Corfu Channel Case (Merits) on 9 April 1949 referred to certain international obligations which are "based on general and well-recognized principles, namely: elementary considerations of humanity, even more exacting in peace than in war," *ICJ Reports* (1949): 4 at 22. Cf. H. Mosler, "General Principles of Law," *EPIL,* Installment 7 (1984); 89 at 102-3; and J. A. Frowein, "Jus cogens," *EPIL,* ibid.: 327-30.

18. See, e.g., R. B. Lillich, "Sovereignty and Humanity: Can They Converge?" in A. Grahl-Madsen and J. Toman, eds., *The Spirit of Uppsala* (Berlin: de Gruyter, 1984): 406-21.

19. See also Declaration on Principles of International Law Concerning Friendly Relations and Cooperation among States in Accordance with the Charter of the United Nations, UN General Assembly Res. 2625 (XXV), 24 October 1970. Cf. G. Fitzmaurice, "The Future of Public International Law and of the International Legal System in the Circumstances of Today," Institut de Droit International, *Livre du Centenaire 1873-1973* (1973), p. 196, e.g., at 324.

20. See, e.g., Universal Declaration of Human Rights, text attached to UN General Assembly Res. 217 A (III) of 10 December 1948, Arts. 3 and 25; International Covenant on Civil and Political Rights, text annexed to UN General Assembly Res. 2200 A (XXI) of 16 December 1966 and entered into force on 23 March 1976, Art. 6(1); and International Covenant on Economic, Social and Cultural Rights, text annexed to UN General Assembly Res. 2200 A (XXI), and entered into force on 3 January 1976, Art. 11.

21. Cf. S. P. Marks, "Principles and Norms of Human Rights Applicable in Emergency Situations," in K. Vasak, ed., *The International Dimensions of Human Rights,* 2 vols. (Paris: UNESCO 1982) 1:175 et seq.; P. Alston and K. Tomasevski, eds., *The Right to Food* (Dordrecht: Nijhoff, 1984); and S. P. Marks, "Emerging Human Rights: A New Generation for the 1980s?" in R. Falk et al., eds., *International Law, A Contemporary Perspective* (Boulder, Colo.: Westview, 1985): 501 et seq.

22. E.g., Second Brussels Convention for the Unification of Certain Rules of Law with Respect to Assistance and Salvage at Sea, 23 September 1910, Art. 11, text in *British and Foreign State Papers,* vol.

103: 434 et seq.; Geneva Convention on the High Seas, 29 April 1958, Art. 12, text in *UNTS*, vol. 450 (1963): 82 et seq.; United Nations Convention on the Law of the Sea, 10 December 1982 but not yet in force, Art. 98, text in *ILM*, vol. 21 (1982); 1261 et. seq.; Treaty of Principles Governing the Activities of States in the Exploration and Use of Outer Space, Including the Moon and Other Celestial Bodies, 27 January 1967, Arts. 5 and 9, see UN General Assembly Res. 2222 (XXI), 19 December 1966; Agreement on the Rescue of Astronauts, the Return of Astronauts, and the Return of Objects Launched into Outer Space, Arts. 2 and 4, see UN General Assembly Res. 2345 (XXII), 19 December 1968; and, more generally, Convention on International Liability for Damage Caused by Space Objects, 29 March 1972, Art. 21, text in *UNTS*, vol. 961: 187 et seq.

23. UN General Assembly Res. 2816 (XXVI), 4 December 1971, paragraph 8 (a)-(f).

24. E.g., Canada and the United States, exchange of notes of 8 August 1967, *TIAS* 6325; Mexico and United States, agreement of 15 January 1980, *TIAS* 10013; France and Federal Republic of Germany, convention of 3 February 1977, Bundesgesetzblatt 1980, Teil II, 33; France and Belgium, convention of 21 April 1981. For further examples, see Council of Europe, Transfrontier Cooperation, International, Interregional and Local Agreements, Doc. Transfront/Office (83) 1 prov. 1983.

25. E.g., Nordic Mutual Emergency Assistance Agreement in Connection with Radiation Accidents, Vienna, 17 October 1963, *UNTS*, vol. 525: 75 et seq.; Convention on Assistance in the Case of a Nuclear Accident or Radiological Emergency, Vienna, 26 September 1986, International Atomic Energy Agency, Doc. GC(SPL.I)/Resolutions (1986): 13 et seq.

26. For many examples, see T. Bruha, "International Rules Designed to Protect against Environmental Emergencies Linked to Technological Development," summary in *Zeitschrift fur auslandisches offentliches Recht and Volkerrecht* (Stuttgart: Kohlhammer), vol. 44 (1984); 1 at 62 et. seq.

27. See Statute of the Office of the United Nations High Commissioner for Refugees, annexed to UN General Assembly Res. 428 (V) of 14 December 1950; Convention Relating to the Status of Refugees of 28 July 1951, text in *UNTS*, vol. 189 (1954): 150 et seq.; and see P. Macalister-Smith, "International Humanitarian Assistance for Refugees: Law and Practice," *Indian Journal of International Law*, 25 (1985): 365-85. The life of the Office is extended by quinquennial General Assembly resolutions.

28. UNICEF was created as the International Children's Emergen-

cy Fund by UN General Assembly Res. 57 (I) of 11 December 1946, and was established on a permanent basis with its present name by Res. 802 (VIII) of 6 October 1953.

29. UNRWA was created by UN General Assembly Res. 302 (IV) of 8 December 1949. See P. Macalister-Smith, "United Nations Relief and Works Agency for Palestine Refugees in the Near East," in *EPIL*, Installment 8 (1985): 519-22.

30. UNDRO was created by UN General Assembly Res. 2816 (XXVI) of 4 December 1971.

31. See UN General Assembly Res. 2029 (XX) of 22 November 1965 and Res. 2688 (XXV) of 11 December 1970. The antecedents may be traced back to UNRRA, see Res. 48 (I) of 11 December 1946.

32. FAO was created in accordance with the Final Act of the 1943 United Nations Conference on Food and Agriculture. For the Constitution, see FAO, *Basic Texts*, 2 vols. (Rome, 1980).

33. WHO's Constitution was adopted on 22 July 1946; for the text see *UNTS*, vol. 14 (1947): 185 et seq.

34. For the text of the statute, see *UNTS*, vol. 276 (1957): 4 et seq.

35. For literature on international humanitarian action in specific situations, with particular reference to the United Nations response, see e.g. the following: L. C. Chen, *Disaster in Bangladesh* (Oxford: Oxford University Press, 1973); T. W. Oliver, *The UN in Bangladesh* (Princeton: Princeton University Press, 1978); M. H. Glantz, ed., *The Politics of Natural Disaster: The Case of the Sahel Drought* (New York: Praeger, 1976); and W. Shawcross, *The Quality of Mercy: Cambodia, Holocaust and Modern Conscience* (New York: Simon and Schuster, 1984).

36. E.g., UN General Assembly Res. 2790 (XXVI) of 6 December 1971; see B. G. Ramcharan, *Humanitarian Good Offices in International Law* (The Hague: Nijhoff, 1983).

37. The Red Cross and Red Crescent constitutional texts and other instruments are published in *International Red Cross Handbook*, 12th ed. (Geneva: 1983). See, e.g., P. Ruegger, "The Juridical Aspects of the Organization of the International Red Cross," *RdC*, vol. 82 (1953-I): 483 et seq.; D. P. Forsythe, *Humanitarian Politics* (Baltimore: Johns Hopkins University Press, 1977); and D. Bindschedler-Robert, "Red Cross," in *EPIL*, Installment 5 (1983): 248 et seq.

38. Twenty-first International Conference of the Red Cross, Istanbul, Res. XXVI; text in *Handbook*, above note 37, pp. 661-62.

39. Principles and Rules for Red Cross Disaster Relief, Twenty-first International Conference, Istanbul, 1969, Res. XXIV; text in *Handbook*, above note 37, pp. 488-94.

40. See P. Macalister-Smith, *International Humanitarian Assistance*, pp. 111-15.

41. International Convention on the Simplification and Harmonization of Customs Procedures, Kyoto, 18 May 1973, Annex F.5; relevant provisions are reproduced in UN Doc. A/32/64, 12 May 1977, Annex II.

42. See UN Charter, Art. 71; UN Economic and Social Council Res. 1296 (XLIV) of 23 May 1968; and Res. 1297 (XLIV) of 27 May 1968.

43. See P. Macalister-Smith, "Humanitarian Action by Non-Governmental Organizations: National and International Law Perspectives," *Bulletin of Peace Proposals* 18 (1987): 119-31.

44. See, e.g., E. M. Kennedy, "International Humanitarian Assistance," *Virginia Journal of International Law* 12 (1972): 299 et seq.; U.S. General Accounting Office, Report to the Congress by the Comptroller General of the United States, *Need for an International Disaster Relief Agency*, Doc. ID-76-15, 5 May 1976; and S. Green, *International Disaster Relief* (New York: McGraw-Hill 1977): 66-67.

45. See Assistance in Cases of Natural Disaster, Comprehensive Report of the Secretary-General, UN Doc. E/4994, 13 May 1971. See also above, note 35.

46. UN General Assembly Res. 2816 (XXVI) of 4 December 1971, paragraph 1(b).

47. Evaluation of the Office of the United Nations Disaster Relief Coordinator, Joint Inspection Unit, UN Doc. JIU/REP/80/11 1980.

48. International Efforts to Meet Humanitarian Needs in Emergency Situations, UN Doc. E/1981/16 of 9 March 1981. See also Doc. A/36/73/Add 1; Doc. A/36/75/Add 8; Doc. E/1981/37/Corr 1 (1981); and A/Res./36/225 of 17 December 1981.

49. For the text of joint recommendations made by UNDRO and the League of Red Cross and Red Crescent Societies in 1977, see UN Doc. A/32/64, Annex II, 12 May 1977. For the text of a draft convention on expediting the delivery of emergency assistance, see UN Doc. A/39/267/Add. 2 - E/1984/96/Add. 2, 18 June 1984.

III. CENTRAL AMERICA

POLITICAL ASYLUM, SANCTUARY, AND HUMANITARIAN POLICY

Doris M. Meissner

On March 9, 1987, the United States Supreme Court ruled that the government must apply a "more generous" standard in deciding claims for political asylum under the Refugee Act of 1980.[1] Called *Immigration and Naturalization Service v. Cardoza-Fonseca*, the landmark decision arose from the denial of political asylum to a Nicaraguan woman who came to the United States as a visitor in 1979. She overstayed her visa and deportation proceedings began. Arguing that her "life and freedom would be threatened" if she were forced to return, she cited as evidence the torture and imprisonment of her brother due to political activities. Although she herself was not politically active, they fled together. She believed her opposition to the government would therefore be known, and she would be in danger if returned to Nicaragua.[2]

These facts are typical of cases of thousands of persons who have emigrated from Central American countries in this decade and been denied political asylum in the United States. The Supreme Court has soundly repudiated these denial decisions. It ruled that the government's requirement that asylum seekers show they are "more likely than not" to be persecuted if returned is wrong. An asylum seeker need only show he has "either been a victim of persecution or can show good reason why he fears persecution."[3]

The Supreme Court's decision raises questions about implementation of the Refugee Act of 1980 that serve as a revealing barometer of humanitarianism and U.S. foreign policy in the 80s. The chapter begins with a review of early experiences implementing the Refugee Act; next is a synopsis of the case of Central American migration since 1980 and the political crosscurrents that have enveloped it; it concludes with an examination of lessons to be learned from contemporary experience if we are to sustain our historical humanitarian traditions as a nation.

THE REFUGEE ACT OF 1980

The Refugee Act of 1980[4] was born of a deeply held consensus that our humanitarian and foreign policy interests call for an orderly and generous system of refugee resettlement in this country and of assistance to persons in first asylum situations in other countries. The debate surrounding its passage centered on constructing a framework for deciding which refugees to bring to the United States from overseas and how many. Scant attention was directed to the problem of political asylum—that is, how to treat people who reach the nation's shores on their own and then claim to be refugees. This was not so much an oversight as a failure of imagination: large numbers of asylum-seekers already in the country had simply not been a feature of our historical experience at that time.[5] However, as a response to known problems, the Refugee Act provided needed solutions and has been the basis for a record of positive accomplishments.

First, it established in statute the process of annual consultations between executive branch officials and Congress to fix refugee admissions ceilings.[6] Consultations have proven a healthy way to assure necessary information-exchange and negotiation over numbers and groups of refugees while preserving adequate flexibility for the government to respond to changes in the refugee picture of unforeseen emergencies.

Second, it incorporated the United Nations definition of *refugee* into U.S. law.[7] This has allowed the U.S. program to complement more logically the efforts of other nations and has helped to solidify consistency of principles and precepts about refugees worldwide.

The third contribution of the act has been coordination of bureaucratic activity among government agencies and the voluntary community. Because refugee affairs have so many actors both within and outside the government, coordination and communication are especially important. As a result, the act's delineation of roles, authorities, and funding provisions has brought about vast improvements in overall program effectiveness.[8]

And finally, the act clarified the legal status of refugees and provided them with a direct path to the rights and prerogatives of legal permanent residents after a year in this country.[9] Therefore, refugee status now leads to eligibility for citizenship after five years. This virtually automatic entitlement, replacing the earlier dependence on special ad hoc legislation to regularize the status of successive groups, signaled an important philosophical and policy commitment to the cause of refugees. In addition, it has eliminated considerable personal hardship and anxiety for the many individuals who had no real status in this country and remained, often for years, in a state of legal limbo.[10]

These improvements have all been to the good. But the act had a deeper purpose. Its underlying hope and promise were to fashion an instrument that would allow this country to carry out the humanitarian ideal to which our nation has been historically committed. That ideal is the offer of liberty and safety to persons from other lands who are persecuted. Achieving it has proven elusive and controversial, particularly where applicants for political asylum are concerned.

Providing for political asylum in the Refugee Act was almost an afterthought. Our historical and policy understanding of refugees and refugee situations was that of an overseas phenomenon. We saw ourselves responding to events that occurred far away, and we saw refugees as persons whom we screened and chose before they could come to the United States.

Regulations for treating political asylum requests by persons already in the U.S. had existed for some years.[11] As they had no statutory base, it seemed tidy to add language to the act providing the requisite authority.[12] An annual number of 5,000 was authorized to allow successful asylum applicants to adjust their status and ultimately be eligible for citizenship.[13] The number was seen as generous and highly unlikely to be needed, since there were just over 5,000 applications, an all-time high, in the system at that time.

The Refugee Act was signed on March 17, 1980. On April 21, just one month later, a storm of boats carrying Cubans from Mariel harbor began arriving in Miami. In one week, 6,000 persons arrived. The boatlift did not stop until five months and 125,000 people later. Among the many problems the boatlift presented was the quandary of how to classify the uninvited newcomers. Earlier waves of Cubans since the 1959 revolution were automatically classified as refugees because they were escaping a Communist regime. Under the new act, the status of the Mariel Cubans was unclear, for their manner of arrival and the reasons they came were never envisioned by the act. Moreover, the Communist imprimatur had been eliminated from refugee law.

Officials responded by instructing the Marielitos to submit individual claims for asylum in order to stop the clock until decisions were made on how to treat this unprecedented influx. Almost 50,000 claims were filed before the president determined that special legislation was needed to establish a new legal status for the entire group.[14] Thus, a substantial political asylum case backlog, generated under the most hostile circumstances in the eyes of the government and the public, appeared virtually overnight.

Two other events added significantly to the political asylum caseload. During the months that Americans were held hostage in Iran, the U.S. declined to return Iranians whose visas had expired. Iranians were encouraged to file claims for political asylum. Because Iranians constituted the largest contingent of foreign students—about one-quarter million—in the U.S. as well as a significant portion of other categories of nonimmigrants, substantial numbers were involved. The second group of claimants were Nicaraguans for whom deportation had been suspended since the fall of the Somoza government in 1979. When the moratorium on deportations was dropped in fall, 1980, Nicaraguans who remained unwilling to return to their country were advised to file claims for political asylum. These applications swelled a caseload that, prior to 1980, consisted mostly of Haitians attempting to use asylum procedures to gain a refugee foothold in the United States.

So, within six months after passage of the Refugee Act, more than 100,000 individual claims for asylum had been filed, largely as a result of the three events described above. A series of ad hoc events in combination with unplanned reactive governmental advice produced a *de facto* safe haven policy for tens of thousands of aliens. Overnight the United States had become a country of first asylum. No machinery had been assembled to handle this workload. No serious thinking or planning had been generated to analyze the implications of the United States as a country of first asylum *and* resettlement. Politically it appeared the government was helpless to control what is generally considered one of the two or three universal attributes of national sovereignty, control of entry of noncitizens. The sense of a loss of control over a fundamental aspect of sovereignty made an indelible image on the public mind. Furthermore, it played a critical part in shaping the policy impressions and ideas of a new administration, under President Ronald Reagan, elected in November of that same year.

This is the framework, then, within which the policies and debate that have surrounded the case of the migration from Central America must be understood.

CENTRAL AMERICAN MIGRATION

In July 1980, while the Marielitos were streaming into Miami, news reports told the grisly story of a group of forty-three Salvadorans smuggled through Mexico into the desert of southern Arizona. They lost their way, were separated, and finally located by Border Patrol agents. Thirteen had perished, and the survivors were at death's door.[15] The tragedy brought to public view the lengths to which desperation can lead people in search of survival and safety. This ill-fated trek was representative of a new but growing aspect of long-standing illegal immigration into the United States across our 1900-mile border with Mexico. The new variable was that these Salvadorans spoke not only of economic despair but of political oppression, killing and disappearances, and fear of return.

The nations of Central America had advanced remarkably in economic terms during the 1960s and 1970s. The five republics of the region—El Salvador, Guatemala, Honduras, Nicaragua, and Costa Rica—despite a doubling of their population to 20 million between 1950 and 1970, accomplished a doubling in per capita income. Yet the historic gulf between rich and the mass of the very poor remained.[16]

Other than Costa Rica, about half of the urban population and three-quarters of the rural could not satisfy basic needs in nutrition, housing, health, and education. With rises in energy costs and the fall in commodities prices during the mid-70s, standards of living, already low compared to the developed world and badly skewed, were cut back across the board. This crisis, which continues today, has a profoundly human dimension. Joblessness is up. Malnutrition and infant mortality have escalated. Poverty, which was pernicious in Latin America even during the growth years, is on the rise throughout the region.[17]

Accompanying the economic crisis has been a profound political challenge: the issue is the legitimacy of government—that is, who shall govern and under what forms. This crisis is probably most clearly illustrated in El Salvador, where the annulment of the victory in 1972 of civilian Christian Democratic candidate José Napoleon Duarte ushered in a period of severely repressive rule. While there were significant national variations, Guatemala and Nicaragua, in addition to El Salvador, went through a roughly parallel process in which a trend toward more open, pluralistic, and democratic societies gave way to oppression and polarization.[18] The result has been aroused expectations followed by bitter frustration.

El Salvador became the focus of the major conflict in the United States over the meaning of the Refugee Act. After the military overturned the 1972 election, guerilla organizations began to proliferate and demonstrations against the government by students, workers, and peasants became increasingly common. Repression increased with political assassination, disappearances and torture becoming common. A new government which took power in 1979 inspired new hope. The United States embraced the regime and resumed military aid that had been cut in the mid-70s. But after a few months, hard-line conservative officers came to dominate the governing junta. Death squads appeared and all potentially in opposition came under suspicion—students, professors and teachers, clergy and lay church workers, village leaders, union organizers, agrarian reform workers.[19]

Guerrilla forces launched a "final offensive" in January 1981 and two-thirds of the country became the scene of major military actions. The guerrillas were forced to fall back but a long, bloody war of attrition had begun. In some provinces, scarcely a family was without death or displacement. The Catholic church of El Salvador reported that over 44,000 civilians were murdered from October 1979 to February 1984. Estimates are that more than one million people, or 25 percent of the population, have been driven from their homes and villages.[20] A comparable figure in the United States would be 60 million people.

Many remained in El Salvador in camps and slums; others went to Honduras and Mexico. Many others went further, managing to slip into the United States. Best estimates are that there are over half a million Salvadorans in this country, the majority of whom have arrived since 1981, when the civil war intensified. Guatemalans are estimated to number between 100,000 and 200,000 and Nicaraguans between 40,000 and 60,000.[21]

These events have been perceived very differently by the two major actors in the domestic drama triggered by this migration, particularly that from El Salvador. Those actors are the government and immigrant advocates.

The attorney general and secretary of state are jointly charged by law with responsibility for the nation's immigration and refugee policy.[22] Refugee policy is administered by the Immigration and Naturalization Service, a bureau in the Department of Justice reporting to the attorney general, and by the Bureau of Human Rights and Humanitarian Affairs, an arm of the Department of State reporting to the secretary of state. The sharp increase in migration from El Salvador was viewed by these government agencies as a flow generated by economic conditions. They believed that the large numbers of this new group applying for political asylum were exploiting a newly found loophole in the immigration system created by the Refugee Act. In filing a claim for political asylum, no matter how lacking in merit, aliens could receive authorization to work during the pendency of the claim and were protected from any immigration enforcement action.

The Salvadorans represented another influx of uninvited persons at a time of record levels of legal and illegal immigration. The perceived inability of the federal government to regulate immigration had created strong public sentiment for more restrictive immigration enforcement practices. Official concerns were grounded in the surge of political asylum applications since passage of the Refugee Act. In 1979 there were 3,000 applications. By 1981 the number was 40,000, and by 1983 it exceeded 140,000. In contrast, in 1981, INS was able to process only 5,000 cases; in 1982 it decided 11,000.[23] There was gridlock in the system. Government officials recognized that a nation has no means to determine the volume, frequency, demographic, or other characteristics of those seeking asylum because they may apply from within the country, circumventing traditional immigration processing. For them the issue was the right of a state to limit immigration and to exercise control over its borders.

Processing the cases became a priority activity in 1983. INS offices and the Department of State's Bureau of Human Rights, charged with issuing individual advisory opinions on each case,[24] mustered the necessary staff to tackle this new caseload. It was, by then, a mixed bag. With the exception of Iran, where country conditions were stark but clear and a history of overseas refugee admissions to the United States had been established, the countries of origin of the largest number of applicants were in the Western Hemisphere, nearby. These countries were sources of significant illegal migration to the United States since the early 1970s. The overriding experience with migration from these nations had been one of controlling an illegal migration flow. That they might also be refugee-producing nations was never seriously addressed by the bureaucracy.

The outlook of government officials mirrored the national experience to date: there were countries of refugee origin—Vietnam, the Soviet Union, Afghanistan—and there were countries of illegal migration—Mexico, El Salvador, Haiti. That some countries might produce both was uncharacteristic. Probing the line separating economically and politically generated flight was a new complexity that was brushed over because officials felt overwhelmed by applications and sensed that aliens were filing for political asylum to stop the enforcement of departure actions and remain here to work. The substantive complexity and new issues presented by the caseload were a secondary, unmet concern.

Although the numbers of Central American migrants were small by immigration standards—INS made at least 1.2 million apprehensions annually during the early 1980s—this new migration triggered another concern among immigration officials. They knew that when an alien invoked the right to a formal deportation hearing, the delays inherent in the immigration administrative review process could stretch out for years. Normal INS operations depend on quick turnaround of large numbers of people. The enforcement system is manageable only because the vast majority of aliens elect not to pursue formal deportation procedures. Instead, they waive a hearing, departing quickly through a construct called "voluntary departure" (VD).[25] Because illegal migrants have traditionally been Mexican, a quick return to Mexico (most trying then to cross the border again), rather than protracted deportation hearings, makes sense. Salvadorans, however, did not want to return quickly to El Salvador. Recrossing the border was expensive and time-consuming. In addition many feared being returned to El Salvador. For them deportation hearings were desirable because they forestalled return and provided the forum where they could raise a political asylum claim.

Persons requesting hearings presented a serious operational problem. They occupied detention space for months which might have been turned over many times by persons departing under VD, allowing much more enforcement activity and numbers of apprehensions. Next to Mexicans, the five largest groups in detention in 1981 were Salvadorans, Guatemalans, Colombians, Nicaraguans, and Hondurans. The Salvadoran number—8,955[26]—was equal to the total of all the others. Thus the pressure to have Salvadorans use the VD process, short-circuiting hearings, was intense.

The larger policy environment established by the new administration reinforced these operational imperatives. White House officials and the attorney general were giving priority to new legislation that would make it unlawful for illegal migrants to work in the United States. They were calling for aggressive immigration enforcement at the border and substantial new resources for INS even as most domestic agencies were absorbing significant spending cutbacks. Immigration agents felt they were receiving high-level support for their mission for the first time in years. They believed that in returning Salvadorans to their country as speedily as possible they were doing the job their government wanted them to do.

To immigrant advocates the picture looked very different. Traditionally comprised of church groups, ethnic lobbies, human rights and humanitarian organizations, and public interest lawyer's groups, immigrant advocates also include civil rights organizations and labor unions from time to time, depending on the issue at hand. These groups are loosely connected at best and have varying degrees of cohesion and resources. Their activities with immigrants have always included both direct services— social welfare and legal assistance—and political advocacy, especially in the Congress.

Immigrant advocates responded to the Central American migration both by offering services and mobilizing advocacy. The direct services activity has been boldly carried out through the sanctuary movement. Sanctuary has also had an active advocacy dimension. In addition, advocacy has been focused upon proposals to achieve a moratorium against returning migrants to El Salvador and, more recently, Nicaragua.[27]

The sanctuary movement arose from within church congregations in the Southwest that had ministries and projects in Central America focused on the poor. Most are bitterly opposed to United States policy toward the region. Friends of the Central American people, they had generally not previously been involved in refugee or immigration activities in the United States. Their work began in earnest in 1980 and 1981, during which they groped their way toward the concept and declaration of sanctuary.

The sanctuary movement was formally launched on March 24, 1982, the second anniversary of Archbishop Oscar Romero's death, at the Southside Presbyterian Church in Tucson, Arizona.[28] The announcement came after more than a year of working at the border with Central Americans who were in detention or had just crossed. These migrants told of their fear of return to El Salvador and, increasingly, Guatemala because of the atrocities they had experienced or witnessed there. The church's work quickly expanded to include helping Salvadorans in Mexico cross the border. Through a series of contact points, mostly clergy and churches within Mexico and in the United States, the migrants were assisted northward to safe destinations.

Sanctuary organizers believed they had made every effort to work within the legal system in behalf of Salvadorans seeking political asylum but that it was impossible. They charged that immigration officials operated in violation of the Refugee Act of 1980 and that State Department officials, through the advisory opinion required on each individual asylum claim, were pursuing foreign policy objectives that precluded a refugee flow from Central America. They reasoned that the government was the lawbreaker, forcing people of conscience to turn to civil disobedience if they were to fulfill their higher duties to God and their fellow beings.

Although the Tucson activists were closest to the border activity, groups in other parts of the country that opposed United States policy in Central America also championed the cause of Central American migrants in the United States. Concentrated in California, Texas, Illinois, and Washington, D.C., many groups coalesced under the sanctuary banner. The Chicago Religious Task Force on Central America assumed a national leadership coordinating role during 1982 with the intent to spread the sanctuary message broadly to other churches and locales.

As these people saw it, the picture was one of El Salvadorans and Guatemalans entering the United States in increasing numbers because of political and military violence in their countries supported and encouraged by the United States. Immigration officials, with the support of the State Department, were detaining them and using heavy-handed tactics to get them to waive their rights to a deportation hearing. Church workers in the Arizona and California groups recounted personally registering, according to prescribed INS procedures, as legal counsel for individual aliens only to find they had been taken from detention and returned to El Salvador. When aliens did get to the deportation hearing stage and the political asylum claim was formally considered, the cases were routinely denied even when exhaustive documentation was provided and compelling accounts of perceived persecution were set forth.

The numbers illustrated the advocates' frustration with the legal process. At the end of fiscal year 1981, the first year that the act was in place, 15,940 Salvadorans were arrested. Of those, 10,473 were returned to El Salvador. Of the 5,570 who requested political asylum, it was granted to 1.4% of the applicants whose cases were reviewed.[29]

The Refugee Act called for the attorney general to establish a procedure for aliens in the United States or at the border, irrespective of status, to apply for asylum. It stated that aliens may be granted asylum at the discretion of the attorney general if he determines the applicant to be a refugee.[30] The church workers felt that Salvadorans were entitled to apply at the border, yet INS had not implemented any procedures to permit it. They saw no middle ground and decided that resistance, even though it meant breaking the law with the possibility of arrest and fines or prison, was a moral imperative.

The sanctuary movement grew quickly, particularly among active, civic-minded groups normally uninvolved in immigration matters. From a base of religious groups—about 300 have formally declared and provide sanctuary[31]—it has come to include Hispanic groups and various legal and political organizations. The activities of the movement include transport and shelter for Central American migrants; projects and resources for lawyers representing political asylum applicants; documentation packets for applicants; computerized lists of victims of abuses in El Salvador and names of organizations providing asylum assistance for Central Americans; policy statements by municipalities regarding enforcement of immigration laws in their jurisdictions; and public appearances by individual refugees telling their stories.

What has distinguished sanctuary activists from traditional immigrant advocacy and assistance has been the underground railroad activity and public sanctuary. The underground railroad—assisting migrants to leave their country or transit Mexico and enter the United States surreptitiously—has caused considerable controversy because it is an illegal activity. Public sanctuary—using appearances by refugees telling their stories to the public and media as an organizing tool to mobilize opposition to U.S. foreign policy in Central America—has been divisive because it represents a fundamental departure from humanitarian activity into politics. Public sanctuary organizers were pursuing a political objective in the name of the Refugee Act, the same crime they charged the government with committing.

Political advocacy in behalf of Central American migrants has been expressed not only through the sanctuary movement but also through a campaign to obtain "extended voluntary departure" (EVD) for Salvadorans. EVD is a discretionary decision which can be made by the attorney general, upon the recommendation of the secretary of state. It bars removal of individuals to a specified country for a specified period due to humanitarian, foreign policy, or immigration reasons.

At first, sympathetic Congressmen wrote letters to the secretary of state and the attorney general requesting an EVD action. Congressional requests were answered by detailed explanations why conditions in El Salvador were improving and case-by-case adjudication of asylum applications afforded sufficient protection to persons subject to persecution.[32] These statements were buttressed by the government's certifications to Congress, as part of the requirement for continued military assistance to El Salvador, that human rights conditions were improving and there was no real justification for a bar to deportations. However, in January 1982 EVD was declared for all Poles in the United States following the imposition of martial law in that country.[33] This action only underscored the conviction of the advocates that immigration and refugee policy was unfair and unjust toward Salvadorans.

With the administration refusing to grant EVD, Congressmen and Senators sympathetic to the position taken by immigrant advocates introduced legislation to bar enforcement of departure of Salvadorans. Several sets of hearings were held and the bill subsequently became broadened to include Nicaraguans. This legislation has not been enacted, though it remains on the Congress's legislative agenda. A major new immigration law, enacted in 1986, established a legalization program for aliens illegally in the country who entered before January 1, 1982. This has been helpful for some Central Americans. But the majority have come since 1982, so that solutions have not been found, either here or in their home countries, for what is now many hundreds of thousands of people.

LESSONS TO BE LEARNED

What can we learn about humanitarianism, as exemplified by our nation's refugee policies, from this recent history?

First, there is the matter of the Salvadorans themselves. In April 1982, just one month after the public announcement of sanctuary, a federal judge in California enjoined INS from returning Salvadorans without fully informing them of their rights. The injunction required INS to provide Central Americans with information in Spanish and English on their right to representation, a deportation hearing, and a political asylum application.[34]

The impact was immediate. The number of voluntary departures dropped by 70 percent; the number of Salvadoran applications for political asylum jumped 56 percent. In 1980, 75 percent of the Salvadorans arrested were returned to El Salvador. In 1981, 67 percent were returned. By 1983, the percentage fell to 29 percent. During the five-year period 1980-1985, about 35,000 people were returned to El Salvador.[35] More than 500,000 are believed to be here. Salvadorans had learned to refuse to leave.

Not that those who applied for political asylum were granted refugee status. Only about 2.6 percent of Salvadoran applications and less than 1 percent of Guatemalan applicants have actually been granted asylum.[36] Still, very few actual deportations of persons denied asylum have been made. The widespread perception that denial of asylum is tantamount to deportation is wrong. Denied asylum cases must be scheduled for deportation hearings. There are not enough immigration officers or judges to handle the deportation caseload. As of January 1987 about 2 percent of denied asylum applicants had actually been deported; 13 percent of the cases were being appealed or adjudicated under other immigration provisions; and 80 percent were at a standstill with no deportation hearing scheduled due to inadequate resources to locate or schedule these aliens.[37] Despite the government's effort to institute more aggressive enforcement and the denunciation of deportations by sanctuary spokesmen, there has been a de facto safe haven policy for Central Americans.

For all its procedural violations, considerable expenditures, and public statements about immigration control, the government has been almost totally ineffective in discharging its law enforcement mission. At the same time, the sanctuary movement, despite its rhetoric and moral outrage, actually assisted only a few hundred people, about one-tenth of 1 percent of the estimated number of Central Americans in the United States.[38]

The battles that made a difference were fought and won in the courts, using the legal process. Capped now by the Supreme Court's finding that the government must be "more generous" in administering the Refugee Act, the judgments of courts have shaped the public policy framework for Central Americans. The irony, of course, is that when the need was greatest—1980, 1981, and 1982—the numbers of people returned were the highest. As conditions have improved, Central Americans and their advocates have learned how to challenge removal actions and asylum decision making.

Even federal prosecution of sanctuary activists has not appreciably strengthened the government's hand nor propelled the movement to have a major impact on policy. Government officials sidestepped legal action against sanctuary movement members for quite some time. They recognized that going after churches, regardless of how illegal their activities might be, could produce martyrs and thereby strengthen the potency of the movement. But as the publicity surrounding sanctuary increased, including a major spread in *People* magazine and a segment on "60 Minutes,"[39] the Service believed it could no longer respond credibly to questions from the press, Congress, and the public on why it was not doing something to stop the transport and harboring of illegal aliens.

At the end of a long and expensive trial, the jury convicted sanctuary workers as the government argued it should.[40] However, the judge declined to sentence them to prison terms, effectively upholding the morality of their position. The outcome was a Pyrrhic victory for each that did nothing to clarify the status or treatment of Central Americans, the underlying issue both were presumably fighting to resolve. What it demonstrates is a severe weakening of the relationship between churches and federal agencies responsible for immigration matters.

At least since World War II, the government and churches have worked together closely on refugee admissions and resettlement. Despite strong disagreements from time to time, they have been able to maintain a constructive relationship because their shared objective was a humanitarian one.

Tension has always existed between the Departments of State and Justice over the issue of who is a refugee. State classically is the refugee apologist and Justice the nay-sayer. Normally, therefore, State seeks high percentages of refugee grants because refugee admissions typically support broader foreign policy goals such as anticommunism or regional stability. Justice, viewing itself as the neutral arbiter of the law and brakeman on the immigration train, errs on the opposite side.

This tension did not come into play with the asylum caseload, because several of the source countries were foreign-policy friends. Toward antagonist nations, political asylum and refugee decisions represent one of many methods for registering disapproval of a nation's leadership or political system. Toward friends and allies, such decisions are trickier. El Salvador is the best case in point. Because the United States was supporting the government of El Salvador, a low percentage of asylum grants served U.S. foreign policy objectives. A high percentage would have conveyed some disapproval behind the vote of confidence being given to its struggle for democracy. So the INS's emphasis on rapid case processing and stemming illegal migration, combined with a lack of incentive for the State Department to dig into the difficult but critical issues of economic versus political flight, resulted in extremely low approval rates at the very time when public awareness of and revulsion over the death squad activity in El Salvador was at its peak.

The patterns between church and government and among government agencies all broke down in the Central American case. The issues became polarized very early and quickly before government agencies could adjust to the unprecedented demands of both a new law and a substantial asylum influx. In addition, the early need to respond to litigation allowed lawyers to take the lead. The adversarial process precluded discussion among all parties of what is the best and proper way to administer an asylum program and respond to asylum emergencies.

Critics of the administration's Central American policy seized upon the anomaly of scant approvals of asylum applications originating from a country gripped by documented death squad terror. They used this theme as a fundamental organizing issue for the sanctuary movement. Sanctuary activists have been successful in developing public awareness of even the most specific details of the asylum decision-making process. Public attitudes about political asylum today are based almost wholly on the controversy and discussion surrounding the Salvadoran asylum caseload. Although the sanctuary movement began as a refugee assistance effort, it came to be dominated by the practice of public sanctuary as a means of mobilizing public opposition to foreign policy. This was not a humanitarian objective and raises serious credibility questions.

Similarly, the government forfeited its credibility in discharging its responsibilities under the Refugee Act. The government saw asylum grants as undercutting its political objectives in the region and its implementation of a tough immigration policy. It refused to act on the overwhelming body of evidence, some of it flowing from its own reports, that real persecution exists in Central America. The Department of State must be especially harshly judged in this regard for humanitarianism is typically seen to support broader foreign policy goals. This commitment has been lacking in United States policy to Central America. It led to a breakdown in the normal executive branch tension that produces a generous refugee admissions policy.

Humanitarian policy cannot be devoid of political overtones but politics cannot be the dominant motivation if true humanitarian objectives are to be achieved. Both the government and the advocates allowed political objectives to overshadow humanitarian imperatives. Where past disagreements between the government and churches would have sparked intense discussion and ultimately some form of pragmatic solution, an honest exchange of views and negotiation did not occur because each correctly suspected the other of having a political rather than a humanitarian agenda. The avenue of trust and good faith that is available when humanitarianism is the shared objective became the casualty of highly charged political priorities.

What, then, is the future of refugee policy as an important component of U.S. humanitarian policies?

Time-honored international principles of protection and *nonrefoulement* are increasingly difficult to maintain in the face of rapid increases in the size of human populations, coupled with economic advances in the West and deteriorating economic conditions in the developing world. These broad, contemporary trends have created profound, endemic income disparities among nations, especially in the Americas.[41] The world today is an unstable place where conflicts that may never produce victories are likely always to produce refugees. We must expect burgeoning numbers of asylum-seekers in the decades ahead.

The United States severely mishandled the Central American migration of the early 1980s. It was neither a 100 percent refugee migration—even sanctuary workers agree on that point—nor purely a creature of economic despair. No one knows the proper approval percentage for Salvadoran cases. It is less than 100 percent, less than 50 percent, and probably less than 25 percent. There is no *right* number. What there is, is a defensible, fair number. It is the number that would have resulted from an honest look at the Salvadoran caseload in an attempt to make distinctions about various types of individuals in it. Special care could have been given to interviewing and assessing circumstances of community organizers, rural health workers, teachers, labor union leaders, doctors, lay religious activists, and others.

Because such an effort was not made, the interested public and careful observers have rendered harsh judgment on the government's good faith and willingness to administer a judicious political asylum policy.

The defect is not limited to the El Salvador case. A story on the front page of the *New York Times* offers a tantalizing new twist. The piece describes a Justice Department review of proposed asylum regulations that resulted from concern that approval rates for Polish applicants, which are about 38 percent, are too low in light of the administration's antipathy for the Communist regimes of Eastern Europe. Certain officials therefore proposed that the asylum regulations state that all applicants from "totalitarian" governments be presumed to be refugees. In explaining the rationale for the proposed change, a staff aide to Attorney General Edwin Meese said, "our asylum policy is inconsistent with our foreign policy."[42]

That is the core issue. Should refugee and asylum policy support and be an adjunct of U.S. foreign policy? Or should refugee policy, based on the humanitarian principle of safety for victims of political persecution in countries of whatever ideological stripe, develop as an equally important national objective in its own right?

The Refugee Act envisioned and provided the framework for the latter. What we have learned since passage, however, is that the act established a *process*, not a *policy*. It codified a framework for refugee admission decision making on an annual basis and the funding mechanisms necessary to support it. These advances were needed, and the process has proven to be a useful and responsive tool. Refugee *policy*, on the other hand, has remained a mirror of our foreign policy and has not developed as a distinct discipline.

Since the Supreme Court's admonition in *Cardoza-Fonseca,*

the government announced that Nicaraguan asylum applicants should resubmit their claims for review under a new standard of proof consistent with the Supreme Court decision.[43] Nothing was said about other nationality groups. Shortly thereafter, INS published proposed regulations to govern the asylum process for all groups.[44] The proposal incorporated a relaxed standard of proof, as called for by the Court. However, other provisions of those proposed regulations have been controversial, causing the government to announce that important portions will be rewritten before final regulations are promulgated.[45] A timetable has not been announced; as of this writing, regulations incorporating the Court's instructions of March 1987 have not been issued. The likelihood, therefore, is that Nicaraguan applicants are being judged on the basis of a more relaxed standard than that used for other groups, again because of foreign policy considerations.

The issues, therefore, remain unsettled, the object of vigorous and continued debate.

The United States has not been alone in its reaction to the asylum phenomenon. Other Western nations, principally Germany and Canada, have seen masses of people, with complex and varied motivations to move, present themselves for asylum. Most Western nations agree that their asylum provisions have been manipulated and abused because asylum offers the chance to circumvent refugee selection processes by filing a claim after fraudulent or clandestine entry to a country. Thereafter, there is recourse to the judicial system through appeals that can take many years during which the claimant works, often failing to appear at hearings. For these reasons, most nations have tightened their systems significantly.

A nation faces imposing difficulties in fashioning a process that works. What is needed is a system that delivers decisions that are impeccably fair but also prompt. Timeliness is the deterrent to use of asylum claims for access to the job market. The system must also produce enforceable decisions to check a spreading sense that immigration policy is out of control.[46] Ultimately it is that perception that threatens a backlash against the entire asylum commitment. Thus, those who favor a generous program of refugee admissions may well have the greatest stake in crafting and supporting procedures that can work.

The taming of the asylum process remains a major item of

business introduced by the Refugee Act of 1980. The Supreme Court's decision in *Cardoza-Fonseca* brings us back to a task that must be done if we are to carry out values that are among the most sacred in our historical traditions and in our hopes for civilization in a troubled world.

NOTES

1. *Immigration and Naturalization Service v Cardoza-Fonseca,* no. 85-782, March 9, 1987, p. 4.

2. Ibid., p. 3.

3. Ibid., p. 16.

4. Public Law No. 96-212, 94 Stat. 102 (codified in scattered sections of 8, 22 U.S.C.).

5. See David Martin, "The Refugee Act of 1980: Its Past and Future," *1982, Michigan Yearbook of International Legal Studies* 91, pp. 91-96.

6. Immigration & Nationality Act (INA) 207(d), 8 U.S.C. 1157 (d) (1982).

7. INA 101(a)(42)(A), 8 U.S.C. 1101 (a)(42)(A)(1982).

8. Section 301 of the Refugee Act of 1980, Pub. L. No. 96-212, 94 Stat. 102, 109-10, establishes by statute the Office of the United States Coordinator for Refugee Affairs. Other portions of the act specify the roles of the Departments of Justice, State, and Health and Human Services. INA 207-209, 411-414, 8 U.S.C. 1157-59, 1521-24 (1982).

9. INA 209(c), 8 U.S.C. 1159(c) (1982).

10. Martin, "The Refugee Act of 1980," pp. 96-97, 109-10.

11. 8 C.F.R. 108 (1978).

12. INA 208, 8 U.S.C. 1158 (1982).

13. INA 209(b), 8 U.S.C. 1159(b) (1982).

14. The administration bill was introduced as S. 3013, 96th Cong., 2d Sess. (1980). It was never enacted, although other legislation incorporated modified provisions for assistance to arriving Cubans and Haitians. Not until November 1986 did Congress enact legislation finally permitting "Cuban-Haitian entrants" to clarify their legal status and become lawful permanent residents. Immigration Reform and Control Act of 1986 (IRCA), Pub. L. No. 99-603, 202, 100 Stat. 3359.

15. Ann Crittenden, *Sanctuary,* (London: Weidenfeld & Nicolson, 1988).

16. U.S. National Bipartisan Commission on Central America, *Report of the National Bipartisan Commission on Central America,* January 1984, p. 23.

17. Ibid., pp. 24-25.

18. Ibid., pp. 22.

19. Ibid., pp. 28-29.

20. Sergio Aguayo and Patricia Weiss Fagen, *Central Americans in Mexico and the United States: Unilateral, Bilateral and Regional Perspectives,* prepared for the Hemispheric Migration Project of the Center for Immigration Policy and Refugee Assistance, Georgetown University, February 1988, forthcoming.

21. Ibid.

22. INA, Sec. 103 (8 U.S.C. 1103) and Sec. 104 (8 U.S.C. 1104).

23. Lars Schoultz, "Central America," in Christopher Mitchell, *Immigration Policy and U.S. Foreign Relations with Latin America,* forthcoming, p. 34.

24. 8 C.F.R. Part 208 (1980).

25. INA, Sec. 244(e), (8 U.S.C. 1254).

26. INS operational statistics, Detention and Deportation branch.

27. U.S. Congress, *Temporary Suspension of Deportation of Certain Aliens* and U.S. Senate, *Temporary Safe Haven for Salvadorans,* Report of the Committee on the Judiciary, June 18, 1987.

28. Schoultz, "Central America," p. 55.

29. U.S. Immigration & Naturalization Service, *Statistical Yearbook of Immigration & Naturalization Service, 1986* (Washington, D.C.: GPO, 1987), p. 48.

30. INA, Sec. 208 (8 U.S.C. 1158).

31. Crittenden, *Sanctuary.*

32. U.S. Senate Report, *Temporary Safe Haven,* pp. 44-47.

33. *Interpreter Releases* 59, no. 5 (January 30, 1982), p. 85.

34. *Orantes Hernandez v Smith,* 541 F. Supp. 351 (C.D. Cal. 1982).

35. Schoultz, "Central America," p. 35.

36. INS, *Statistical Yearbook, 1986,* p. 48.

37. U.S. General Accounting Office, *Asylum: Uniform Application of Standards Uncertain—Few Denied Applicants Deported* (B-224935), January 1987.

38. Crittenden, *Sanctuary.*

39. Ibid.

40. *Washington Post,* July 2, 1986, p. 3.

41. Michael Teitelbaum, *Latin Migration North: The Problem for U.S. Foreign Policy* (New York: Council on Foreign Relations, 1985).

42. *New York Times,* March 30, 1986, p. 1.

43. U.S. Department of Justice, Press announcement, July 8, 1987.

44. *Federal Register,* vol. 54, no. 167, August 28, 1987, p. 32552.

45. "Political Asylum Revision Dropped," *Washington Post,* October 30, 1987, p. 23.

46. Martin, "The Refugee Act of 1980."

A VIEW FROM THE
SANCTUARY MOVEMENT

Michael McConnell

> There comes a time when force attempts to sub-
> due the mind. . . . It is then that true humanists
> recognize their role. Refusing to give in, they
> oppose brute strength with another, invincible
> power: that of the spirit.
>
> André Gide, 1937

At the heart of foreign policy and refugee questions lies the definition of humanitarian. What does it mean to be truly humanitarian? Is it possible to separate politics from the plight of refugees? *Humanitarianism* according to *Webster's Dictionary* means "asserting the dignity and worth of the human person." Thus, to be humanitarian means to stand on the side of life and opposed to all that brings degradation, misery, and death.

Over the past eight years the U.S. government has engaged in policies and actions that have caused unimaginable suffering and death, not only to refugees from El Salvador and Guatemala but to those who have remained behind. What is missing from the worldview of many so-called humanitarians is an understanding of the United States government's relationship with Central America. In this setting, the primary humanitarian question is not one of charity but of justice.

Justice in the biblical Hebrew is *mishpat*, which translated means defense of the weak, the liberation of the oppressed, doing justice to the poor (Exodus 21:1; Exodus 15:25; Exodus 18:13-27). True humanitarianism, like biblical justice, demands life for the most vulnerable and works against needless death.

Politics deals with power relationships, which can either be life-giving or death-dealing, just or unjust. The goal is not to avoid politics, but rather to participate in the politics of life rather than the politics of death.

Just before his assassination Archbishop Oscar Romero laid out the choice very clearly:

> the church, like every person, is faced with the most basic option of its faith, . . . life or death. It is very clear to us that on this point there is no possible neutrality. We either serve the life of Salvadorans or we are accomplices in their death. . . . We either believe in a God of Life or we serve the idols of death.

The sanctuary movement emerged in 1982 to dramatize the choice between life and death in Central America. Its members have chosen to risk possible imprisonment and fines to stand with the most vulnerable—those in forced exile from their homeland who speak a strange language and whose rights were systematically denied both here and in their countries of origin.

Refugees do not drop from the sky. They flee their homes for specific reasons, and, for the most part, the fears and persecutions of refugees from El Salvador and Guatemala are well documented. Since 1979 these two small countries have lived through a litany of abuse and terror. Since 1980, 60,000 civilians have been killed in El Salvador, the majority by right-wing death squads and the Salvadoran military itself. One-fourth of the population has been displaced. According to human rights groups, aerial bombardments in rural areas have killed thousands and dislocated hundreds of thousands. More tonnage of bombs has fallen on El Salvador in the last four years than on any country in the history of the Western Hemisphere.

In Guatemala 38,000 people have disappeared since 1980. The Guatemalan military admits to committing 440 village massacres, although human rights groups put the figure much higher. Forty thousand civilians have been killed since 1980 and there are at present 120,000 orphans.

Behind all of the statistics are people like Pedro and Silvia, Daniel and Albertina, who have witnessed the terror in their countries and seek safe haven in the United States. Some bear the physical signs of torture or burns from napalm or phosphorous bombs. Others are withdrawn, barely able to whisper of the atrocities they have lived through. There are also the less visible scars—insomnia, heartache over dead children, unhealed ulcers, arthritis aggravated by lying on the damp ground during harried border crossings—and the memories, always the memories. Children wake up screaming in the middle of the night, not from nightmares of imagined fears, but from the memory of real horrors still lodged in their minds. It is all part of the tragedy of forced exile.

U.S. census figures verify the cause of the exodus. The U.S. Census Bureau states that in 1980 there were 45,000 undocumented Salvadorans in the United States. Refugee groups now put the number at 500,000 to 750,000. That increase corresponds directly to the increase of violence in the Salvadoran civil war and the increase of U.S. military aid to the government of El Salvador. El Salvador has been poverty-stricken for decades and yet only 45,000 came to the United States prior to the war.

In Guatemala the same argument can be made concerning the Mayan Indian population who consider their land sacred. Hundreds of thousands fled, not for financial gain, but in the face of the most ruthless counterinsurgency campaign in the history of modern terrorism. They were forced from their land; they did not choose to leave.

Since 1982 the sanctuary movement has held that those fleeing from El Salvador and Guatemala are *bona fide* refugees under international law who have a right to stay in the United States temporarily until the violence in their countries subsides. The Refugee Act of 1980 was passed by Congress to bring the United States into compliance with international law so that ideological claims did not determine the definition of who was a refugee. According to Gil Loescher and John A. Scanlan in their book *Calculated Kindness*, well over 90 percent of those admitted to the United States as refugees since 1945 have fled Communist countries. The Refugee Act of 1980 was designed to change that trend, but it did not. Loescher and Scanlan write:

> Today, in a markedly more restrictive era, the Reagan administration has responded to more restrictive voices. It has begun to limit the opportunities for refugee migration. At the same time it has continued to maintain—and indeed, has strengthened—the double standard which began emerging in the aftermath of World War II. Thus, like all of its predecessors, it has extended special wel-

come to the victims of the "evil empire"—those facing persecution from Communist regimes. More openly and absolutely than its predecessors, however, it has chosen to ignore the claims of other refugees and to define suffering in rigid ideological terms. That choice reveals how calculating America's response to refugees has become, how far it has strayed from Emma Lazarus' vision.[1]

Under international law the principle of *nonrefoulement* forbids countries to deport a refugee if his/her life would be threatened because of a well-founded fear of persecution in the country of origin. Thus, by providing refuge in the United States, the sanctuary movement has acted to fulfill international law and enforce the Refugee Act of 1980 in the way it was intended. In 1986 the movement received unsolicited support from Amnesty International when eleven sanctuary workers were on trial in Tucson, Arizona. That support served as one more proof that refugees from El Salvador and Guatemala were indeed refugees and sanctuary workers were acting in accordance with international law. The U.S. government had indicted the eleven sanctuary workers on charges ranging from harboring and transporting "illegal aliens" to conspiracy. Some faced up to thirty-five years in prison. Eight of the eleven were convicted. Amnesty International's International Secretariat wrote to the judge in the case saying in part:

> While not disputing the USA's right to enforce its own immigration laws, Amnesty International is concerned at the U.S. government's inconsistent compliance with certain international legal standards which provide that governments may not return refugees to countries where they risk death, "disappearance", torture or imprisonment. . . . Amnesty International's research on El Salvador and Guatemala suggests that, owing to the state of civil and political unrest in these countries, refugees who are returned to them are put in grave danger of being subjected to human rights violations.
>
> Amnesty International considers that the defendants have been convicted of violating laws which, in their current practice, directly facilitate the violation of human rights to which this organization is opposed. In the event of their being sentenced to terms of imprisonment, Amnesty International will, consequently, adopt them as "Prisoners of Conscience" and its members will campaign for their unconditional release.[2]

The eight convicted sanctuary workers were not imprisoned, but another sanctuary worker, Stacey Lynn Merkt, was imprisoned in Texas on similar charges. Amnesty International adopted her as a prisoner of conscience and began a successful worldwide campaign for her early release. She was the first U.S. prisoner of conscience Amnesty International had designated since 1979.

When these *bona fide* refugees reach the United States they are hunted down by the Border Patrol, intimidated into signing voluntary departure papers and/or imprisoned in barbed wire enclosures. Some of these same detention camps used for Central Americans housed Japanese Americans during World War II. The Immigration and Naturalization Service (INS) has used children as "bait" to capture their parents; one INS official in San Francisco said that if the refugees had carried a photocopy of their death threat with them, then they might obtain asylum. Another INS official cynically said that one refugee's torture marks were no different than scars from falling off a bicycle.

In 1984 the Chicago NBC affiliate took the testimony of a family who had fled El Salvador. The Salvadoran National Guard had entered their house at 1 A.M. and at gunpoint forced the family to watch the rape of their two teenage daughters. The soldiers then kidnapped the two young women. At that point the father searched for seven days for his daughters. He finally found the body of one of them in a graveyard, her arm severed from her body and a dog chewing on her hand. The body of the other daughter was found burned. They fled for their lives and went into sanctuary in a Catholic church in Milwaukee. When NBC questioned the Chicago District INS office about their chances for obtaining political asylum, they were told that unfortunately the family could not receive asylum because they had no written proof of why the soldiers had acted in this way toward them.

These anecdotal stories are verified by studies and statistics that show a systematic denial of political asylum to Salvadorans and Guatemalans since 1980. These denials are based on U.S. foreign policy, not on justice for immigrants. Over the last eight years the U.S. government has sent billions of dollars in military equipment and advisors to the governments of El Salvador and Guatemala. A large approval rate for asylum-seekers from those countries would only confirm a failed foreign policy which arms governments that kill their own people. The refugees are the living witnesses to the atrocities; they must be intimidated into hiding or deported into silence. That is why the sanctuary movement has proven so "dangerous" to those behind present U.S. policy. It has made the connection between a cruel immigration record and an immoral foreign policy.

Recent studies have pointed to this double standard. A Government Accounting Office (GAO) report from January 1986 compared political asylum approvals for Poles and Salvadorans. They found that among those who supported their asylum request by claiming to have been tortured, the approval rate was 4 percent for Salvadorans and 80 percent for Poles. Moreover, the INS changed its decisions to agree with State Department advice in 100 percent of the cases involving Salvadorans. Senator Arlen Spector (R., Pa.) said, "This indicates to me that these decisions are not being made on the basis of merit but on what is considered best for foreign policy. This study and hearings held on these refugee cases have definitely convinced me that Central American refugees are not being treated fairly."

The 1987 Supreme Court decision of *INS vs. Cardoza-Fonseca* has been no landmark but rather business as usual for the Reagan administration. In fiscal year 1987 the political asylum approval rate shows that the Reagan administration has continued to deny asylum to Salvadorans and Guatemalans at a 97 percent rate, in spite of the Supreme Court decision loosening the requirements to prove persecution. However, during that same year Nicaraguans received asylum at an 83 percent rate. In FY 1987, 1,867 Nicaraguan cases received asylum, but only 7 Guatemalan cases and 29 Salvadoran. INS reports approval figures on a case basis rather than reporting the number of individuals accepted or rejected. A case could represent several individuals in the same family. On an individual basis the Salvadoran percentage drops to 1.7 percent.

In FY 1987 the worldwide average for asylum approvals was 54 percent. Nicaraguans alone accounted for 46 percent of all approvals. Asylum applicants from just three countries, Nicaragua, Poland, and Iran, accounted for 80.8 percent of all approvals.

In FY 1987 Poles received asylum at a 47.3 percent rate,

despite the fact that Poles have been receiving extended voluntary departure (EVD) status for the last several years (EVD status means they will not be deported and have a legal right to work and temporarily stay in the United States). For over four years various groups, including the sanctuary movement, have supported legislation that would grant EVD status for Salvadorans and Guatemalans, but the Reagan administration has vowed to veto it even if passed.

The GAO study and the post-*Fonseca* case statistics for FY 1987 conclusively prove what the sanctuary movement has been saying since 1982: immigration policy is a function of foreign policy. Political asylum denials are simply one part of the larger power relationships of domination by the United States over the smaller Central American countries. Humanitarianism for refugees is inextricably linked to justice for Central Americans. Justice requires a thorough analysis of the situation in Central America. What causes refugee flight? How will it stop? What will bring true peace to Central America?

The Central American Context

It is impossible to understand the refugee exodus, the sanctuary movement, and the government's indictment of religious workers without understanding the war in Central America. Colonel John Waghelstein, former U.S. head of advisors in El Salvador, describes the type of warfare being waged in Central America: "The term 'counterinsurgency' has been replaced by the less controversial 'low-intensity conflict.' . . . It is total war at the grassroots level."[3]

This military strategy is an undeclared war that is intense, continuous, and deadly. It utilizes the full range of U.S. economic, political, psychological, and military power, and can be escalated and shifted with incredible speed and coordination. The word *low* only refers to the low number of U.S. combat troops and the low visibility of this type of warfare to the U.S. public.

In "total war" civilians are the targets because the opposition forces are too elusive. As Americas Watch reported in September 1985 about El Salvador: "It is apparent from the testimony of those fleeing Guazapa over the past few years that the civilians and their means of subsistence have been the true targets of the Army in that area."

This has resulted in a variety of human rights abuses (also documented by Americas Watch) which destroy the myth that the human rights situation in El Salvador has been improving.

> In seven supplements of reports (we) have chronicled many changes in the human rights situation, including significant reductions in some forms of abuse; at no time has it been possible to assert that there was a general improvement in human rights. To our regret that remains true. President Duarte's government notwithstanding, the human rights situation in El Salvador remains terrible.[4]

The report goes on to name those practices of the government of El Salvador that violate human rights, including aerial bombardments, strafing, mortaring, and army ground operations that kill, maim, and terrorize the civilian population. In addition, the army engaged in forced relocation of civilians. The report also documented the resurgence of death squads, the continuing, selective use of torture by security forces, including electric shock, hanging by the arms and legs, beatings, and the use of the *capucha* (hood) that makes breathing impossible. This continuing terror is a calculated part of the total war being waged against the people of Central America. The killing of civilians and the creation of refugees are the linchpin of total war. The elimination and/or dislocation of the population is seen as crucial to a Salvadoran (i.e., U.S.) military victory.

Refugees fleeing El Salvador and Guatemala are not victims of random violence, people "caught in the middle" of a bloody war; they are the real targets. The killing and dislocation of the civilian population is the real purpose of the bombing campaigns. The creation of refugees is crucial to the U.S. military strategy. This is why U.S. deportations of Salvadorans will either decrease or remain at low levels. The U.S. government does not mind that they are here, but will do everything possible to keep their presence from proving the existence of continued human rights violations in El Salvador. Thus, they are denied asylum and intimidated into remaining silent. Those who help them to speak out, like the sanctuary movement, are prosecuted, branded as criminals, and intimidated. Evidence abounds that the sanctuary movement and other organizations opposed to the present administration's Central American policy have been put under heavy and illegal surveillance.

Over a dozen sanctuary churches have been broken into. Nothing of value is stolen, but records and files are taken or disturbed. The pattern of break-ins in sanctuaries and scores of other offices of Central American organizations fits the counter-intelligence style of the FBI during the antiwar protests of the 1960s and 1970s. Such operations were designed to disrupt these movements through a variety of intrusive techniques. The committee headed by Frank Church in the U.S. Senate in the mid-1970s condemned these tactics. Recent revelations concerning a sweeping and intrusive FBI investigation of the Committee in Solidarity with the People of El Salvador (CISPES) will spark more congressional investigations. Sanctuary congregations and organizations were mentioned in the FBI files on CISPES, suggesting even broader abuse of first amendment rights by the FBI. This FBI surveillance and the use of undercover informants in the Tucson sanctuary trial show the lengths to which the U.S. government will go to stop grass-roots criticism of U.S. foreign and immigration policy. It also demonstrates how churches and synagogues can be effective and prophetic witnesses to the truth, countering the disinformation and cover-ups produced by the administration. The sanctuary movement has been "dangerous" to those in power because it has consistently unveiled the truth and offered the refugees a platform to tell their stories.

This ministry has proven compelling to many. Over 400 congregations throughout the country have declared public sanctuary and hundreds of others have joined in support. In addition, nearly every major Protestant denomination has passed national resolutions supporting sanctuary and encouraging their local congregations to seriously consider becoming sanctuaries. The Conservative Rabbinical Assembly and the Union of American Hebrew Congregations have both endorsed sanctuary, and several Catholic bishops have written pastoral letters encouraging their congregations to prayerfully consider it. Nearly thirty city councils have declared their cities as sanctuaries, many instructing city workers not to aid immigration agents in determining the status of a person's documentation.

The sanctuary movement has also brought a new theologi-

cal rigor to the Judeo-Christian community in its refusal to separate faith from politics, or the political from the humanitarian. If
a killer were loose in any of our communities, injuring and
killing our neighbors, the response of people of faith would be
twofold. We would certainly find medical help for the wounded
but we would also try to disarm the killer. Why is it considered
humanitarian when churches help the victims of the war in Central America but not humanitarian when they try to stop the
bullets and bombs killing and wounding them in the first place?
The U.S. government would like the progressive religious community to stand silently by while the government chooses who
will die in Central America. The sanctuary movement has refused this role of compliant pallbearers and silent witnesses to
atrocity.

As theologian Dietrich Bonhoeffer said during the Nazi
reign in Germany, the church must certainly bind up the wounded being crushed beneath the wheel, but there comes a time
when the faithful must be like a stick in the spokes, grinding the
wheel to a halt. For the sanctuary movement, this is such a time.

NOTES

1. Gil Loescher and John A. Scanlan, *Calculated Kindness* (New
York: Free Press, 1986), p. xviii.

2. Quoted in *Sanctuary: A Justice Ministry* (Chicago Religious Task
Force on Central America, Spring 1987), p. 25.

3. Quoted in Sara Miles, "The Real War: Low Intensity Conflict in
Central America," *NACLA: Report on the Americas,* April-May 1986, p.
19.

4. *The Continuing Terror: Human Rights in El Salvador* (New York:
Americas Watch, 1985).

HUMANITARIANISM AND POLITICS IN CENTRAL AMERICA

Gil Loescher

Humanitarian work is generally perceived to be somehow separated from politics. This perception has persisted to some extent in the field of refugee protection and assistance. Yet, as other authors in this book have amply demonstrated, humanitarian activities, including refugee work, are deeply intertwined with politics. Refugees are, in fact, an intensely political issue. Their existence affects both foreign and domestic policy, exacerbates inter-state conflicts, and influences international attitudes.

In an earlier chapter, Peter Macalister-Smith traced the evolution of international law and institutions governing humanitarian action. In the aftermath of World War II, a special international regime comprised of UN agencies, governments, churches, and voluntary agencies evolved to aid and protect refugees. When the Office of the United Nations High Commissioner for Refugees (UNHCR) was established in 1951, its work was required to be humanitarian and nonpolitical. However, the postwar period is full of examples where political considerations have influenced international and governmental responses to refugee crises. The cold war in Europe facilitated the reception and care given to Eastern European refugees in the 1950s and 1960s. UNHCR officials have realized for some time that whatever power they exercise is largely dependent on the financial and political support of the United States government and other large donor countries. As David Forsythe argues in another chapter in this book, it has been common for the United States to link humanitarian concerns to strategic national interests. For example, refugees have been used both symbolically and instrumentally to serve larger American foreign policy concerns.[1] "Freedom fighters" from Eastern Europe, Cuba, Indochina, and Nicaragua have been welcomed with open arms in the United States. For the United States, these refugees demonstrate the concrete failings of Communist societies. Refugee have also been used to undermine and destabilize enemy regimes; some refugees have been armed and their counterrevolutions supported, both materially and ideologically.

Today, pressures to politicize refugee crises are increasing everywhere in the world. Humanitarianism has become a political tool used to justify the arming of refugee camps in Pakistan, Thailand, and Honduras, aiding insurgencies in Nicaragua, Ethiopia, and Angola, and suppressing insurgencies in El Salvador and elsewhere. The practice of using refugees in the service of foreign policy or military objectives is by no means limited to the United States, as indicated by the activities of the PLO; Algerian support of Polisario guerrillas claiming the western Sahara; use by Libya of the northern Chadians in operations against Chad; the activities of SWAPO in southern Africa; the sanctuary offered to antigovernment Ethiopian groups by Sudan and to Sudanese secessionists by Ethiopia; and in numerous other cases. Depending on circumstances and its own regional and global strategic objectives, the Soviet Union may lavish assistance or choose to desert groups it has long sponsored. Through such developments, any independence of the humanitarian "space" on the landscape of politics among nations has evaporated.

The fate of efforts to build a "space" for humanitarian work is perhaps best exemplified by examining refugee policy in Central America. Since 1980, war and political persecution have uprooted several million people in Central America. Statistics on displaced persons in Central America are difficult to obtain given the fact that this population is dispersed or wants to remain anonymous. Nevertheless, as of early 1988, approximately 500,000 persons were displaced and unable to live in their home communities within El Salvador, another 500,000 were displaced within Guatemala, and at least 250,000 within Nicaragua.[2] Some of these persons live in recognized camps or settlements, but the majority are dispersed among the marginal population on the fringes of towns and villages. In addition, large numbers of Guatemalans, Salvadorans, and Nicaraguans have left their home countries as refugees and have sought safety in neighboring countries, where they are now playing an increasingly influential role in the politics of the region. Since the intensification of the Central American conflicts between guerrillas and armed forces began, approximately a million Salvadorans and 150,000 Guatemalans have fled their countries, going mostly to Mexico and the United States but also to neighboring nations.[3] In addition, since the advent of the Sandinista revolution and the contra war effort, about 100,000 Nicaraguans have left for neighboring countries and the United States.[4] This article is concerned with the latter groups, particularly those refugees in Mexico, Honduras, and Costa Rica. It examines the political dimensions of recent Central American refugee movements and analyzes the ways in which the perceptions of refugees and the treatment they receive from different governments have been politicized. In particular, this case study of refugee policy in Central America illustrates the different objectives and moral priorities of governments and voluntary agencies and seems to support the earlier contention of Rogers Smith that in such circumstances it is inevitable that the two groups will clash.

As persons outside of their country of origin, refugees are entitled under international law to protection by the UN High Commissioner for Refugees and should be safe from being returned home against their will. Refugees are also entitled to a range of human rights and social and material assistance. Not only the UNHCR, but also the U.S. government, by virtue of being the hegemonic power in Central America, has a direct stake in refugee situations in every country in the region. The level of protection and assistance rendered these refugees is greatly affected by geopolitics and ideology, the interests of a wide range of social actors, and internal security concerns. When discussing refugee issues, it is necessary not just to focus on international legal standards, but also to look at the various actors, their interests, and the way in which geopolitics, ideology, and ethnic politics factor into refugee policy.

For Central American governments, like governments elsewhere, refugees are intimately linked to their nations' security problems.[5] Governments walk a tightrope trying to balance economic, national security, and humanitarian interests. Most are extremely reluctant to accord legal status to refugees from neighboring countries for fear of damaging diplomatic relations, encouraging a mass influx of people seeking refuge, or offering protection to an ideologically incompatible group of persons. Refugees place unacceptably high burdens on Central American governments which are facing severe problems during one of the worst economic crises in the region's history. Refugees require jobs and social services at a time when an increased number of nationals within host countries are also in desperate need of such jobs and services, creating popular resentment toward the refugees and pressures on governments to restrict immigration. Often refugees are vulnerable because they are living on, or very near, disputed borders, and are either residing among combatants in an ongoing conflict or are perceived to be materially assisting guerrilla forces attempting to overthrow the government from which they have fled. Central American governments have viewed refugees as illegal immigrants, guerrillas, or subversives, and have even accused the host governments which provide refuge and the voluntary agencies which work for refugees as "leftist sympathizers" or "contra supporters." As a consequence, on various occasions some host governments have closed their borders to refugees, treated all who attempted to cross as illegal immigrants, expelled new arrivals, incarcerated and harassed those in border camps, and denied journalists and voluntary agencies access to refugee camps.

MEXICO

In 1981–83, when tens of thousands of Guatemalans fled the counterinsurgency campaigns of General Rios Montt, the Mexican authorities initially tried to stem the outflow from Guatemala by forcibly turning back already weak and famished refugees across the border.[6] Emergency assistance was needed simply to assure the survival of the refugees, but the UNHCR and the Mexican government were slow to respond to the crisis. The Catholic Diocese of San Cristobal de las Casas and the already impoverished local peasant communities struggled to fill monumental needs. The Mexican military and migration authorities harassed the refugees and even illegally deported large numbers back to Guatemala.

Eventually, it became clear to the Mexican authorities that
the Guatemalan army's "scorched earth" campaign profoundly
changed the Guatemalan countryside and accepted the fact that
Guatemalans would continue to flee to Mexico for refuge. The
Mexican Commission to Aid Refugees (COMAR), an interagency
office within the Ministry of Interior, which had been established
in July 1980, but had functioned badly and was alleged to be
corrupt, was reorganized in 1983, and empowered to direct a
comprehensive response to the influx of Guatemalan Indians.
With funding from the international community (UNHCR), over
eighty camps were set up in the Mexican southern state of Chiapas to house 45,000 refugees, many of whom were women and
children.

Nevertheless, even today, several years later, living conditions in the camps in Chiapas are poor.[7] Mexico discourages
further refugee migration by providing only minimal services in
the camps and by refusing assistance to new arrivals. Mexican
officials argue that providing adequately for refugees could trig-
ger further resentment on the part of local Mexican populations
who suffer from hunger, disease, and high infant mortality rates.
It is unlikely that local integration will ever be allowed to take
place officially in Chiapas. Most refugees cannot legally take
jobs; when they do find employment, wages are much lower that
those offered to Mexicans. Officially, refugees have no freedom
of movement. Claiming that refugee camps in Mexico harbored
guerrillas and "subversives," the Guatemalan military in the past
crossed the border and ruthlessly attacked refugees with impunity.

Despite these attacks, Mexico was unwilling to protest
strongly the incursions across its border or to take any actions
that the Guatemalan government could interpret as hostile.
Historically the two countries have had difficult relations over
border incidents and over profound differences in political orientation. Chiapas is territory which has strong historical and cultural ties to Guatemala and in the past the region has been
contested by Guatemala. Under these delicate and dangerous
circumstances, Mexico was especially sensitive not to unduly
antagonize its southern neighbor, fearing that a deterioration in
its relations with Guatemala could lead to a militarization of their
common border.

The presence of Guatemalan refugees in Chiapas, therefore, is a source of tension for Mexico's relations with Guatemala and has been perceived by some Mexican officials as a national security risk. Nevertheless, Mexico is willing to offer limited protection to the refugees by allowing them to stay in its territory, but is unwilling to recognize them officially as refugees, since this would allow them permanent residence and would imply a negative judgment on Guatemala's political system. Mexico handles the problem of the Guatemalan Indians' legal status by placing them in the category of "border visitors" and granting them temporary, renewable visas. At the same time, Mexico has attempted to defuse the tension in Chiapas by moving the refugees away from the border.

Since June 1984, about 20,000 refugees have been relocated from Chiapas to the states of Campeche and Quintana Roo in the Yucatan Peninsula, where they live in four refugee centers on land donated by the Mexican government.[8] Certainly these refugees are safer and more economically secure in the Yucatan, but understandably refugees have been extremely reluctant to leave the border area.[9] The terrain and population in Campeche and Quintana Roo are quite different from Chiapas. The climate is hot and dry and there is a persistent problem with having access to sufficient supplies of water. Moreover, there is not enough available land to farm and opportunities for employment outside the centers are minimal. Chiapas, on the other hand, is similar to those parts of Guatemala the refuges left behind. The geography is almost identical and many of the refugees share parts of a common sociocultural heritage with the local Indian population. In Chiapas, the Guatemalans are still close to their former homes. They only have to lift their eyes to the horizon to see the Guatemalan highlands.

In the past, however, COMAR has insisted that, if possible, all the Guatemalans should relocate to the Yucatan Peninsula.[10] They argued that only by moving from the border could the refugees be physically safe from further attacks by the Guatemalan army. In addition to such practical considerations, the Mexican government believes the relocation of Guatemalans from the strategically important border also serves politically useful ends.[11] Population pressure on available arable land and the rapid deforestation of the region has led to a deterioration of living conditions. The Mexican authorities fear that the Guatemalan refugees will strain the existing sociopolitical situation and create fertile ground for political conflict. Chiapas is a politically unstable region which has more than its share of university strikes, political killings, and land tenure problems,[12] and some Mexican officials fear that the Central American revolutions might extend into southern Mexico, which, although poor and underdeveloped, is rich in natural resources. Just as important, Mexico wants to reduce friction with Guatemala by removing a significant source of that friction, the refugees, from the border areas.

All means of persuasion have been used to get the refugees to move from Chiapas. In the past, COMAR cut off supplies to certain camps. Mexican soldiers and border police verbally assaulted the refugees and there were repeated allegations of physical intimidation. The army occasionally burned camps after they were vacated in order to prevent refugees from returning.[13] There is a long tradition of disagreement between national government authorities and the Catholic Church in San Cristobal, and the presence of refugees in this region exacerbates these tensions. Bishop Samuel Ruiz of San Cristobal has routinely criticized the government's rights violations against refugees. The controversy over relocation has tended to polarize the positions of the Mexican government, on the one hand, and the refugees, the local Catholic Church, and voluntary agencies on the other. The UNHCR position is that it opposes the use of violence by Mexican authorities in transferring refugees who refuse the relocation to Campeche and Quintana Roo, while conceding Mexico's sovereign right to decide to move refugees away from border areas. At the same time, UNHCR has made it clear additional relocations would be unsuccessful unless Mexico provides more land for the refugees. Such political decisions are likely to be taken only after the 1988 presidential election in Mexico.

The issue of relocation has been recently superceded in importance by the possibility that some or all of the Guatemalans might be repatriated. With the inauguration of the civilian regime of Vinicio Cerezo in Guatemala in January 1986, hopes were raised for the possible repatriation of thousands of Guatemalans outside the country. During the rule of former military regimes, only a few thousand Guatemalans had returned home from Mexico. Information about the fates and whereabouts of Guatemalan returnees in inadequate. However, at least some of them were reported to have been forced to live in army-run "model villages" or "polos de desarollo" where, it is said, many of the inhabitants were virtual prisoners subjected to roll calls, compulsory labor, and reeducation sessions.

The new president is the first civilian to lead Guatemala since a brief interlude in 1966, and he heads what is effectively the first popularly elected government since 1954. There were hopes that Vinicio Cerezo would take advantage of this wave of support to consolidate civilian power and push through a program of political and economic reforms after decades of repression and military rule.[14] In particular, hopes have been raised regarding an improvement in the human rights situation in Guatemala. Reports on political violence in Guatemala by the U.S. State Department, the Guatemalan government, and human rights organizations give contrasting views of Guatemala's human rights situation since President Cerezo took office. For example, the 1987 State Department Country Report on human rights in Guatemala claimed: "In 1986, political killings and kidnappings dropped to the lowest level in this decade."[15] The Guatemalan government claims there is virtually no political violence. Human rights organizations dispute these findings. According to voluntary agencies working in the field and human rights organizations, the new president is having difficulty ending violent repression and restoring civilian rule in the Guatemalan countryside. Although the controversial secret police force (Departamentos de Investigaciones Tecnicas) was officially disbanded in February 1986, human rights violations, including political assassinations, continue to occur.[16] The "polos de desarollo" have increased in number and compulsory participation of all men between the ages of eighteen and fifty in civilian patrols under army control persists despite the new president's promise to end this practice. The military maintains full control of the rural areas, and displaced persons, returnees, and the few voluntary agencies allowed to work with these groups remain under the strict supervision of the Ministry of Defense.[17]

Despite this controversy over the human rights situation in Guatemala, discussions between the Guatemalan and Mexican governments and UNHCR were initiated in order to determine the possibilities for the safe return home of Guatemalan refugees. At the same time, a visit by the president's wife, Mrs. Cerezo, to refugee camps in Mexico and bilateral discussions between Guatemala and Mexico regarding repatriation occurred on different occasions throughout 1986 and 1987. President Cerezo personally invited all Guatemalan refugees abroad to return home and he set up a Special Commission on Repatriation (CEAR), which has significant military representation to supervise the reception and transportation of returning Guatemalan refugees. In March 1987 the UNHCR established a chargé de mission in Guatemala City and in July 1987, opened a repatriation office in Huehuetenango to receive the returnees. Huehuetenango is a department bordering on Mexico which has little available arable land and which is plagued by land tenure problems. In order to ease the repatriation process, the UNHCR and the European Economic Community have initiated a $898,000 rehabilitation project to cover reception costs and immediate assistance and to pay to upgrade schools, build health clinics, and dig wells in Huehuetenango.[18] In addition, repatriates are given short-term assistance by UNHCR and the World Food Program before they leave Mexico. Upon their arrival in Guatemala, further assistance is provided by CEAR.

Although during 1987 approximately 800 Guatemalans returned with UNHCR assistance and many more returned spontaneously and without official UNHCR sponsorship, the majority of Guatemalan refugees are reluctant to repatriate while the domestic political situation remains unsettled and the army maintains undisputed control of the rural areas. Nongovernmental organizations at work in the area, the Catholic Church of Guatemala,[19] and the refugees themselves do not consider the situation in Guatemala safe for repatriation at this time. While UNHCR and CEAR can supply transport and basic material assistance, they cannot provide physical protection to returnees in the isolated areas to which they return. In March 1987 Guatemalan military forces in Huehuetenango voiced their opposition to repatriation from Mexico of Guatemalan refugees, particularly those from Chiapas. The army believes the refugees have been penetrated by the guerrillas and cannot be trusted. Some military officers hold that refugees who are not accepted by their home communities should be resettled in "polos de desarollo" and subjected to psychological operations. No one in the army is anxious to see refugees return in large numbers but, for the present, acquiesce in the repatriation of small groups they feel they can control.[20] Also there is reported to be local oppositions to the return of refugees in Huehuetenango. There have been complaints from repatriated refugees who say that when they do return to their villages, their land has often been expropriated by squatters and that they are harassed by the civil patrols established by the army. They also complain that they are forced to sign the government amnesty decree and are subsequently viewed with hostility by their neighbors who suspect them of being linked to the guerrilla movement.[21] Apparently other refugees have reintegrated successfully although, all returnees are faced with the same economic and security restraints as the rest of Guatemala's rural population. The condition of returnees varies from one community to the other, but internal turmoil is the rule and not the exception in Guatemala. In these circumstances, the position of UNHCR in mid 1988 is to facilitate voluntary repatriation of Guatemalans whenever it is clear that individual refugees have asked to go home but not to actively promote repatriation. At the same time, UNHCR is identifying UN agencies, such as the United Nations Development Program (UNDP), and voluntary agencies with programs in Guatemala whose collaboration in reintegration assistance could be sought either as an implementing partner or resource organization should the conditions for voluntary repatriation dramatically improve.

The huge numbers of undocumented persons from Central America currently residing in Mexico present an additional intractable refugee problem. On the Pacific Coast, around Tapachula, the entry point into Mexico from Guatemala and the rest of Central America, there are tens of thousands of Guatemalans and an indeterminant number of Hondurans who are seeking refuge.[22] There has always existed a traditional flow of migrant workers from Guatemala who have worked on the coastal coffee, sugar, and cotton plantations in Mexico and who, after the harvests, have returned home. Today, however, the economic situation is so bad in the Guatemalan highlands that the Indian workers simply remain on the fringes of the plantations in Tatachula or go on to the United States after the harvest season. These people are largely unassisted by the international agencies and

COMAR, although they are helped by the local Catholic diocese and by some voluntary agencies, principally CODAIF (Diocesan Committee to Aid Immigrants at the Frontier).

Perhaps the most vulnerable refugee population in Mexico is the Salvadorans. Mexico competes with the United States in having the largest numbers of Salvadorans outside El Salvador. Estimates as to their numbers range from 100,000 to 200,000.[23] Most Salvadorans arrive by air on tourist visas and overstay their time, or enter illegally through the coastal corridor at Tapachula. Since 1983, Mexico has tightened its visa requirements for Central Americans in an attempt to reduce the influx of illegal aliens. The Salvadorans living illegally in Mexico find it increasingly difficult to blend into the national society because of the continuing economic crisis and the consequent high unemployment. Unlike the Guatemalans who are basically Indian peasants from impoverished rural areas. the Salvadorans come from urban areas or small towns. Many are young men who have fled to Mexico out of fear of being pressed either into government military service or into the guerrilla forces. They come individually or in small groups and are dispersed among the most marginalized populations in Mexico's urban "barrios," where they are vulnerable to extortion and exploitation by some corrupt Mexican officials. Although Mexico has been forced by national and international pressure to provide a temporary solution to the plight of Guatemalans in Chiapas, no such similar pressures exist in the case of Salvadorans in the interior. Their plight has received little attention and COMAR does not provide direct social services to the Salvadorans. Only a handful of voluntary agencies, chiefly SEDEPAC (Service for Justice and Peace A.C.), and Catholic and lay missionaries offer minimal help and programs. Also, UNHCR does provide assistance, educational grants, and administrative and social services to many individual Salvadorans in Mexico.

In addition to their precarious economic situation, Salvadoran refugees have virtually no legal protection and live in constant insecurity. The UNHCR can offer them only limited protection. Mexico has not yet signed either of the two principal international refugee instruments, the 1951 UN Convention on Refugees and the 1967 Protocol, and Mexican law does not recognize the status of refugee. However, Mexico is a signatory to several inter-American conventions on asylum and does recog-

nize asylees' status. Unfortunately the protection offered under
these conventions is limited, and flight solely because of personal
safety is not sufficient grounds to warrant asylum. In Mexico,
asylum requires political persecution as the main cause of exodus.

For Salvadoran refugees it is difficult to make a case for
political asylum, since persecution must be proven on an individual basis. The majority of Salvadorans cannot adequately document their cases, and only a small minority can prove direct
political involvement as the cause of their flight. Because very
few Salvadorans can prove individual persecution and because
many are perceived as "economic migrants," the UNHCR office
in Mexico City recognized only a small number of Salvadorans
as asylees. Until recently, the Mexican government granted legal
status of security to only a handful of the candidates for asylum
presented by UNHCR.[24] By 1987, this situation had changed
significantly for the better.

North of Mexico City, Salvadorans and illegal immigrants
are easy prey to Mexican officials and the bands of human smug-
glers ("coyotes"). Harassment, intimidation, imprisonment, and
deportation are common for refugees unable to pay the necessary
bribes. In the early 1980s, the Mexican government deported
between 600 and 1000 illegal immigrants weekly, but there was
no way of determining who were refugees and who were economic migrants.[25] Today's figures are not available. Mexico cooperates with U.S. border officials in returning Central Americans
apprehended at the U.S. border back to Central America. According to voluntary agencies working in the area, approximately
600 Central Americans are detained each month in Mexican
border cities where they are subjected to abuse and extortion.[26]
Mexican agencies intervene to protect many of the most vulnerable cases. The Centro de Investigacion y Estudios in Tijuana has
secured the release of hundreds of such Central American refugees imprisoned by Mexican authorities.[27]

It is U.S. deterrence policy to stop the flow of Central
Americans to the United States by capturing potential refugees
before they cross the border. Mexico has tightened its control
over Central Americans attempting to cross the northern border
into the United States but prefers not to publicize such actions.
Although both governments want to reduce the flow of Central

Americans into their countries, bilateral cooperation on immigration matters has been limited by international and domestic policy factors. Mexico and the United States have widely different perspectives towards the conflicts in the region. The Central American refugee issue exacerbates tensions over U.S. treatment of Mexican nationals, who still outnumber the Central American arrivals, and there exist significant internal Mexican pressures against any actions that appear to subordinate Mexican policies to U.S. pressures.[28] Those Salvadorans who manage to evade the Mexican authorities but are seized by the U.S. Border Patrol after entering the U.S. are confined to detention centers and deported.

Each month about 500 Salvadorans are deported from the United States directly back to San Salvador.[29] The Intergovernmental Committee for Migration (ICM) cooperates with the United States in the Salvadoran deportation program. ICM receives the returnees upon their arrival in San Salvador airport, registers the returnees, and provides them with identity papers and funds for initial transport and lodging.[30] ICM attempts to maintain contact with those registered with it by distributing a questionnaire to returnees. Those who have returned the questionnaire have indicated that they have experienced no problems. This information is used by the U.S. government to justify further deportations. ICM is by no means an international protection agency and cannot provide protection to the returnees. Information on the questionnaires regarding the plight of Salvadoran returnees is extremely limited, and about half of them do not respond at all. The Political Asylum Project of the American Civil Liberties Union claims that in the past there were large numbers of cases of returnees allegedly imprisoned, tortured, or killed,[31] but the U.S. State Department disputes this finding. There remains an urgent need for a credible international or regional agency such as UNHCR, the International Committee for the Red Cross (ICRC), or the Inter American Human Rights Commission to monitor Salvadoran returnees.

As a result of the deliberate U.S. policy to keep out Salvadorans and to refuse them even temporary haven, primarily on the grounds of national interest and immigration control, a serious rift has occurred between church and state over the issue of humanitarianism and U.S. foreign policy in Central America. These issues are discussed in detail in the chapters by Doris

Meissner, Michael McConnell, and Henry Shue. However, U.S. policies toward Central American asylum-seekers reflect official American attitudes toward the region as a whole and the propensity on the part of U.S. policymakers to place national security interests above humanitarian goals.

HONDURAS

The refugee situation in Honduras is even more complicated than that existing in Mexico and is intimately tied to the geopolitics of the region. The actors are numerous and include not only the Honduran government and military, but also the Honduran Refugee Commission (CONARE), the U.S. government, the UNHCR, the Honduran Catholic Church, voluntary agencies, the contras, international human rights and religious groups, and the refugees themselves. Honduras has refugees from all three refugee-producing countries in Central America: El Salvador, Guatemala, and Nicaragua. Since the early 1980s, the number of officially recognized refugees include about 20,000 Salvadorans, about 500 Guatemalans, about 15,000 Miskito, Sumo, and Ramos Indians and other Atlantic coast refugees from Nicaragua, and about 11,000 Ladino or Spanish-speaking Nicaraguan refugees. Among the Atlantic coast refugees, there are numerous factions, each with its own political agenda.

There are several strategic, historical, and legal influences on refugee policy-making in Honduras. Real decision-making power remains in the hands of the military commanders in Honduras, who, in turn, are directly influenced by the U.S. government.[32] Honduras regards the refugee problem as a matter of national security rather than a humanitarian issue. Thus, the treatment and protection accorded refugees are determined largely by geopolitical and strategic consideration, in particular by Honduran relations with the U.S. and Salvadoran governments. Although refugees are a microcosm of the geopolitical struggle in the region and are viewed by the Honduran military and the United States in East-West, Communist versus non-Communist terms, history, geography, and border tensions also have their impact on policy and to a certain extent moderate the effect of ideology on policymaking.

Traditionally, Hondurans perceive El Salvador as posing the principal threat to their security. This is partly the result of demography. El Salvador is the most densely populated country in the region and Honduras has far fewer people per square mile. For some time there has been a traditional migration of agricultural workers from El Salvador to Honduras. Salvadorans are viewed as industrious and aggressive, and Hondurans don't want them to settle in their country. The so-called "Soccer War" in 1969 between the two countries was a result of these migration tensions. The recent wave of Salvadorans began in 1980, and settled precisely in this conflictive region of historical migration. Nicaragua, on the other hand, is not viewed as a traditional threat to Honduran security. Although there were border clashes in the 1950s and 1960s, and problems during the Sandinista insurgency in the 1970s, the Honduras-Nicaragua relationship has been more harmonious than the Honduras-El Salvador relationship. Thus, the Honduran military is divided over how to treat Nicaragua. The American-trained soldiers share the U.S. geopolitical view of the Sandinistas and consider the Communists the principal threat to Honduran security, while the "Soccer War" veterans see El Salvador as the danger. These soldiers resent the training of Salvadoran soldiers on Honduran territory and view such efforts as enabling El Salvador to one day more easily achieve its ambitions and seize Honduran territory.

In addition, Honduras is not a signatory to the 1951 UN Refugee Convention or the 1967 Protocol. Honduran migration authorities issue identity cards to refugees in camps and recognize Salvadorans and Guatemalans as refugees legally in the country. However, Salvadoran refugees are restricted to the camps and have no right to work or travel. Moreover, there is no guarantee of physical safety for these individuals, because they are either in camps which are located only a few kilometers from the militarized border zone or in camps which are surrounded, controlled, and harassed by the Honduran military. Honduras treats refugees as an essentially political problem to be resolved outside any legal framework and has formulated policy using chiefly ideological and geopolitical considerations rather than legal considerations. This development has had a powerful impact on the level of protection accorded refugees of certain nationalities in Honduras and has resulted in a double standard being applied which discriminates against Salvadorans and Guatemalans and favors Nicaraguans.

To date, the response of Honduras to the Salvadorans and Guatemalans seeking refuge in the country has been to place them in camps under strict military guard. Violent crimes against the refugees have been committed with apparent impunity.[33] The worst such attack occurred on August 29, 1985, when the Salvadoran camp at Colomoncagua was surrounded by Honduran military forces, while a division of the COBRAS, an elite counter-insurgency force, entered the camp and terrorized the refugees. In the violence that followed two refugees were killed, one a three-month-old baby, reportedly kicked to death. Thirteen were wounded, one of whom subsequently died as a result of injuries suffered during the attack.[34] It was the first time in Latin America that a host government army killed and wounded refugees in a United Nations-run camp. Ten Salvadorans were detained and confined in small prison cells in Tegucigalpa until their release for resettlement abroad in January 1986. Attacks against individual Salvadoran refugees continue, and local and international voluntary agency personnel daily risk their lives to perform their duties in these camps.

This policy of persecution of Salvadoran refugees stands in marked contrast to the policy applied to refugees from Nicaragua. Unlike the Salvadoran refugees who are sympathetic to the forces fighting against the U.S.-backed government of El Salvador, many Nicaraguan refugees either are opposed to Nicaragua's Sandinista government or are fleeing the violence in their country. Nicaraguan refugees are not subjected to the same strict monitoring by the Honduran army. Although the freedom of movement previously accorded Nicaraguan refugees has been curtailed, they enjoy much greater freedom of movement than the Salvadorans and can work outside their camps. Until recently, contra commanders entered Nicaraguan camps and openly recruited young refugee men into the armed forces. This contrasts sharply with the officially sponsored campaigns of vilification depicting the Salvadoran refugees and the voluntary agencies which help them as threats to Honduran national security.

Tensions between the Honduran authorities and the Salvadorans continue because of the Hondurans' belief, shared by the U.S. government, that the refugee camps along the border provide direct support for Salvadoran guerrillas.[35] The refugees in these camps originate principally from the border departments of Morazan, Cabanas, and Chalatenango, where guerrilla activity is intense. Therefore, sympathy for the FMLN forces among the refugees is great, but according to UNHCR and voluntary agency staff who actually live in the camps, the Salvadoran refugees provide moral, not strategic, support to the guerrillas.[36] The refugee camps at Colomoncagua and San Antonio house, for the most part, women, children, and old men and are unarmed. As a result, refugees have not been able to defend themselves against the Honduran army during previous attacks and harassments. The voluntary agencies which distribute food and medicine to the refugees and oversee the camp workshops which produce clothes and boots also completely disagree with Honduran and U.S. allegations that the refugees are channelling a significant amount of supplies (boots, clothes, food, medicine) to guerrillas fighting inside El Salvador.[37] Moreover, the camp is surrounded by an aggressive Honduran military patrol. An on-site investigation of the security situation at Colomoncagua by the author in early 1986, confirms the UNHCR–voluntary agency view that it would be physically impossible to smuggle any significant amount of aid through that encirclement patrol. However, the U.S. and Honduran governments remain adamant that their positions are correct and believe that large-scale assistance to Salvadoran refugee constitutes help to forces hostile to their interests. The issue symbolizes the intensity of the conflict with Honduras and the U.S., on one side, and the refugees and certain voluntary agencies on the other.

There have also been attempts to relocate and repatriate Salvadoran refugees. The Honduran military (and the U.S. government) have in the past pushed hard for relocating the Salvadoran refugees encamped along the border, by force if necessary, to Mesa Grande or to other suitable sites further inland. Relocation, it was believed, would cut the guerrilla life-line and clear the border for military maneuvers.[38] The refugees, backed by the voluntary agencies, believed that they should be allowed to stay where they are with improved protection and greater opportunities for self-sufficiency. These contrasting positions illustrate once again Roger Smith's earlier contention that governments and humanitarian agencies are most likely to clash in circumstances where national security interests override humanitarian objectives. Voluntary agencies were also concerned that, regardless of the merit of the move from the border, it could not be accomplished without violence. The UNHCR supported an earlier relocation of Salvadorans which took place in late 1981. This move was forcible and involved considerable hardship and loss of life.[39] No buildings were prepared prior to the refugees' arrival at the relocation site at Mesa Grande and there was a severe shortage of water. Food supplies were cut off to those who refused to relocate, and numerous refugees and Honduran voluntary agency workers were murdered or injured. Conditions were so horrible that an estimated 4,000 Salvadorans repatriated to El Salvador rather than remain in Honduras. Because UNHCR supported the relocation, relations between it and the voluntary agencies deteriorated significantly.

When Honduras announced its plans for a second relocation in December 1983, UNHCR affirmed the right of the Honduran government to determine the location of the refugee settlements but made it clear that it would support further relocations only if they could be carried out without violence and only if the refugees were given land to farm, were allowed to become self-sufficient, and could obtain work and have freedom of movement. Government efforts to establish a new relocation program faltered because of vociferous local opposition from the population at proposed relocation sites in Olanchito in northern Honduras and in other states. The Honduran populace deeply resented giving over large tracts of land to Salvadoran refugees when they themselves had little or no land to till. Moreover, the Honduran army was divided over the relocation issue and did not want to see Salvadorans as permanent settlers. International human rights and religious groups also criticized the relocation plan. In light of this opposition, the Honduran authorities were forced to publicly abandon relocation after the August 1985 attack on Colomoncagua. José Azcona Hoyo, the president of Honduras, affirmed that relocation is no longer a priority for Honduras and that refugees will not be moved against their will.[40] Instead, the Honduran authorities are escalating their military presence around the camps and have assumed more direct administrative control over the refugee programs inside the camps.[41] The objective of such maneuvers is to make conditions inside the camps as austere as possible so as to discourage new arrivals and to encourage repatriation to El Salvador.

Repatriation has always been an option for Salvadoran refugees in Honduras.[42] In late 1981, 4,000 Salvadorans spontaneously returned home rather than relocate to Mesa Grande in Honduras. During the past several years, several thousand more Salvadorans have repatriated. Most of these refugees were accompanied to the border by UNHCR officials in Honduras, who gave them basic subsistence aid for the first few weeks upon their return. Because UNHCR had an extremely limited presence in El Salvador, it could not possibly monitor returnees adequately. Nevertheless, the possibility of large-scale repatriation was kept alive through the existence of an official tripartite commission comprising El Salvador, Honduras, and UNHCR.

In August 1986, UNHCR opened a chargé de mission in San Salvador in order to assist returning refugees. Since February 1987, the UNHCR has received returnees at the border and has helped them obtain birth certificates, national identification cards, and other documentation needed to travel within the country. As a result, the number of organized repatriation movements from Honduras to El Salvador have continued at a steady rate. In October 1987, 4,500 Salvadorans repatriated en masse to El Salvador from Mesa Grande. Most of these refugees had been in camps for six years and were increasingly frustrated by the harsh conditions of camp life and by the total lack of possibility for local integration in Honduras. The refugees had set certain conditions for their repatriation, including the promise by Salvadoran officials that returnees could go back to their places of origin, that they would not be drafted into military service, that there would be no military posts in their communities, that they would have freedom of movement and the right to work, that they would have a right to assistance from international agencies and free access to the media.[43] The Social Secretariat of the Salvadoran Catholic Archdiocese as well as national and international agencies within El Salvador have mobilized themselves to coordinate assistance to the returnees and to monitor, along with UNHCR, their safety upon return.

Repatriation poses considerable problems for the government of El Salvador. Since the passage of the Immigration Reform and Control Act of 1986 in the United States, the Duarte government has been apprehensive about the possible return home of nearly half a million Salvadorans living illegally in the United States and subject to deportation. Moreover, the armed forces of El Salvador perceive the refugees as guerrilla sympathizers and are reluctant to permit a mass return to their original areas where the guerrilla opposition is most active. Therefore, returnees cannot be certain of their physical safety. In September 1987, for example, six returnees were wounded and one died when Salvadoran planes bombed a small village in one of the areas of El Salvador selected for repatriation. Despite these problems, reports from the returnees in early 1988 indicate that the repatriation was an initial success and may lead the way for other groups of Salvadorans to return home later in the year.

Although it is common for Salvadoran refugees to have their human rights abused and their physical safety threatened, Nicaraguan refugees also have security problems. In the past, problems of protection arose from the activities of the Nicaraguan armed opposition forces (contras) who were frequently given free reign by the Honduran military. Nicaraguan refugees served convenient symbolic and instrumental purposes in U.S. foreign policy. Symbolically they have been perceived by anti-Communists as fleeing a repressive totalitarian regime. By "voting with their feet," they are sending a clear message to the world that life inside Nicaragua is intolerable.[44] Nicaraguan refugees have also been instrumentally useful. They are "freedom fighters" who can be trained and used to wage revolutionary war against Nicaragua, America's principal adversary in the region. Thus, U.S. humanitarian aid to these groups and to the contras is perceived to have become an open political tool to arm refugee camps and to aid insurgencies. The Honduran position is more complicated because the authorities have to placate internal Honduran resistance to the presence of contras on Honduran soil and at the same time respond to external pressures from Washington to allow the contras a base for their guerrilla activities. Until recently, Honduras maintained an official policy of not openly admitting to the presence of contras within its territory while quietly cooperating with U.S. efforts to supply them. However, by mid 1988, the military position of the contras had considerably worsened and Honduran support waned.

Nicaraguan refugees, particularly Ladinos, have been

served solely by the Honduran Red Cross and by conservative Protestant evangelical agencies that are anti-Sandinista and openly support the contras.[45] The influx of Ladinos began in 1982, and there has been a continuous increase in numbers since that time. Many of the refugees are peasants fleeing fighting in the Nicaraguan countryside; others are young men fleeing conscription into the Sandinista military. Moreover, as the domestic economic situation in Nicaragua has steadily deteriorated further under American sanctions, still more Nicaraguans have fled to Honduras. In recent years, the size of the Ladino camps has nearly doubled as large numbers of Nicaraguans associated with the contras have sought safety further inland.[46] Because of the partisan political setting, many voluntary agencies have shied away from working in these camps. The lack of a more neutral international presence in these camps has made it easier for the refugees themselves to be exploited by the contras and the United States for political and military purposes.

As counterinsurgency forces brought war to the border areas and as groups of Atlantic coast Indians became discontented with the Sandinista regime and its political indoctrination, thousands of Miskito and Sumo Indians fled Nicaragua during 1981–1983.[47] The 20,000 Miskitos and other Atlantic coast refugees who took refuge in the sparsely populated region near the Honduran Caribbean coast have been particularly exploited for political purposes. Miskito and Sumo Indians have been manipulated ideologically and subjected to forced military recruitment by militant Nicaraguan Indian groups allied with the contras, particularly along the Rio Coco between Honduras and Nicaragua.

The militarization of the border provided a significant barrier to effective relief and protection work by UNHCR, which began a program in the Honduran Mosquitia in 1982. In order to offer better protection and relief, UNHCR relocated refugees away from the troubled border in 1983 to dispersed settlements further inland. Over the next two years, conditions for these refugees improved and the number of settlements increased. In contrast to Salvadorans in western Honduras, Nicaraguan Miskito and Sumo Indians enjoyed freedom of movement, access to markets and adequate material assistance. However, problems of protection continued as refugees were harassed and forcibly recruited by militant Miskito Indians (Misura), who controlled the infrastructure of the camps and directly benefitted from refugee aid.[48] The Honduran army, which is responsible for security in the Mosquitia, seldom intervened on behalf of the refugees and was perceived to be in close collaboration with the contra forces. Until early 1985, UNHCR did not have protection officers based in the region, and World Relief, the principal voluntary agency contracted by UNHCR to carry out relief operations, placed inexperienced North American personnel in key positions in the refugee settlements.

In 1985, new problems occurred. The World Relief/ UNHCR effort to make the refugees self-sufficient was hampered by severe restrictions on the cutting of wood for land clearance and domestic use by the Honduran Forestry Commission. As a consequence, rice production fell drastically in 1985. The Miskitos also complained that the soil around the inland settlements didn't produce a good bean crop, a staple of the Indian diet. In late 1984 and 1985, these conditions encouraged a mass movement of refugees back to the border where land was more fertile and government wood cutting restrictions did not apply.[49] At about the same time, during the period of a congressional ban on aid to the contras, the U.S. Congress voted to provide $7.5 million in "humanitarian" aid to Misura. These projects were administered by USAID and by a partisan evangelical organization, Friends of America, on the Honduran-Nicaraguan border. These refugee camps became a base for Miskito-contra operations and pulled refugees away from UNHCR settlements in the Honduran Mosquitia. During the past several years, the Nicaraguan government has issued several amnesty decrees for rebel Indian groups in an attempt to attract home all Miskito and other Atlantic coast refugees.[50] In 1985 wide-ranging negotiations were initiated with some of the armed Indian opposition on the subject of regional autonomy. Limited peace accords between the government and indigenous groups made possible the return of 12,000 internally displaced Miskitos and Sumos to the Rio Coco. During the same year, some 2,000 Miskitos who had taken refuge on the Honduran bank of the river returned to Nicaragua on their own, and another 500 to 600 Miskitos were also repatriated from the inland settlements in Honduras. According to UNHCR,[51] the numbers of returnees would have been much larger had the refugees been allowed to travel directly from the refugee settlements to their former homes, a distance of about two hundred kilometers. Instead, UNHCR was required to move refugees in small groups a distance of about 1,500 kilometers, out of the Honduran Mosquitia to Tegucigalpa, by bus to Managua, and then by small plane to the Nicaraguan Atlantic coast. This costly and complicated procedure was eased considerably when UNHCR finally won the approval of the Honduran authorities to transport the refugees by air from the Atlantic coast of Honduras directly to the Atlantic coast of Nicaragua in May 1987. By early 1988, approximately 4,000 Miskitos had been assisted by UNHCR to return home via this air corridor and another 7,000 had returned by land unassisted.[52]

Hopes for an early mass repatriation, however, are complicated by grave security and economic problems in this war torn region of northeastern Nicaragua. Much of the Indians' former land is militarily contested, and entire villages have been destroyed by military action or natural decay since the early 1980s. The provision of social services to the Atlantic coast by the government is made difficult by poor transport and the lack of other infrastructure in the region. In the past, government health and education workers sent to help resettle refugees have been murdered or kidnapped. Periodic conflict continues between the Sandinista forces and militant Indian groups who are just across the Rio Coco in Honduras. The Nicaraguan government and the international community are, nevertheless, making considerable efforts to ensure a successful repatriation of Miskitos and other Indians to Nicaragua. Since late 1986, UNHCR, ICRC, and World Food Program have provided assistance for returnees and the EEC has pledged $1.5 million for a reintegration program for the Nicaraguan Indians.

Thus, the situation for Nicaraguan Indian refugees remains in a state of rapid transition and is highly complex. In mid-1985, the militant Indian group Misura was officially dissolved and replaced by a new organization called Kisan, which was firmly in the contra organization in Honduras. Operations by Kisan in northeastern Nicaragua in early 1986 caused considerable instability and resulted in the flight of thousands more Indians across the Rio Coco into Honduras.[53] Despite these events, a considerable number of Miskitos applied for the Sandinista amnesty during 1987.[54] Alarmed at the rapid decline in the Indian resistance movement, the U.S. State Department organized a meeting of Kisan and other exile groups in June 1987, to form yet another new organization, Yatama or FACA (armed forces of the Atlantic coast). One of its objectives was to prevent the return of the Miskito Indians from Honduras to Nicaragua. In February 1988, the Nicaraguan government and Yatama signed an accord agreeing to halt all military actions and to continue talks aimed at ending the war and working out a new policy for Nicaragua's Atlantic coast. Nicaraguan Indian groups in Costa Rica are monitoring the situation carefully before deciding whether or not to return. A successful mass repatriation of Miskitos to Nicaragua, therefore, will depend on the ability of Miskito groups and the Sandinistas to maintain a ceasefire in the region.

Costa Rica

Although the refugee situation is not as acute as that which exists in Honduras or Mexico, political and foreign-policy considerations have also played a part in shaping Costa Rica's response to refugees. Costa Rica is the recipient of refugees from the three principal refugee-producing countries in the region: El Salvador, Guatemala, and Nicaragua. There are approximately 23,000 Nicaraguan and 5,000 to 6,000 Salvadoran refugees officially registered in the country since 1980, and the Nicaraguans have been arriving since 1983, with 6,000 coming in 1985 alone. Seventy percent of the refugees in Costa Rica live in urban areas, principally in San Jose, and 30 percent in refugee camps in rural areas. The reception and transit camps are administered by the Costa Rican Red Cross and the Center of Socio-Political Analysis (CASP), a national nongovernmental organization which also provides assistance to refugees in urban areas. The country's increasing international indebtedness and local economic problems limit assistance and employment opportunities for refugees. In the rural camps there is no land to farm, and although refugees can obtain work permits, only a small percentage of them actually find jobs on a permanent basis. Urban based refugees receive limited training and education. However, given the educational level of many of the refugees and the restrictive legal provisions regarding employment, they find it difficult to obtain work and are unable to compete with Costa Rican nationals. The so-called "active center" at Achiote which is administered by the International Rescue Committee provides small plots of land to farm but accommodates only relatively small numbers of refugees.[55]

In addition to the registered refugees, Costa Rica has at least tens of thousands of undocumented immigrants.[56] There is a long history of migration from Nicaragua to Costa Rica. Former president Luis Alberto Monge has termed this problem a "migratory time bomb."[57] Public perception that jobs are being lost to these newcomers, while large amounts of assistance are also being provided them, has given rise to an intense and emotional debate over refugees within Costa Rica. Growing popular resentment against refugees is evident almost daily in the Costa Rican press and xenophobic and racist comments about refugees have been made in the past by Costa Rican officials responsible for refugee and migration affairs.

Costa Rica is renowned for its democratic traditions. Although situated in a region where armed conflict has recently been the rule, Costa Rica has not had a standing army since 1948. With the intensification of military turmoil in Central America during the late 1970s, however, Costa Rica was inevitably drawn into the conflict in the region. U.S. military aid to Costa Rica rapidly increased during the early 1980s and many U.S. economic projects in Costa Rica appeared to serve military ends.[58] Near its northern border, Costa Rica in the past played host to two contra forces: Arde, led by the former Sandinista leader Eden Pastora, and the CIA-backed Uno group. Cross-border clashes between these groups and Sandinista forces were common. As the Contra-Irangate hearings have now made clear, the United States assisted the contras in Costa Rica through the American embassy in San José and supplied the contras inside Nicaragua from a secret airstrip built by Americans in northern Costa Rica. According to testimony made public through these hearings, the United States had a virtual free hand in Costa Rica to pursue its military objectives for the region prior to the Oscar Arias administration.[59]

The militarization of Costa Rica policy directly affected the protection of refugees. The UNHCR provides the funds for the refugee program but has no permanent presence in these camps. Until late 1985, a national organization, Socorro Internacional, ran the camps for Nicaraguans in an inefficient, corrupt, and politicized manner.[60] Some of them were found to have paid themselves excessively high salaries, and to have had direct links to the contras, and to have run paternalistic programs. The camp for Atlantic coast Nicaraguan refugees at Limon, which I visited in January 1986, had the worst physical conditions of any camp I saw in Central America. Although the refugees were apparently well fed and had adequate health care, the housing was inferior and the camp inhabitants appeared despondent and apathetic for lack of anything to do. There was no land to farm and no workshops, and the refugees were entirely dependent on the outside assistance provided them. The camp infrastructure was under the control of an ex-commandante Miskito contra. Conditions in other camps for Nicaraguans were somewhat better. A large number of the inhabitants were single young Ladino men, many of them teenagers, who had fled forced conscription or bad economic conditions. The camps provided little activity for the refugees and were badly overcrowded.

In late 1985 Costa Rican authorities and UNHCR began to reconstruct the refugee programs for Nicaraguans and to make the camps more participatory and less paternalistic. In September 1985 Costa Rica created the National Council for Refugees, which consolidated refugee policymaking in the office of the presidency. With the election of Oscar Arias Sánchez, Costa Rica reached a tentative agreement with Nicaragua to neutralize the border and to try to establish a civilian monitoring team to prevent contra raids into Nicaragua.[61] The revelation in late 1986 of the transfer of millions of dollars of clandestine aid to the contras from sales of arms to Iran by the Reagan administration and the politically damaging Contra-Irangate hearings further strengthened the ability of Arias to resist U.S. pressures to aid contra efforts in Costa Rica. As a result, Arias demonstrated his determination to stem the militarization of his country and to criticize the U.S. determination to pursue a military solution against Nicaragua. In particular, Arias emphasized the advantages of political rather than military pressure on Nicaragua and publicly called for ending U.S. aid to the contras.

The Costa Rican president's peace initiatives culminated in a regional peace accord signed by five Central American governments on August 7, 1987, in Guatemala City. The central features of the accord require the Central American governments to stop aiding the U.S.-backed contras in exchange for the Sandinista government negotiating a cease fire, issuing an amnesty, ending press censorship, and guaranteeing full political freedom. The agreement also addresses the conflict in El Salvador and Guatemala, but the provisions relating to ceasefires and aid to irregular forces cannot be implemented without the consensus of other interested parties, particularly the United States.

Since the signing of the peace accord, the presidents, ministers, and various technical staffs have met several times to implement the agreement and to ensure that the Committees of National Reconciliation established in most of the Central American nations were functioning properly. Although the Reagan administration initially opposed the Arias plan, the political and economic costs of waging a protracted war in Nicaragua weighed heavily on both the Sandinistas and their contra opponents. For President Daniel Ortega, the war has devastated much of Nicaragua and has helped to bankrupt its economy. For the contras, the will and means to continue the fight were rapidly deteriorating as a result of a string of losses at the hands of government troops, together with the refusal of Congress to grant any more military aid. For the United States too, the prospect of a long-term commitment to a low intensity conflict which involved frequent tussles with Congress over funding and constant appeals for support from an American public deeply divided over the war was not greatly appealing. At talks in Sapoa, Nicaragua in March 1988, the two Nicaraguan combatants agreed to a sixty-day truce while negotiating an end to the war. The initiation of direct negotiations between the contras and the Sandinistas remains the most solid achievement of the peace process so far and hopefully signals the possibility of an end to the conflict in Nicaragua. Unfortunately, the same willingness to negotiate and make political compromises is not present in either El Salvador or Guatemala. Therefore, in mid 1988, many observers remained skeptical of the immediate prospects for peace throughout all of Central America.

THE STRUGGLE FOR HUMANITARIAN SPACE

Humanitarianism in Central America has by and large fallen victim to political and ideological conflict. This development bears significance not only for American foreign policy, but also for intergovernmental and private humanitarian efforts supported by the United Nations and the voluntary agencies. The activities of UNHCR and the voluntary agencies are directly affected by the geopolitical and ideological context in which the United States and local governments perceive the refugee issue. The UNHCR has been criticized by voluntary agency officials, as well as by representatives of governments which finance the UNHCR program in the region, for its inability to protect refugees from harassment and for its failure to provide an adequate level of assistance to all groups of refugees. As the principal donor to UNHCR programs in the region, the United States has used its financial leverage to improve conditions for Nicaraguan refugees in Honduras and Costa Rica and has exerted pressure to influence UNHCR decisions about such issues as the relocation or repatriation of Salvadoran refugees in Honduras.

U.S. influence aside, the institutional capacity of UNHCR to ameliorate the refugee situation in Central America is also limited by the willingness of national governments to cooperate with it. UNHCR can call attention to the legal obligations undertaken by governments that have adhered to the UN Refugee Convention and Protocol, but it is without the ability to change the course of a determined government that intends to violate treaty commitments to protect and aid refugees or to ignore the policies of the United Nations with regard to refugees.

Honduras and Mexico are not signatories to the UN Refugee Convention and Protocol, and although the 'nonrefoulement principle' (no forcible return to country of origin) is confirmed in their domestic laws, neither country has formal procedures to determine refugee status. In both countries UNHCR operates large-scale refugee programs, but there are disagreements over how the UNHCR exercises its protection mandate. There have also been tensions over the management of refugee assistance programs in all three countries, Mexico, Honduras, and Costa Rica.

Caught between its general function to offer protection to

refugees and the necessity to work closely with the country of first asylum, UNHCR is reluctant to irritate local authorities or the United States by pressing too hard on protection problems in Central America. As noted, the limited effectiveness of UNHCR to guarantee protection is also partly due to UNHCR's special relationship with the United States. Dependent on the United States for a large percentage of its annual budget, UNHCR simply lacks the financial independence and institutional strength to challenge its largest benefactor.

Voluntary agencies, ranging from international NGOs to churches, have also discovered that their ability to operate independently of the United States is limited and at the mercy of events which remain largely under the control of military and strategic planners. In Central America these institutions, simply by virtue of working in certain refugee camps, are often regarded by the security forces of local governments and by the United States as subversives or sympathizers with the opposition forces. In this kind of ideologically charged environment many voluntary agencies find it extremely difficult to carry out humanitarian programs of assistance. Thus churches and voluntary agencies have met with many difficulties which have ranged from economic pressures to hostility, threats, kidnappings, deportation, and even the deaths of many workers. In Salvadoran, Nicaraguan, and Guatemalan refugee camps in Honduras, Costa Rica, and Mexico, voluntary agency representatives have had to assume protection functions at considerable personal risk to themselves. The presence of international agency staff should serve to reinforce the security of the refugees and of the local national workers in the camps. In many instances, respect for the basic human rights and personal security of refugees depends on the whim of junior military officers or migration officials locally in command of the camps. Not only do voluntary agencies and churches provide local protection but these institutions are also particularly influential in shaping international public opinion. Concerned churches and human rights organizations provide information on refugee conditions to the public and monitor human rights abuses and violations of international agreements. The extent to which *nonrefoulement* is even minimally respected in Central America is probably due to the vigilance of these private and international groups who have raised loud objection to past border incidents in Mexico and Honduras, when refugee camps were attacked by military forces and refugees forcibly repatriated. As Rogers Smith argues, humanitarian agencies act in this way as valuable critics of U.S. and other governments' "excessive parochialism" and call on policymakers "to conform to [their] own best principles." Voluntary agencies, in other words, can act as a healthy corrective to governments' tendencies to pursue realpolitik at all costs.

However, although voluntary agencies view themselves as the "world's conscience for refugees," they are themselves rarely totally neutral in a political sense. Some agencies take pride in being able to work on both sides of a political fence, but most voluntary agencies are selective about the places they choose to work and the refugee groups they choose to assist. In their effort to counteract U.S. regional policies, some voluntary agencies have emphasized their commitment to Salvadoran and Guatemalan refugees but have shied away from assuming a similarly strong protection role for Nicaraguan refugees. Conservative religious voluntary agencies, on the other hand, are very forthright in their support for Reagan administration policies in Central America and many of them target their assistance toward Nicaraguan camps while excluding Salvadorans. As we have seen, some voluntary agencies have contributed to the treatment of refugees as political and military objects. Friends of Americas, for example, opened new programs in Honduras close to the Nicaraguan border in order to attract refugees from established and safer camps so that they could more easily be recruited by their contra allies. Local governments reinforce this selectivity by making it difficult for voluntary agencies to have a presence in refugee camps of all political and ideological persuasions. Such selectivity increases the risk of voluntary agencies being used for narrow political interests and makes some of them appear to be as discriminatory as the U.S. government policies they oppose or as mere extensions of American military policy. In particular, the use of humanitarian assistance to promote American political and strategic interests in the region has sharply divided the voluntary agency community. Some agencies believe the contras deserve their active support, while others perceive aid to the contras to be neither humanitarian nor appropriate. In these instances humanitarian agencies need to be reminded of the immediate material needs of individuals irrespective of their political ideology or their relationship to U.S. foreign policy in the region. Clearly both governments and voluntary agencies need to engage in what Smith terms an "open-ended critical dialogue with each other." However, in the case of Central America, conflict over what constitutes genuine humanitarianism has to date formed insuperable obstacles to any such dialogue.

While refugees are pawns in relations between states, they are not always the helpless victims intergovernmental and voluntary agencies often picture them to be. Such stereotyping is usually not only inaccurate but encourages paternalism. Refugees and their leaders are seldom passive. Over the past decade some of the refugee groups in Central America have patiently built up, under incredibly difficult circumstances, the major elements of the infrastructure required for their communities. These groups request that these attempts to rebuild their lives be respected and their human rights not be violated. Other refugee groups are factionalized and have been intimately involved in politics. As we have seen, there are instances where some refugees have used their countries of asylum as a base for guerrilla warfare and are alleged to even be supplied with arms, while still receiving refugee assistance. Moreover, their actions may help to shape the terms of any future political settlement in the region.

Many of the refugees in Central America live in impoverished circumstances, often herded together in camps in which they are virtual prisoners because of the extreme danger they would face if they attempted to leave. Other groups of refugees are subject to forced recruitment and are dealt with as expendable pawns in an effort to overthrow the Sandinista regime in Nicaragua. None of these refugees have any prospect of rebuilding normal lives until the conflict is over.

From Humanitarianism to Reconstruction

This chapter has examined the political dynamics of the refugee crisis in Central America and has analyzed the factors that influence government and international agency policies toward refugees, beyond legal or humanitarian concerns. Protection for refugees in Central America is quite precarious and is dependent on a variety of geopolitical and ideological factors, the interests of a variety of state and nonstate actors, internal security concerns, and foreign policy interests. There exists today an urgent need to maintain a separation between military and humanitarian activities in Central America and to elevate the needs of refugees above the limitations or immediate political concerns. The politicization of humanitarian aid undercuts the effectiveness of intergovernmental and private agencies as aid providers and protectors of refugees, whether such aid and protection is treated as an extension of U.S. foreign policy or as a device for critiquing American policy. At the same time, solutions to refugee problems in the region ultimately depend on political actions taken by regional and extraregional states and actors.

The successful implementation of the Central American Peace Plan of August 7, 1987, could have a significant impact on the refugee problems in the region. The heads of governments agreed to care for refugees and displaced persons through the provision of protection and assistance. They also agreed to facilitate their repatriation, resettlement, or relocation, provided it is voluntary and decided on an individual basis. In addition, the governments agreed to negotiate with the international community with a view to obtaining assistance for refugees and displaced persons, either directly or through UNHCR or through other organizations and agencies. The agreement also acknowledged the potential problems regarding repatriation or relocation posed by the contras and other members of armed guerrilla groups and envisaged a political solution to these problems. The governments explicitly mentioned the need for outside assistance for reintegration of these persons to normal life. In the meantime, a special commission set up after the Cartagena Declaration to work on possible solutions to Central American refugees is planning a regional conference in 1988 to highlight and promote a resolution to these problems.

While the return of peace to the region will help resolve the problems of international protection of refugees in Central America, the problems caused by war and massive displaced populations in the region are long-term and will not suddenly disappear. The entrenched war between the right and left in El Salvador, the Guatemalan army's counterinsurgency campaigns, and the external aggression against Nicaragua have profoundly affected the societies and economies of the rural and urban sectors of these countries. Generalized violence and repression, combined with economic inequality, have contributed to a serious deterioration in basic living and security conditions. During the past decade, Central America has experienced a deep and prolonged recessions which has made the situation of the poor even more desperate. As a result of shortfalls in production and exports, large unmanageable imbalances have appeared in the fiscal, monetary, and balance of payments accounts of the countries of the region. In an effort to soften the impact of the economic crises, most Central American countries resorted to huge external borrowing which further increased their dependence. Clearly, given the depth and duration of the humanitarian and economic problems facing Central America, it will be unfeasible for Central America to pull out of its current crises without considerable international assistance. It will be insufficient for the international community to attend solely to the arrival and reintegration of repatriated refugees and internally displaced persons. Rather, to the extent possible, the international community will have to provide infrastructure and basic services to areas that have been depopulated and devastated by the war. Only through such means will the refugee problems of Central America ever really be resolved.

NOTES

I am grateful to Lowell Livezey, Tom Lent, Elizabeth Ferris, Barbara Harrell-Bond, Kai Ambos and to the anonymous reviewers and UNHCR staff who read this manuscript in draft form. I have tried to incorporate their suggestions for changes but I am responsible for any existing shortcomings. In early 1986, I traveled to Central America and Mexico with three other researchers. Before leaving for Central America, we traveled to Washington, D.C., and New York where we interviewed officials from the U.S. Department of State, the Inter-American Commission on Human Rights, Amnesty International, Americas Watch, Freedom House, Catholic Relief Services, Refugee Policy Group, and Oxfam-USA, among other agencies. In Central America, we visited twelve refugee camps where we interviewed hundreds of refugees either singly or in groups. We also interviewed sixty officials from the Office of the UN High Commissioner for Refugees, the Intergovernmental Commission for Migration, the Mexican, Honduran, Nicaraguan, and Costa Rican governments, voluntary agencies, and several Catholic and Protestant bishops and clerics and lay workers. Since my trip to Central America, I have interviewed officials at the UNHCR and voluntary agency headquarters in Geneva and have presented my findings at seminars at Notre Dame, Oxford, and in Geneva. Field research for this article was supported by a travel grant from the Kellogg Institute for International Studies at the University of Notre Dame. The article was written while I was a Visiting Fellow of the Refugee Studies Programme at Queen Elizabeth House, Oxford University.

1. Gil Loescher and John Scanlan, *Calculated Kindness: Refugees and America's Half-Open Door: 1945 to the Present* (New York: Free Press; London: Macmillan, 1986). For a fuller treatment of the foreign policy aspects of refugees, see: Gil Loescher, "Refugee Issues in International Relations" in Gil Loescher and Laila Monahan, eds., *Refugees and International Relations* (Oxford: Clarendon Books, 1989).

2. See Frank Shary, "Displaced Persons: Humanitarian Challenge in Central America," *World Refugee Survey 1984* (New York: U.S. Committee for Refugees, 1984), pp. 24-17; U.S. Committee for Refugees, *Aiding the Desplazados of El Salvador* (New York, Fall 1984); Mike Gatehouse, *Uprooted: The Displaced People of Central America,* Oxford: British Refugee Council/Queen Elizabeth House Working Papers series, vol. 3, no. 3 (May 1986); Lawyers Committee for International Human Rights and Americas Watch, *El Salvador's Other Victims: The War on the Displaced* (New York, April 1984); and U.S. General Accounting Office, *Central American Refugees: Regional Conditions and Prospects and Potential Impact on the United States* (Washington, D.C.: GAO, July 20, 1984).

3. Universidad Centroamericana, *Desplazados Y Refugiados, Version Preliminar* (Displaced and refugees, preliminary version) (San Salvador, 1985) and International Council for Voluntary Agencies (ICVA), *Consultations* (Geneva, 1986-1988).

4. ICVA, ibid.

5. See for example, Elizabeth Ferris, "Central America: The Political Impact of Refugees," *The World Today* 41, no. 5 (May 1985): 100-101.

6. For background see Beatrice Manz, *Guatemala: Community Changes, Displacement and Repatriation* (Cambridge, Mass.: Harvard University Press, 1986); Elizabeth Ferris, "The Politics of Asylum: Mexico and the Central American Refugees," *Journal of Inter-American Studies and World Affairs* 26, no. 3 (August 1984): 357-84; Sergio Aguayo, *El Exodo Centroamericano* (Central American exodus) (Mexico: Secretaria de Educacion Publica, Foro 2000, 1985); Suzanne Fiederlein, *Central American Refugees in Mexico: The Search for a Policy* (Austin: University of Texas at Austin, 1985).

7. The author visited refugee camps in Chiapas and in Campeche, Yucatan Peninsula in January 1986.

8. See Sergio Aguayo Quezada and Laura O'Dougherty, "Los Refugiados Guatemaltecos en Campeche y Quintana Roo," *Foro Internacional* 106 (October-December 1986): 266-95.

9. Author's interviews with Guatemalan refugees in Chiapas and Campeche, Mexico, January 1986.

10. Author's interviews with UNHCR and COMAR (Mexican Commission to Aid Refugees) in Chiapas, Campeche, and Mexico City, January 1986.

11. Author's interviews with Mexican government and Catholic Church officials and lay workers, Chiapas and Mexico City, January 1986. See also Americas Watch, *Guatemalan Refugees in Mexico, 1980-1984* (New York, September 1984); Aguayo, *El Exodo Centroamericano*, and Ferris, "The Politics of Asylum."

12. See Amnesty International, *Mexico: Human Rights in Rural Areas* (London, 1986); Ferris, "The Politics of Asylum," p. 366.

13. Author's interviews with Guatemalan refugees in Campeche, with Bishop Samuel Ruiz of San Cristobal, and with Catholic Church officials, January 1986. Past COMAR activity has also been detailed in Aguayo, *El Exodo Centroamericano*.

14. Jonathan Power, "Guatemala: Stirrings of Change," *The World Today* 42, no. 5 (February 1986): 31-35.

15. U.S. Congress, Senate Committee on Foreign Relations, House Committee on Foreign Affairs, *Country Reports on Human Rights Practices*, 100th Cong., 1st Sess., 1987, pp. 509-10.

16. See for example, the written statement submitted by the International Federation of Human Rights before the UN Subcommission on Prevention of Discrimination and Protection of Minorities (UN E/CN.4/Subject 2/1987/NGO/8, 12 August 1987). See also Amnesty International, *Guatemala: The Human Rights Record, 1987*; Americas Watch and British Parliamentary Human Rights Group, *Human Rights in Guatemala* (New York: Americas Watch, 1987); and Catholic Institute for International Relations and Latin America Bureau, *Guatemala: False Hope, False Freedom* (London: CIIR, 1987).

17. Patricia K. Hall, "Military Rule Threatens Guatemala's Highland Mayan Indians," *Cultural Survival Quarterly* 10 (Summer 1986), 48-52, and Minutes, ICVA, Subgroup on Mexico and Central America, New York, March 3, 1986, pp. 3-4, and San Jose, Costa Rica, November 21-23, 1985, p. 5.

18. See Sidni Lamb, "Guatemalan Exiles and Returnees," *Refugees*, no. 44 (August 1987), p. 31.

19. The Guatemalan Catholic Bishops believe that security conditions are not good enough for them to endorse repatriation, but they are

under considerable pressure to cooperate in assisting returnees. The local Church in Hueheutenango does help implement assistance programs to those who choose to return but maintains a low profile. Author's interviews with UNHCR, International Catholic Migration Commission, and World Council of Churches, Geneva, September 1987.

20. Author's interviews with UNHCR staff and voluntary agencies, Geneva, September 1987.

21. Americas Watch Committee, *Guatemala News in Brief,* no. 15 (July 1987), p. 11.

22. Edelberto Torres-Rivas, *Report on the Condition of Central American Refugees and Migrants* (Washington, D.C.: Georgetown University, Center for Immigration Policy and Refugee Assistance, July 1985), p. 39.

23. Ibid., pp. 24-16; General Accounting Office, note 2 above, p. 26; U.S. Congress, *Refugee Problems in Central America,* staff report, 98th Cong., 1st Sess. (Washington, D.C.: Government Printing Office, 1983).

24. Author's interview with UNHCR officials in Mexico City, January 1986, and with Patricia Weiss-Fagen, Washington, D.C., December 1985.

25. Ferris, "The Politics of Asylum," p. 368.

26. ICVA Consultation on Refugees and Displaced Persons in and from Central America and Mexico; San Jose, Costa Rica, 11-14 September 1986, p. 17.

27. Jose Luiz Perez-Conchola, "Refugiados Centro-Americanos en Mexico: La Frontera del Norte," *Refugees* (World Council of Churches), no. 81 (November 1986); author's interview with Jorge Bustamante, University of Notre Dame, April 1987.

28. Author's interview with Patricia Weiss-Fagen, Washington, D.C., December 1985, and with Sergio Aguayo, Mexico City, January 1986.

29. Author's interview with UNHCR official, Washington, D.C., December 1983; Loescher and Scanlan, *Calculated Kindness.*

30. Author's interview with Albert Corkos, Intergovernmental Committee for Migration, San Salvador, January 1986.

31. American Civil Liberties Union Fund, *The Fates of Salvadorans Expelled from the United States* (Washington, D.C.: ACLU Political Asylum Project, September 5, 1984).

32. James LeMoyne, "U.S. Role Grows in Honduras," *International Herald Tribune,* July 14, 1986. This observation was confirmed by on-site interviews with Honduran politicians and voluntary agency officials.

33. Americas Watch and Lawyers Committee for International

Human Rights, *Honduras: A Crisis on the Border* (New York: January, 1985).

34. A detailed account of the attack on Colomoncagua can be found in *Canadian Church Task Force on Salvadoran and Indigenous Nicaraguan Refugees in Honduras, August 29-September 5, 1985* (Toronto: InterChurch Committee on Human Rights in Latin America, October 1985). See also *New York Times*, September 5, 7, 8, 1985.

35. Author's interviews with U.S. Senate Department officials in Washington, D.C., December 1985, and with Honduran government and U.S. State Department officials in Tegucigalpa, Honduras, January 1986.

36. The author visited and stayed overnight in the camp in Colomoncagua in January 1986 and interviewed UNHCR and voluntary agency staff and Salvadoran refugees.

37. Ibid.

38. Author's interviews with U.S. State Department officials in Washington, D.C., December 1985, and in Tegucigalpa, January 1986.

39. See Americas Watch and the Lawyers Committee for International Human Rights, *Honduras: A Crisis on the Border*, note 33 above; Patricia Weiss-Fagen, *Refugees and Displaced Persons in Central America* (Washington, D.C.: Refugee Policy Group, March 1984); and Bruce Nichols, *The Uneasy Alliance: Religion, Refugee Work, and U.S. Foreign Policy* (New York: Oxford University Press, 1988), pp. 117–31.

40. Author's interviews with UNHCR officials, Geneva, May 1986.

41. Minutes, ICVA Subgroup on Mexico and Central America, New York, March 3, 1986, p. 2.

42. For background see Sidni Lamb, "El Salvador: Next Stop: Home," *Refugees*, no. 44 (August 1987), pp. 20-22.

43. These conditions were set out in at least two letters sent by the refugees at Mesa Grande to government and international officials on January 10 and April 2, 1987.

44. See for example: U.S. Department of State, *Human Rights in Nicaragua under the Sandinistas* (Washington, D.C.: Department of State, December 1986), p. 64.

45. Author's interviews at the Nicaraguan Ladino refugee camp at Teupasenti, January 1986.

46. Author's interviews with UNHCR and voluntary agency staff members, Geneva, 1987.

47. For background see Organization of American States, Inter-American Commission on Human Rights, *Report of the Situation of Human Rights of a Segment of the Nicaraguan Population of Moskito Origin* (Washington, D.C.: General Secretariat, OAS, 1984); Amnesty

International, *Nicaragua: The Human Rights Record* (London, 1986); and Roxanne Dunbar Ortiz, *La Cuestion Miskitia en la Revolucion* (Mexico City: Editorial Linea, 1986).

48. U.S. Committee for Refugees, *World Refugee Survey: 1985 in Review* (Washington, D.C., 1985), p. 59.

49. Author's interview with David Befus, World Relief, Tegucigalpa, Honduras, January 1986.

50. Author's interviews with Nicaraguan government representatives and leaders of the Moravian Church, Managua, Nicaragua, January 1986.

51. Author's interviews with UNHCR officials, Tegucigalpa, Honduras and Managua, Nicaragua, January 1986.

52. Author's interviews with UNHCR staff, Geneva, January 1988.

53. Americas Watch, *With the Moskitos in Honduras* (New York, April 11, 1986).

54. Stephen Kinzer, "Indians Return in Nicaragua," *New York Times*, April 18, 1987.

55. For a detailed analysis of Costa Rican refugee policy see Kai Ambos, *The Central American Refugee Crisis*, Refugee Studies Programme, Oxford University, October 1987.

56. Estimates of the number of illegal immigrants inside Costa Rica vary widely. There exists a traditional migration from Nicaragua to Costa Rica. The former minister of the interior claimed that there were 200,000 to 250,000 illegal immigrants, but that figure is not considered reliable by many people.

57. Michael S. Barton, "Influx of Refugees from Nicaragua to Costa Rica," *Refugees*, no. 20 (August 1985), p. 20.

58. Author's interviews with international and voluntary agency officials in San Jose, Costa Rica in January and February 1986.

59. See, for example, Joel Brinkley, "As Ex-Ambassador Says U.S. Ordered Aid for Contras," *New York Times*, May 3, 1987.

60. Author's interviews with camp officials at Limon, Costa Rica, January 1986.

61. "U.S. is Reported to Press Costa Rica to Cooperate over Use of 'Contras,'" *International Herald Tribune*, April 14, 1986.

PVOS, HUMAN RIGHTS, AND THE HUMANITARIAN TASK

Lowell W. Livezey

That the humanitarian dimension of international affairs is thoroughly intertwined with political realities is not only a central theme of most of the essays in this volume, but increasingly clear from direct observation. It may well be that there is no such thing as purely humanitarian action, if by that one means action without political consequences. While the motives of some actors may be "pure"—and even this is doubtful—humanitarian action invariably affects not only the living conditions of persons and groups, but the balance and structure of political power within and among their countries.

The dense fabric of relationships, both governmental and voluntary, between the United States and the countries of Central America illustrate the intricate relationships between humanitarian action and political power. The other essays in this section explore a number of these relationships, particularly those which arise in the sustenance of displaced people, refugees, "refugees not recognized as such," and illegal aliens. Even the selection of these terms entails the adoption of a political stance toward the governments involved and critical judgment about the legitimacy of their policies toward the people being helped. Indeed, those essays suggest that there is simply no way to be involved in the care of Central Americans away from their homes without supporting or opposing the policies of governments, or without enhancing or challenging their capacity to govern.

The same basic reality is also illustrated in this essay, in which an examination of nongovernmental organizations that promote internationally recognized human rights in the region provides a perspective on humanitarian politics. The most notable conclusion here is not the pervasiveness of the political consequences of humanitarian action as such, but the fact that humanitarian action seems to contribute to *both* sides of a highly polarized political situation. It would have been no less political, but a lot simpler, if nongovernmental agencies working for humanitarian goals were unified in their positions on such issues as U.S. aid to the countries—and the insurgencies—in the region, the legitimacy of U.S. military intervention, and the working relationships between the voluntary agencies themselves and the governments and opposition groups. But such unity does not exist, and the disagreements are not limited to extremists of the right and left. Rather, the humanitarian work of nongovernmental agencies in the United States reflects the deep divisions present in the public at large.

Human rights issues bring out the political contentiousness of humanitarianism. Advocacy of human rights is a more explicitly political form of humanitarianism than the care and feeding of refugees, disaster relief, community and economic development, and even the protection and sustenance of war victims. This is not to say that such advocacy is more politically significant but that the political significance is more obvious, more difficult to neutralize.

Human rights are, in and of themselves, political ideas, and the claim that there are human rights at all is a political act of no small moment. Human rights means that persons have dignity and worth simply by virtue of being human, and not as a result of action or authority of the state (or any other institution, for that matter). The consequences of this idea are enormous; it means that the state and society are limited with respect to the individual, and that the state or the society may have obligations to individuals or groups within it. Indeed, part of the current disagreement about the legitimacy of the government of Nicaragua derives from conflicting judgments about the compatibility of Sandinista ideology with a limited state.

The notion of the *international recognition* of human rights carries us a step further, for it means that persons are to be taken into account in the relations among states. The notion seems plausible enough from a humanitarian point of view, and despite the important differences between Henry Shue and Rogers M. Smith[1] argued in this volume, each articulates a principled basis for making the welfare of human beings an aim of the international action of states. Yet they are both challenging the dominant motifs in international relations. The prevailing notion of state sovereignty has meant that, whatever accountability a state may have to its people, that accountability is in no way a concern of the international community or, indeed, of any state besides the one in question. Shue's "cosmopolitan" perspective has had respectable support among philosophers since Kant, but in the world of diplomacy and modern international relations scholarship it has been thoroughly eclipsed by the "realist" school. And while Smith's argument reclaiming the national interest from the amorality to which it has been assigned by the other realists is persuasive, it is also an argument yet to be won.

Organizations advocating the international recognition of human rights are therefore not only advocating proper treatment of specific people, but are putting forth ideas about the proper nature of the international system and of state responsibility within it. Thus, in a world where human rights are recognized internationally, the sovereignty of each state is qualified not only by the independent standing of individuals within it, but also by the competence, indeed the duty, of states to concern themselves with the well-being of the citizens of all states.

Generally speaking, American organizations promoting international human rights accept, at least implicitly, these understandings of states and of the international system. There are important differences, however, concerning the point at which the principle of state sovereignty is overridden by the principles of human rights. The most controversial actions are those—such as U.S. military pressure on Nicaragua—in which states seek to influence the behavior of other states without accepting the limits or going through the procedures established by the human rights treaties. In effect, such states are "taking the (international) law into their own hands."

Because some rights are explicitly political, such as the right to vote, to stand for office, or to be represented in government, the recognition of these rights amounts to the claim that there ought to be a political order of a certain character. Other rights, such as the right to food, the right to due process of law, and the right not to be tortured or arbitrarily killed, are not political in the sense of specifying the structure of government, but they entail judgments about the essential responsibilities of government. Obviously the disagreements over the legitimacy of Central American governments derive partly from emphasis on different rights. The serious attempt by Sandinista Nicaragua to distribute basic food and shelter to all looms large (and positive) to those who emphasize subsistence rights, while its restrictions on non-Sandinista political activity loom large (and negative) to those who emphasize political rights.

In addition, actors for human rights must make choices about which victims to defend, which violators to challenge, and which strategies to pursue, because their resources are limited. Their choices may be based on political judgments and always have political consequences. In El Salvador, for example, the difference is enormous between defending an organizer for a union affiliated with the Duarte's Christian Democrats and defending a displaced person who recently fled from a war zone and is suspected of having aided the insurgency—even if both were threatened by right-wing death squads.

All of these political factors are present in the humanitarian work of nongovernmental organizations in Central American and in their efforts to influence U.S. policy toward Central America. Taken together they lead to a lively pluralism among humanitarian agencies, which results in both a complementarity of functions and a measure of conflict. Although disaster relief (help for victims of earthquakes or floods) does not normally reflect these political considerations, the care for refugees, assistance in community development programs, and defense of human rights victims often does. Different organizations care for different refugees. In development work, they cooperate with different governments. In the defense and promotion of human rights, they challenge different governments and, sometimes, insurgencies.

This "division of labor" has a certain practical value to those in need of assistance. Refugees fleeing Nicaragua may be recognized and protected by different agencies than those fleeing El Salvador or Guatemala, but there are agencies to support each group.[2] Similarly, a number of voluntary agencies work cooperatively with the Nicaraguan government in community-level agricultural and economic development, but maintain a critical distance from the governments of El Salvador, Guatemala, and Honduras—either by staying out entirely or by limiting their work to what they can do in cooperation with associations that are themselves thoroughly independent of the governments. Yet for other agencies, the range of cooperation and dissociation is reversed, and the result is that North American voluntary agencies work in development projects throughout the region, in support both of governmental programs and of nongovernmental efforts intended to make people and communities more self-sufficient.[3] And while it would be difficult to say that all Central American human rights victims have North American advocates, it is clear that all Central American governments have critics among the array of North American human rights advocacy organizations.

Yet even though all the humanitarian issues are "covered" and no important category of victim may be without its advocate, the very diversity of approaches to humanitarian action that makes this possible also means that in extremely important ways the political directions of humanitarian actions are contradictory and mutually destructive. This is particularly obvious in the application of human rights principles to U.S. foreign policy and the implications of other humanitarian action for that policy. However beneficial the political diversity of humanitarian action may be, and even though it may be the inevitable reflection of American pluralism, one must acknowledge that it creates problems for the development, promotion, and public support of a U.S. humanitarian policy.

Beginning in the late years of the Vietnam War, a new wave of international human rights activity began to emerge in the United States that was to reflect the distaste for U.S. military intervention that Americans had developed during the Vietnam ordeal. The idea of human rights seemed to be genuinely humanitarian, both in the cosmopolitan sense urged by Shue and in the sense of expressing the humanitarian element in American self-interest argued by Smith in this volume. If guided by human rights, the United States would not only remain free of complicity in atrocities like those of Saigon—El Salvador, Guatemala, and Somoza's Nicaragua came readily to mind—but we would avoid the military and political quagmires into which such complicity had been shown to lead. Successive amendments of the Foreign Assistance Act between 1974 and 1977[4] to make most U.S. economic and military assistance subject to a standard of human rights performance by the recipient provided a focus for lobbying and educational activities by nongovernmental humanitarian organizations. And since many of the larger service agencies received substantial government funding and distributed government commodities, their work was directly affected by any curtailments in assistance to human rights violators.

The Coalition for a New Foreign and Military Policy is probably the clearest example of the identification of the promotion of human rights with opposition to U.S. intervention. Because its over fifty national affiliates include most mainline Protestant denominations and several Catholic religious orders, Jewish associations, and peace and human rights groups, its positions are a good clue to the perspectives of a large sector of voluntary humanitarian agencies. The Coalition was formed in 1976 at least partly as the result of efforts by organizations (and caucuses within organizations) that had united in opposing the Vietnam War to redefine and to extend their agenda for the post-Vietnam era.

The Coalition exercises a great deal of its influence by virtue of the strength and prestige of its affiliates, including several that are very important in the delivery of humanitarian services in Central America—American Friends Service Committee, National Council of Churches (parent organization of Church World Service), and a number of Roman Catholic religious orders. Although it should not be taken simply as a reflection of its member organizations, its positions normally do not contradict those of its members in any important respects. Its professional staff work closely with the Washington representatives of many of the organizations in the Coalition, forming a network of working relationships among professional policy analysts and advocates.

The Coalition was formed just a few months before the Carter administration came into office, a time when there were significant constituencies both in government and in the public for advancing international human rights through U.S. foreign policy. The Washington Office on Latin America (WOLA), founded two years earlier, was already serving as a voice in Washington for human rights activists throughout the hemisphere. Older humanitarian organizations such as the American Friends Service Committee and the Fellowship of Reconciliation were beginning to identify their ongoing efforts for social justice as part of the human rights movement. Amnesty International was rapidly gaining international recognition and would shortly receive the Nobel Peace prize.

During the years of the Carter administration, the agenda of these and other like-minded organizations was "given" to some extent by the way the human rights issue emerged. First, it was a matter of U.S. law that economic assistance and military assistance were supposed, under normal circumstances, to be withheld from countries that practiced "a consistent pattern of gross violations of internationally recognized human rights. . . ." The Coalition and other human rights lobbies monitored the compliance of the United States and advocated withholding of assistance to Central American countries other than Costa Rica (as well as to such countries as the Philippines, South Korea, Zaire, Chile, and Argentina). Second, during 1977 and 1978, the Coalition supported efforts to extend the human rights legislation to cover U.S. assistance through the international financial institutions, the Export-Import Bank, and Public Law 480 (known as "Food for Peace").

The other major objective of the human rights lobby during this period was the ratification of the two International Covenants on Human Rights. The material produced to promote these Covenants highlighted the role of the United States in human rights abused by other countries. While the Covenants material made it clear that the Covenants would apply to all countries and that countries throughout the world were violators, the examples of violators were nearly always recipients of U.S. aid or close military allies of the United States. Thus the educational effort on behalf of the Covenants reinforced the political efforts on behalf of the extension and implementation of the human rights legislation affecting U.S. foreign policy.

Perhaps the most basic notion advanced by work on the Covenants was the understanding that it would be in the best interest of the United States to seek allies that had the support of their own people, rather than to identify with those that were able to stay in power only by force of arms against their own people. Sooner or later, the Coalition said, such governments would fall—and the United States would have been on the wrong side. Vietnam and Iran were cases in point. Nicaragua, it said (a year before the Sandinista revolution), was likely to follow.

The first years of the Reagan administration brought a significant change of tone and emphasis in the programs of the Coalition, its members, and similar organizations. Whereas it had sought to support the human rights and anti-interventionist factions within the Carter administration and the Congress, it now sought to defend against the Reagan administration's policy overall. As it reported to constituents in the summer of 1981, "we believe the honeymoon is over and battle lines clearly drawn."[5]

The first example of the new battle lines was to be found in the new administration's reticence to appoint an assistant secretary of State for human rights and humanitarian affairs, and then in its nomination of Ernest Lefever to the post. In the successful battle to oppose the nomination of this self-avowed opponent of the very idea that human rights had a substantive place in foreign policy, the liberal Washington lobbies established the political impossibility of excluding human rights from foreign policy consideration, and forced the Reagan administration to redefine the human rights issue in terms compatible with its approach to foreign policy. This was a Pyrrhic victory; as redefined by the administration, human rights became part of its anti-Soviet strategy and of its rationale for military intervention in the third world. The human rights issue was kept on the foreign policy agenda, but in a form directly opposed to the anti-interventionist commitment of those who had led the struggle against the Reagan administration.

It was perfectly logical, therefore, that under the conditions of the Reagan era, opposition to U.S. military intervention and assistance in the third world would often be associated with support for human rights. The Coalition for a New Foreign Military Policy's "Campaign against U.S. Intervention" became the principal context of its human rights work, with the Coalition's human rights coordinator in charge of the campaign's masthead. The pacifist premise of the American Friends Service Committee assured its opposition to U.S. military intervention, and this cohered with its work for social change in countries receiving military support. The "liberal" Protestant churches, generally associated with the National Council of Churches and supporting humanitarian work through Church World Service, had become increasingly critical of U.S. foreign policy during the 1960s and early 1970s. The human rights issue became an integral part of their effort to oppose U.S. support for repressive governments and the projection of U.S. power by military means. The role of the Roman Catholic Church and its humanitarian agency, Catholic Relief Services, is more complex because of the collegial relationship between the U.S. bishops and the episcopal conferences of foreign countries. Yet while the bishops did not always actively oppose U.S. military assistance in the region, they supported the principle of subjecting assistance to the criterion of human rights performance by the recipient countries. Finally, the Americas Watch Committee came into existence with the Reagan administration and, while occasionally issuing a report critical of Cuba or Nicaragua, added evidence and publicity mostly detrimental to the humanitarian claims of American policy in Central America. In sum, a very large part of the community of humanitarian organizations have long been opposing U.S. military involvement in Central America and severely criticizing human rights violations by regimes dependent on the United States.

Yet there have been other nongovernmental agencies engaged in humanitarian services and advocating human rights in Central America that have taken quite different positions on U.S. policy. This is not to say that many humanitarian agencies openly and explicitly appeal, as does the Reagan administration, to human rights as a justification for American intervention. But the identification of American ideals with U.S. interests and the defense of those ideals with the containment of Soviet influence had undergirded the foreign policy consensus that had prevailed for over two decades following World War II. Although the consensus broke down in the Vietnam era, these premises continued to guide both the foreign policy itself and a substantial portion of the humanitarian service community. Thus the "new wave" of human rights activity that emerged in the 1970s ran counter not only to the prevailing foreign policy but to the work of many humanitarian organizations already in existence. These included evangelical churches and relief agencies (especially World Relief and World Vision), the labor movement (most importantly for

Central America, the American Institute for Free Labor Development of AIFLD), refugee agencies like the International Rescue Committee, the largest U.S. Jewish organizations, and various advocacy organizations such as Freedom House and the World Without War Council.

Freedom House, founded in 1941, embodies many of the most significant political characteristics of these older humanitarian organizations. While it does not engage in relief or development programs, it applies the criterion of "freedom" in its advocacy of U.S. policy, and it serves as a voice and an amplifier for people it considers oppressed by foreign governments.

The major components of the Freedom House program are the monitoring of elections in countries where their openness and fairness are in doubt, the continual monitoring of national and international news media, the publication of a "Survey of Freedom" in which all countries are assessed in terms of political freedom and civil liberties, publication of *samizdat* literature from countries in which it is suppressed, shipment of books to youth in the third world, and provision of information to the Freedom House constituency, primarily through the periodical *Freedom at Issue*, the newsletter "Freedom Monitor," Freedom House Books and occasional papers. Freedom House occasionally testifies to Congress and frequently advises U.S. government officials and agencies on a range of foreign policy questions.

The importance of elections to Freedom House is illustrated first by the fact that it monitors and reports on them, and second by the fact that reasonably fair elections have constituted sufficient grounds for Freedom House to recommend support for governments that were guilty of other serious human rights violations. It sent a team to observe El Salvador's election of a Constituent Assembly in March of 1982 and reported in detail on the procedures that were followed and on the available evidence of both fairness and fraud in the election process. It concluded that the election was as open and fair as could reasonably have been expected, that the high level of participation reflected genuine popular support for the process, and that in sum the elections were a significant step toward democratization. Later that year, the quality of the elections formed an important part of the Freedom House case that, despite continuing human rights violations, El Salvador should be certified for further U.S. military and economic assistance.[6] The progress of the land reform program, the movement toward an independent judiciary, and government efforts to reduce the level of violence were also appealed to, but they were assessed in the context of the recent elections and the movement toward democratization the elections made possible.

Freedom House's position on El Salvador (as on other issues) also reflects its attention to geopolitical factors. El Salvador is important to Freedom House not only because of the freedom of its people, but because of the interrelationships of the political forces in the Caribbean Basin—in particular, the influence of Cuba and Nicaragua and, through them, of the Soviet Union.

During the 1980s Freedom House has sponsored a Center for Caribbean and Central American Studies to address the major issues of the region. Although not a declared purpose of the center, its activities point in the direction of a sustained, if not increased, U.S. role in the region. The Center gave early exposure to Nicaraguan abuses of the Miskito Indians and helped the Miskitos to get a hearing at the UN Human Rights Commission. Later on, it helped former Sandinista Eden Pastora reach the press and public throughout the Americas and Europe. In *The Democratic Mask*[7] and other publications, Freedom House countered the positive interpretations of the Sandinista revolution offered by the human rights movement discussed above, emphasizing its more repressive characteristics and its ties to Cuba and the Soviet Union.

While Freedom House has not explicitly endorsed U.S. sponsorship of the insurgency in Nicaragua, it has clearly provided some of the evidence and argument used by others to support that policy. And at the more general level, Freedom House views military power as a major and nonproblematic instrument of the power of states, so military assistance and intervention are among the means by which freedom may be advanced.[8]

The evangelical churches are another significant force promoting active U.S. involvement in Central America. Leaving aside the new Christian right of Jerry Falwell and Jimmy Swaggert—which is also involved in the region but in work more difficult to define as humanitarian—one must consider seriously the work of the National Association of Evangelicals (NAE) and its member churches in their sponsorship of World Relief, their lobbying in Washington for religious freedom and other human rights, and the education and publication programs conducted with other organizations such as the Institute on Religion and Democracy, the World Without War Council, and the recently formed Central America Peace and Democracy Watch.

American evangelicals have long conducted missionary programs in Central and South America, and the current vitality of the region's indigenous evangelical churches has increased the NAE's attention to human rights violations there. Following a 1982 mission to Guatemala at the invitation of President Rios Montt, NAE spokesmen noted improvements in the security of the people and in the responsibility of the military, and expressed concern for those still threatened by the guerrillas. They did not address the question of violations by the government.[9] A 1985 mission to Nicaragua of evangelical leaders, organized and led by NAE, was designed to express solidarity with the evangelical churches there. Reporting on the trip, NAE President Billy Melvin said the churches were "hurting and harassed" even as they were growing in strength and numbers, though he said he observed no direct evidence of religious persecution.[10] Without taking a specific policy position, NAE commentary has suggested support for the Duarte government of El Salvador and is critical of the government of Nicaragua. The Institute on Religion and Democracy, created by conservative factions within the liberal Protestant churches as a counterweight to the policies of those denominations, builds a similar picture of Central America.

Although American labor unions are frequently omitted from the lists of humanitarian agencies, in places like Central America they are engaged in extensive activities to promote economic development and social welfare. By advocating freedom to organize unions and cooperatives they become part of the human rights movement. When their organizers are detained, tortured, and killed, they find themselves fighting the same battles as other organizations identified explicitly as humanitarian.

In Central America, by far the greatest part of the humanitarian work of U.S. labor unions is undertaken by AIFLD, a branch of the AFL-CIO, and AIFLD generally supports a role for the United States that is actively opposed to Soviet and Cuban influence and actively supportive of independent unions. On the

ground, AIFLD provides funds and technical assistance to worker and peasant unions it considers to be relatively democratic. In
their recent Central American experience, this has included support for organizations associated with the Christian Democratic
parties in the region, but not those associated with the FSLN in
Nicaragua or with the opposition forces in El Salvador and Guatemala. AIFLD has generally supported U.S. aid to governments
threatened by Communist-supported insurgencies.

The cleavage within the human rights and humanitarian
movement is of considerable importance politically and internationally because it contributes to the ambivalence of U.S. foreign
policy. Because that policy is so crucial to forging solutions ultimately required to alleviate the dire circumstances to which humanitarian agencies respond, the agencies have a substantial
stake in the conduct of policy. The U.S., after all, is deeply involved in the wars that generate most of the region's refugees. Its
decisions on trade, aid, and debt service directly affect the economies that generate hunger and economic migration. A memo by
a middle level Washington bureaucrat may have more effect in
the region than a year's work by a voluntary agency. So the
agencies cannot be indifferent to U.S. policy toward Central
America. And they are not. Yet neither, apparently, can they agree
on what the policy should be—especially on the major policy
choices affecting the U.S. role in the region and its relations with
the Central American governments.

The polarization among the humanitarian agencies is deeply
rooted, not a superficial reflection of the divisions within American public opinion on foreign policy. It is rooted in differences in
the understanding of human rights and humanitarian principles,
and in different understandings of the roles of states—especially
of the United States itself—in international relations.

With only occasional exceptions the approach to humanitarianism identified in this essay as opposed to Soviet and Communist influence and generally supportive of an activist U.S. involvement in Central America is one in which political rights and
civil liberties are seen as the bedrock of a good society and a
proper criterion of foreign policy. The approach identified as
skeptical of U.S. involvement and opposed to military intervention is one that emphasizes the rights of the security of the
person and, to a lesser extent, rights of subsistence. Most of the

organizations involved, if pressed for a general perspective on human rights, acknowledge that which is now embodied in the Universal Declaration of Human Rights and the human rights Covenants and Conventions, which incorporate all of these categories as one body of rights. Yet the difference in emphasis amounts to substantial difference in program.

Freedom House is most explicit. What it means by freedom is best expressed in terms of political rights and civil liberties. As Raymond Gastil put it in the 1984 Freedom House yearbook, "political rights . . . are primarily rights directly of through freely elected representatives in the determination of the nature of law and its administration in society. In a large modern state this apparently requires competing political parties and ideally several tiers of government."[11] He goes on to explain that civil liberties include the freedoms that make possible the "organization and mobilization of new, alternative, or non-official opinions." These include especially freedom of the news media, of voluntary associations (including unions), of religion, and of movement. Within this general framework, some organizations are even more selective. Evangelical Christians often cite religious freedom as the foundation of the other freedoms. Unions stress the rights of association as practically necessary to monitor and secure the other rights. Jewish organizations have cited freedom of movement, especially the right to leave one's country, as most fundamental because it may be the only escape from tyranny and the means of access to the other freedoms.

This is not to say that these organizations consider other rights, particularly the rights of the security of the person, unimportant. Quite the contrary. But the fundamental idea is that such rights cannot be secure except through legitimate government. As the Founding Fathers put it, "To secure these rights, governments are instituted . . ." and the government that they did institute now serves as a model for humanitarians operating from this premise.

The other humanitarians, those skeptical of the U.S. role, generally emphasize rights pertaining to the tangible welfare of individuals and groups. This emphasis does not exclude the importance of personal liberty or political participation as a part of welfare, but it tends to focus on what is happening to the individual rather than on the structure of government and society that may have caused the individual's condition to come about.

The work of the National Council of Churches illustrates the point, for the rights of the security of the person are by far the most frequently the subject of its actions, in Central America and worldwide. In Latin America, to most frequent targets have been Argentina (before the 1984 election), Chile, Paraguay, Uruguay, Guatemala, Honduras, El Salvador, and Haiti. Victims defended are often activists for social and economic change, so their defense may be a means of promoting subsistence rights or greater economic equality as well. On the other hand, the absence of Nicaragua from the list does not necessarily imply satisfaction with the Sandinista record on human rights in general, but rather support for its performance on the particular rights the Council (and its affiliated denominations) consider most important.[12] Similarly, Church World Service and related denominational mission programs cooperate actively in development and relief efforts sponsored by the government of Nicaragua, while preserving as much autonomy as possible in the other countries of the region.

The American Friends Service Committee's focus on human rights victims in El Salvador, Honduras, and Guatemala, combined with its largely positive view of the Nicaraguan government, is also correlated with direct attention to arbitrary killing, political assassination, illegal detention, and disappearances. The AFSC is also much more explicit than most North American humanitarian organizations in its commitment to subsistence rights and in its interpretation of humanitarian service work as enabling people to overcome economic exploitation. Like Church World Service it sees the Nicaraguan government as much more congenial to these purposes than the governments of El Salvador, Honduras, and Guatemala. The work of the Coalition for a New Foreign and Military Policy, the Washington Office on Latin America, and most of the affiliates, follows a similar pattern.[13] While one must stop short of concluding that these organizations' understandings of human rights fully explains their fervent opposition to U.S. policy in the region, there is an obvious congruence between the two.

Other important underlying differences among humanitarian organizations pertain to their views of the place of humanitarianism, and particularly of human rights, in U.S. foreign policy. And this in turn involves judgments both about the way the international system works (what academics call the theory of international relations) and about the degree to which humanitarian concerns cohere with the national interest. Both of these appear to be present in the argument between Henry Shue and Rogers Smith in the introduction to this volume. While humanitarian organizations rarely express themselves explicitly in these terms, their actions and rhetoric often presuppose political judgments at this level.

For the evangelical churches and certain factions within liberal Protestant churches, for organized labor, and for advocacy organizations with the political orientation of Freedom House and World Without War Council, the principles undergirding international humanitarianism are also the bedrock principles of American democracy. Moreover, the actual experience—not just the ideal—of American democracy stands as the best historical example of the embodiment of those principles. Therefore, there is no shame in promoting for others the system of government and structure of society that we have attained for ourselves. If American power can prevent the spread of Soviet influence, then that is good for human rights and humanitarianism, because "freedom" (in the sense defined by Freedom House) is defended against its most serious threat. While some of these organizations approve or welcome the fact of international agreements codifying these freedoms in treaties and law, the international instruments are unnecessary, for freedom is a universal value. It has been validated by the American experience and that of other democracies, and American action to preserve and promote it should not be subject to review or limitation by the international community. Moreover, in this view the United States has an important interest in preserving and strengthening states constituted on similar premises and, failing that, in preventing the rise of states that deny or oppose those premises. While it is still debatable whether governments like those in power in El Salvador, Guatemala, and Honduras are the kind of allies that serve American interests, this is a separate matter from the purpose of using American power to preserve conditions favorable to an American notion of freedom. It is that use of power for which Rogers Smith's essay seeks to provide a humanitarian justification.

The other set of the humanitarian agencies discussed here are both more skeptical of American values and more doubtful about the convergence of American self-interest and universal norms. Disenchanted with the America of Vietnam and Watergate, these organizations welcomed the formulation of humanitarian principles that did not derive exclusively from Western political thought and of the development of international humanitarian law and institutions based in part on the experience and values of other countries and peoples.

While different agencies have their various ultimate authorities for human rights and humanitarian principles—natural law, "that of God" in every person—it is the appeal to the United Nations formulations and institutions that serves to dissociate these principles from national self-interest. Moreover, the appeal to these principles as grounds for criticizing U.S. foreign policy and the behavior of other governments is a way of expressing the underlying belief that states can be restricted by cosmopolitan values and/or by international law—even if their own interests are at stake. For the churches, and for religiously based organizations such as AFSC, it is theologically significant to have some practical means of expressing the limits of the authority of states (else states view themselves—and be viewed—as gods). Thus the rejection in principle of the final authority of the state, and of an international system expressing the anarchy of equally sovereign states, is a part of the basis upon which humanitarian organizations oppose U.S. intervention. But it is difficult to determine the extent to which this factor is decisive.

These observations about the perspectives of humanitarian organizations on human rights, humanitarian principles, and the nature of the international system are only suggestive of possible explanations for the political character of nongovernmental humanitarian action and its relationship to U.S. foreign policy. Whatever the explanatory factors may be, however, it should be clear that, among humanitarian agencies concerned with Central America, there is a deep division concerning the legitimacy of its governments and concerning the proper role of the United States in the region. This division is relatively harmless with respect to the ability of the agencies to deliver assistance to needy people in—and refugees fleeing from—Central America. Political disagreements are reflected in a division of labor, so the various programs complement one another. The same cannot be said, however, with respect to U.S. foreign policy. On these crucial issues the humanitarian movement has been polarized for nearly two decades and remains so today.

NOTES

1. See their essays in Section I of this book, "The Humanitarian Ethic in U.S. Foreign Policy."

2. The political dimensions of refugee issues in Central America are discussed insightfully in the preceding essay by Gil Loescher.

3. These observations are based primarily on interviews with voluntary agency personnel, conducted in Central America (all countries except Guatemala) in January 1986 and August 1987.

4. The most important of these were Section 116, initiated in 1975 and adopted in 1977, and Section 502B, adopted initially in 1974 and strengthened in 1976.

5. *Human Rights Working Group Letter,* Summer 1981.

6. *Freedom at Issue,* September 10, 1982, p. 6; also, U.S. Congress, Senate, Committee on Foreign Relations, *Presidential Certifications on Conditions in El Salvador,* testimony by James Finn on behalf of Freedom House (p. 98), August 3, 1982.

7. Douglas W. Payne, *The Democratic Mask: The Consolidation of the Sandinista Revolution* (New York: Freedom House, 1985).

8. Raymond D. Gastil, ed., *Freedom in the World 1980* (New York: Freedom House, 1980). In his own essay, pp. 193ff., Mr. Gastil argues for the legitimacy of U.S. intervention on the side of repressive regimes.

9. NAE press release, December 31, 1982.

10. "Tensions Between Church and State in Nicaragua Pose Dilemma for U.S. Christians," *Christianity Today,* September 6, 1985, pp. 54ff.

11. Raymond D. Gastil, *Freedom in the World 1983-84* (Westport, Conn.: Greenwood Press, 1984), p. 4.

12. For a more complete discussion of this aspect on the human rights work of the National Council of Churches, see Lowell W. Livezey, *Nongovernmental Organizations and the Ideas of Human Rights* (Princeton: Woodrow Wilson School of Public and International Affairs, 1987).

13. These points are also discussed in *Nongovernmental Organizations and the Ideas of Human Rights,* under the sections devoted to the various organizations.

IV. THE HORN OF AFRICA

CATHOLIC RELIEF SERVICES IN ETHIOPIA: A CASE STUDY

Lawrence A. Pezzullo

Controversy over humanitarian assistance is a type of foreign policy debate that has arisen time and again in our recent history. In our relations with the world we have traditionally sought to meld high purpose—moral rectitude, if you will—with self-interest. The tensions that have arisen in such attempts have been greater or smaller according to circumstances. At times there has been wide national consensus that the marriage of goals has been successful; at others, it has engendered the most intense and divisive disagreement. The basic impulse, however, has generally made it impossible for American governments, regardless of party, to see the world as a place where there are "no permanent friends, no permanent enemies, only permanent interests."[1] We have, as a people, tended to be suspicious of foreign policy goals framed in terms of unalloyed self-interest. Americans, it seems, do not simply want to do well for themselves, but also to do right by others.

This is a current that runs very deep in American life and consciousness. To simplify somewhat, I would suggest that its principal source is in that particularism which we have always seen in our history: the belief that the American experience is something new under the sun, to be fostered at home and shared with the rest of the world. Whether led by John Winthrop, Lord Baltimore, or William Penn, the early settlers on these shores saw themselves involved in new and holy undertakings. As the Puritans set about establishing a "Holy Commonwealth" in the "howling wildernesse" of New England, Winthrop declared that "we must consider that we shall be as a city on a hill, the eyes of

all people upon us." Thomas Jefferson enunciated American independence in terms of "certain unalienable rights" with which
"all men" are endowed by the Creator. In the midst of the terrible
trail of the Civil War, Lincoln held out the American experiment
which was then in jeopardy as "the last best hope of earth."
(Anyone who doubts the potency of the past as an influence on
the present should recall that Ronald Reagan used Winthrop's
words to give what is perhaps the most memorable expression of
his own political vision.)

Such ideas, such a sense of purpose, resonating down
through the years have had significant moral implications for the
ways in which the United States views and responds to the wider
world. Among other things, the persistent influence of this strain
of thought has meant that foreign policy debates in this country
have tended to be expressed in terms of values as well as of
interests. Indeed, it is accurate to say that appeals to the moral
goals which policies are presented as aiming toward have often
been the most critical factor in gaining public support. There is
ample opportunity for hypocrisy in such a framework, of course,
as friends and adversaries alike have frequently complained.
Clemenceau's acid comment that Woodrow Wilson insisted on
fourteen points while God Himself made do with ten suggests
the exasperation with which other countries have often greeted
the moral dimension in American policies. Nonetheless, those
who have failed to appreciate this expectation have suffered
considerable discomfort. Henry Kissinger, to cite a recent example, learned this with some pain when, in the Ford administration, he faced a barrage of criticism alleging that the heavy doses
of *realpolitik* he had injected into the policy-making process were
draining out traditional American values, especially in terms of
concern for human rights on the international scene.

Americans have been concerned with humanitarian issues
for most of this country's history. The concept of disinterested
response to human need has been well understood and accepted
as a principle. For most of our life as a nation, however, chiefly
because of constitutional interpretations which prevailed until
recent times, humanitarian response was undertaken through
private channels—the most important and enduringly influential being the extensive overseas missionary efforts of the nineteenth century.[2] But as the United States' role in the world

evolved from one of relative isolation and inward direction to one of world leadership, so too there developed official expressions of humanitarian or charitable concern. The real impetus to worldwide humanitarian response as a matter of national policy—and the mingling of private and governmental action—came during World War II. It was then that many of the major relief agencies like Catholic Relief Services and Church World Service were formed.

Initially, these agencies directed their efforts to war relief and refugee care in Europe, first among our allies and then among the people of the countries that had formerly been our enemies. There was a cooperation with the government in these efforts which at the time seemed perfectly appropriate. The military was still engaged in fighting the war and, while the armed forces did engage in civic action programs that involved aid to civilian populations, that was necessarily subordinated to their primary mission. Given the American tradition of voluntarism, it seemed natural to look to private organizations, particularly church groups with strongly established constituencies in this country and institutional ties in Europe, to undertake a large share of the humanitarian work that so clearly needed doing—albeit with substantial support from American tax dollars. In the context of the prevailing attitudes at that time, there was nothing incongruous, or seemed not to be, in this partnership of government and private entities. As one student of this relationship has noted, "The United States' primary world leadership position encouraged a belief that virtually all of mankind's problems could be solved by the use of U.S. power, influence and money. . . . "[3] For a brief moment, the popular piety of this overwhelmingly religious people was blended into the popular patriotism of the time.[4] There was a consensus on the nature of the needs that existed and a corresponding consensus that both private and official channels should be used to meet those needs. The period "marked a new stage in American foreign policy, in which charitable, fiscal, political, ideological and military motives would be more confused than ever."[5] Confusion there may have been, but there can be little doubt that this agenda, infused in equal measure with altruism and pragmatism, was an accurate reflection of the aspirations of the American people as the country set out to define its new international leadership role. In the euphoria and optimism of the time, many of the implications inherent in such an agenda were little appreciated.

It is in many ways remarkable that relative stability among potentially conflicting policy goals should have lasted as long as it did. It was not until Vietnam, I think, that the tensions and conflicts present in the mixture became fully apparent in a public sense. The war in Vietnam produced many casualties at home and in the rice paddies, and one of them was the notion that political and humanitarian goals could be uniformly pursued in harmony. From the sixties onward, we came to see the world and our place in it as substantially different from the post-World War II era. Both the government and the private agencies shed their innocence to one degree or another and often found themselves in opposition as to the goals the country should pursue in the conduct of its international relations. That did not mean that the humanitarian agenda was removed from the foreign policy debate. By any measure, such concerns are a permanent part of the fabric of those discussions. It did mean, however, that the close identity of view and purpose that official organizations and the private humanitarian groups had largely shared came into serious question and was not infrequently rejected outright. As a result, there has been a general tendency on the part of official policymakers to attempt to more closely integrate humanitarian programs into conventional areas of political and economic focus. Advocates of humanitarian issues, for their part, have intended to assert for those programs a separate and increasingly independent role relatively free of the political calculus.

It is against this background that the current controversies have been played out. The disagreements are not cast in straight shades of black and white. There are, of course, zealots and single issue diehards on both sides, but most of those involved share a genuine regard for the value of humanitarian action and do not seriously dispute that the government should give expression to American values through policies which seek to achieve humanitarian goals. How such policies should be formulated and conducted and their relation with other national goals is quite another matter. In this context, the debate over humanitarian aid to the contras is depicted, according to one's point of view, as a logical extension of aid to people in need that is consistent with American values and practice, or, on the other hand, as a callous attempt to pervert the very meaning of the term "humanitarian" in order to pursue political goals that have failed the test of the congressional and public marketplace. We should not be surprised that the advocates of each position claim the moral high ground. Nor should we be surprised that, as happens all too often in political discourse, the langauge itself is the first casualty.

I am not one who accepts the rough equivalence of these two positions. In my view, the attempts that have been made to put humanitarianism at the service of military strife are deplorable. Humanitarian concern is, by definition, disinterested and aimed at victims rather than combatants. It is deeply unfortunate, I believe, that the administration has undertaken to clothe itself in a moral rhetoric that is devoid of substance. It is unfortunate, too, that these efforts have extended to encouraging self-styled "humanitarian" groups to provide materials of war in a hypocritical parody of real humanitarian action. It is a sad day when, having failed to gain support through the civil arts of persuasion, a foreign policy can be pursued by what amount to vigilante methods.

While I have stated my views on an issue with which I have had long acquaintance and which has a direct bearing on my current position, my purpose is not to examine American policy in Central America. As executive director of a major relief and development agency, my only interest is in attempting to preserve the integrity of humanitarian assistance as it has been traditionally understood in international law and custom; the wider issues must be debated in appropriate political forums. I have been asked to present a case study of a humanitarian program in action, drawing on the experience of Catholic Relief Services. In doing this, I want to examine the practical realities of undertaking such an effort, the areas of tension and cooperation that exist between private and governmental bodies and to draw some conclusions for the future from the example. While many possibilities present themselves, it seems to me that the case of Ethiopia is timely, complex, and instructive for this kind of discussion. In many ways, the extensive relief effort carried out in the 1980s in Ethiopia is larger than life and thus not typical. But the very size of the effort there may magnify and clarify the variety of often complicated issues that such programs entail.

The appearance of the Ethiopian famine on the American scene can be precisely dated. It was on the evening of October 23, 1984, that NBC News aired BBC film footage which showed the ravages of hunger among the residents of a camp at Korem in northern Ethiopia. With the entry of those graphic images of hollow eyes and emaciated bodies into millions of American homes, Ethiopia became overnight a major news story and a major humanitarian issue on the public agenda. Once the story broke, it elicited an unprecedented response from the world press and public opinion for the next six months. News organizations from the United States, Canada, Europe and Australia rushed reporters and camera crews to the scene, as television, radio, and the print media focused on the unfolding tragedy in which as many as eight million people were at risk of starvation. Private agencies were deluged with calls and donations on a scale that none had ever experienced before. At Catholic Relief Services we had received 80,000 individual contributions by mail in all of 1983, yet in the two months following the NBC story 250,000 flooded into our offices.[6] Even as attention turned to the serious conditions elsewhere in Africa, Ethiopia stood as an emblem of suffering humanity that captured world attention with gripping intensity.

While world awareness of conditions in Ethiopia began in late 1984, the reality of the famine extends back to 1982. In that year, crops failed in the northern provinces of Eritrea and Tigray for lack of adequate rains, and the food situation became ever more acute. The drought extended into 1983, ravaging harvests and spreading hunger through more and more regions of the country. By the time of the first extensive news reports, millions of people were in imminent danger of starvation. CRS had been active in Ethiopia for over a generation, and at the time of the first crop failures, we were one of only sixteen European and American private agencies working in the country. Virtually the only officially sanctioned American assistance being provided to Ethiopia passed through CRS hands in the form of some 11,000 tons of foodstuffs made available through the Food for Peace Program. These commodities were used to support mother and child nutrition programs in Addis Ababa and other sites in which about 100,000 recipients were enrolled. As the situation worsened in the north, we applied for and received small additional amounts of U.S. government food supplies to open emergency operations in both Eritrea and Tigray along with funds to cover inland transport costs. In late 1983, we sought 16,000 additional tons to further extend our efforts. This request was delayed for seven months, but was finally approved and, by late 1984, CRS had a significant relief program in operation through which a total of 36,000 tons of food had been distributed to over 700,000 people. At the time NBC aired the footage from Korem, we were already making plans to mount a massive countrywide effort which would eventually reach two million people using 225,000 tons of commodities annually.

The early stages of the Ethiopian relief effort were marked by a complex set of circumstances, some of which have persisted to the present day. For one thing, it was at that time almost impossible to attract the attention of governments or public opinion to conditions in Ethiopia. CRS and other agencies, both here and in Europe, attempted to sound the alarm in appeals, congressional testimony, publications, press interviews, and other means. None of these efforts was successful in any significant degree. The peculiar chemistry between event and receptivity that apparently needs to operate to grasp hold of public attention was lacking. Before the BBC film footage, dramatic images of imminent death and catastrophe were not yet available and, in retrospect, it seems that without their impetus the reality was virtually mute. Those reporters who evinced an interest in learning more about the situation were only occasionally permitted entry into Ethiopia by the government and, even then, were not allowed to travel freely in the countryside. News reports in the *Washington Post* and the *New York Times* in the late summer of 1983 failed to stimulate a wider awareness, though they helped to speed approval of a CRS emergency food request through the Agency for International Development (AID). There was, in any case, no follow up, and the story passed by as the extent of the famine grew apace in Ethiopia.

The lack of receptivity to such early warnings as there were was in part due to political factors. On the official level, the U.S. and Ethiopia had been at odds since 1977. The military regime, the Dergue, which emerged after the fall of the Emperor Haile Selassie a little over a decade ago, placed itself squarely in the Soviet camp. Russian advisors and Cuban troops were invited to

Ethiopia, and the government seldom let an opportunity pass to criticize the United States in the most strident terms. Washington reacted accordingly, supporting Somalia in the 1977 Ethiopian/ Somali war. The aid that had been so generous during the years of the emperor had, by the eighties, been reduced to the small CRS food program. With the coming to power of the Reagan administration there was a new hard line toward Communist governments in Washington, and the already strained relations between the two countries worsened. By late 1984 there were virtually no substantive contacts between Washington and Addis Ababa; such communications as there were came in the form of mutual recriminations.

On the American side, distrust of the Ethiopian regime was openly and strenuously expressed. The frank hostility of the Dergue, taken with the large infusions of Soviet military assistance Ethiopia was receiving, made the Reagan administration little inclined to spend tax dollars that might aid its continuation in power. U.S. officials pointed out that most forms of development assistance to Ethiopia were legally precluded because of the Dergue's failure to meet past financial obligations to the U.S. government and American commercial firms. Even the small CRS food program, which was not operated through the Ethiopian government, was scheduled to be phased out. Washington denounced the Dergue's policies of collectivization in agriculture and claimed that it was inflicting widespread human rights abuses on its own citizens. As the regime celebrated the tenth anniversary of the revolution in September of 1984, the United States charged that millions of dollars had been devoted to a vainglorious ideological excess while countless Ethiopians in the countryside went hungry. In some quarters of the administration and the Congress, the belief was expressed that the regime had created the problems it was facing and should look to its friends in the Eastern bloc for help in trying to retrieve its failures. Even those urging moderation were frequently dismayed at Ethiopian political rigidity and harshness at home and the Dergue's pugnacity toward the West in its foreign relations.

The Ethiopians, for their part, felt that they had ample reason to return such feelings in full measure. Quite apart from any ideological considerations, the country had a centuries-old tradition of proud isolation from the outside world. The Marxist government of Lt. Col. Mengistu Haile Mariam, which had emerged after a period of often sanguinary struggle within the military following the fall of the emperor, was committed to rooting out the vestiges of a malign past, including a longstanding history of close relations with the United States and the West. Officials in Addis Ababa argued that the country, one of the poorest in the world, had enormous obstacles to overcome, not the least of which was the history of corrupt and ineffectual administration that had been the principal legacy of the imperial regime. The United States, they pointed out, had been the emperor's chief prop, but was unwilling to help the new government defend itself or undertake badly needed reforms. Instead of accepting the new revolutionary consensus that emerged with Selassie's downfall, it was charged, the United States was openly desirous of its overthrow. Adding significantly to Mengistu's anxieties was the ongoing presence of two tenacious insurgencies which he was no better able to deal with than the emperor had been. The government was incapable of imposing its will on the insurgents in Eritrea and Tigray and they, in turn, were unable to force a settlement on their terms. The regime was regarded by its neighbors in the Horn of Africa with misgivings because of its ideological orientation and suspicion regarding its political intentions. Only the eastern bloc, it was claimed in Addis Ababa, was responsive to Ethiopia's needs. In Mengistu's view, the revolution that had occurred ten years before was a historical turning point for the heretofore suppressed people of his ancient land. Finding little in the way of positive reception to the establishment of his vision of a new order in the region or in the west, Ethiopia replied with an attitude of defiant distrust.

As CRS and other private agencies in Ethiopia began to seek food and other resources to help cope with the growing hunger in the country, the influence of these factors was keenly felt. After initial approval of small amounts of food from the United States, subsequent requests met with long delays. It was apparent that they were being held up in part for political reasons, reflecting the administration's disinclination to aid such an outspokenly unfriendly country, and in part for bureaucratic reasons imbedded in an approval process that required the assent of several different government agencies whose often differing views had to be reconciled before final action could be taken.[7] In

Ethiopia, on the other hand, the government was unwilling to acknowledge or did not yet fully appreciate the magnitude of the growing problem. Though the respected Relief and Rehabilitation Commission (RRC), the official agency involved with the issue, began making appeals as early as 1982, the government did not declare famine relief a priority until after the tenth anniversary celebration in September of 1984. Thus, the first steps in moving to meet the needs created by the famine were slow and faltering, with both Western donors—the only realistic source of food in the quantities needed—and the Ethiopian government reluctant to face the full extent of the problem for quite different reasons. The situation was perhaps best described by a *Newsday* reporter who visited Ethiopia in mid-October of 1984:

> . . . the atmosphere is one of charges and countercharges; Ethiopia says that the western donor nations responded with too little, too late; western nations counter that the Ethiopian government has ignored the plight of its own people. But from interviews with relief agencies, western diplomats, Ethiopian government officials and others, it becomes clear that there is blame enough to go around.

There can be no disagreement with that conclusion. On the ground, however, the problem was not to assess blame, but to get the huge amounts of resources that would be needed to the millions facing starvation. The private agencies found themselves in a unique position whereby, though foreign-based and apolitical in character, they became for a time virtually the only advocates for famine relief to Ethiopia. To judge by the record, their efforts in this unaccustomed role might have fallen short had it not been for the international media's "discovery" of famine in Ethiopia. From late October on, with growing momentum, news organizations put the story before the world. The effect on public opinion in the Western donor nations was dramatic, swift, and decisive. Whatever the political considerations that might have applied before Ethiopia became an international symbol of suffering and starvation, they were swept away by a rolling tide of public compassion. Public opinion drove policy and politicians bowed to the unmistakable demand for a clear, unambiguous humanitarian response.

In the United States, with our deep humanitarian traditions

and pervasive media culture, the effect of these revelations was palpable. As I have described, the private agencies like CRS were well nigh overwhelmed by what seemed to be an almost universal desire by countless individuals to do something to help. This powerful current in the public consciousness was quickly felt in Washington, where such signs are closely watched. As received there, the message was plain: Americans wanted something done to avert the impending disaster; they were willing to contribute their own funds to the effort; and they wanted their government to take prompt action as well. Even the harshest critics of the Ethiopian government, while not failing to deprecate the shortcomings of the regime, lent their support to the relief effort. In early November of 1984, AID Administrator M. Peter McPherson visited Ethiopia and made preliminary commitments of food and funds. As the Congress came back into session in January of 1985, legislation was immediately introduced for a supplemental appropriation for famine relief and rehabilitation in Africa. Though the administration had advocated lower levels, the final bill appropriated $400 million in food aid, $137.5 million in emergency funding, and created a $225 million emergency food reserve. The measure became law in April and, by that time, the United States was committed to African relief on a scale that would make it the largest single donor in the worldwide effort that was then taking shape.

In late 1984, we at CRS looked to a dramatic expansion of our ongoing relief efforts. It was clear that the government would not itself be able to meet the full extent of the need through existing infrastructures and that, in any case, some donors, notably the United States, would be reluctant to commit substantial resources to official Ethiopian entities. Thus, we joined together with three other church-related groups—the Lutheran World Federation, the Ethiopian Evangelical Church Mekene Yesus, and the Ethiopian Catholic Secretariat—to form a nationwide network of feeding centers operated by private organizations which would run parallel to and complement government efforts. By year's end, this consortium was distributing 10,750 tons of food each month. The goal for 1985 (which was reached) was to distribute 225,000 tons to over two million recipients. In addition to CRS efforts, the restrictions that had previously made private agencies chary of working in Ethiopia were relaxed and other organizations from Europe and the United States set up operations to distribute food and provide medical care. There were, of course, certain delays because of the need to start fresh, but the community of private agencies that developed in late 1984 and early 1985 has helped to carry a significant part of the famine relief burden up to the present time. There were also considerable difficulties in mounting such a large-scale effort. The transportation network was not adequate to meet the heavy new demands being placed on it, the terrain was often forbidding, the three available ports had limited capacity, and it took time to open a pipeline that would provide a smooth and regular flow of food in the amounts required. In spite of such obstacles, however, the relief effort grew steadily and, by the spring of 1985, it was estimated that most of those needing assistance were being reached.

There was, however, one important exception. From the beginning of the relief effort, it was important that populations in the disputed areas of Eritrea and Tigray were not being reached. Some charged that the Ethiopian government was attempting to achieve by starvation what it could not do by force of arms in these regions. The U.S. Government was supporting a cross-border feeding program from Sudan, but the lack of adequate roads and ongoing hostilities limited the amount of food that could be moved by this route. CRS and other church groups joined in appeals from Geneva twice during 1984, urging the Ethiopian government to permit some sort of safe-passage to allow humanitarian assistance to be provided in the areas of conflict. We also raised the matter privately with government officials and sought access to the regions in question. None of these efforts produced the desired results. The focus of world attention on Ethiopia, however, elicited sharp criticism of the government's position on this issue. International concern being expressed by the principal donor countries, particularly the U.S. government, put pressure on the regime in Addis Ababa that it could scarcely ignore. Matters apparently came to a head in June of 1985 when Vice President Bush and other American officials met with the Ethiopian Foreign Minister in Geneva and the latter agreed to permit relief efforts to operate from government-held territory into the disputed areas through private agencies.

With a pledge of food and transport funding from the U.S.,

CRS began to organize an initiative in Eritrea, while another agency, World Vision Relief Organization, undertook to do the same in Tigray. In Eritrea, we looked to our counterpart, the local Catholic Church, which had access on both sides of the lines, to undertake actual distribution of commodities. Working with the local clergy, we set up a series of feeding stations along the forward areas of conflict. The government guaranteed access to the centers without molestation and food was provided to carry away to all who came, with no questions asked. This "northern initiative," as it came to be called, promised to be precarious. It involved a considerable degree of danger, since hostilities were never suspended. It also involved a certain critical element of mutual trust in a situation where trust was in short supply. In the event, the effort got under way in August of 1985 and was successful. Originally designed to feed 200,000 people a month, the network eventually reached out to 400,000.

Up to this point, I have largely confined myself to describing the various tensions that existed between governments and private agencies in attempting to develop a humanitarian response in Ethiopia. While such differences of view often went very deep, they were to a degree understandable given the different natures of the protagonists. The situation in Eritrea and Tigray and the Ethiopian government's resettlement program, however, provoked conflicts within the community of private agencies involved in one way or another with the relief effort. In each case, some groups, while asserting a humanitarian status, have been advocates for political positions critical of the Ethiopian regime's policies. The general charge has been that the government has used the famine and the relief effort to pursue its war aims against the resistance groups or to forcibly relocate large numbers of people. The remedy that these groups have urged is to suspend all assistance until the Ethiopian government changes its policies. For CRS and most of the other operational private agencies such a position is untenable. In our view, a political agenda is incompatible with the humanitarian principle, which aims at providing assistance to all those in need regardless of race, creed, or politics. Advocacy groups have every right to hold and advance political positions and often play an important role in the debates that surround emergency responses, but that role is essentially different from that of humanitarian aid agencies. The latter must focus on those in need impartially, whatever the cause of their need, commensurate with the resources and access that they can command. The goal is to alleviate suffering to the maximum extent possible among the victims of emergencies. If we at CRS were to pull out of Ethiopia to make a political point, the over two million people we are feeding would bear the very human costs of such a gesture. Thus, while we have privately and publicly sought access to the disputed areas and urged that no program of resettlement be undertaken that is not entirely voluntary and adequately prepared, we have seen our humanitarian role as one of extending our access to those in need wherever they are, rather than becoming political partisans.

Once the initial period of hesitation was passed, food, medicine, tents, blankets, and other items of obvious need began to move rapidly. There were, however, and remain significant differences of opinion as to the extent of assistance that should be provided in Ethiopia. The U.S. government made it clear early on that its policy, while allowing for some flexibility in application, would be aimed at meeting needs caused by the emergency and that, once the emergency had ended, so would most or all U.S. assistance. This has meant that throughout the relief effort the United States has been both the major supplier of assistance to Ethiopia and the harshest critic of the Ethiopian regime. Washington has made it plain that its antipathy to the Mengistu government has not lessened and has, if anything, been deepened by such programs as resettlement and villagization which have been carried on while relief operations were in progress. The Ethiopian government has remained firm in its allegiance to Moscow and has continued to bristle at American criticism, making only the tardiest and most grudging acknowledgements of the extraordinary levels of U.S. aid.

In 1987–88 famine once again struck Ethiopia. Though press attention has been less comprehensive than in 1984–85, it is reliably estimated that as many as six million people will be in jeopardy in the course of 1988. In responding to this new wave of hunger, some of the delays and tensions that I discuss concerning the earlier period were, I am pleased to say, avoided. The United States government, again the major Western donor, moved quickly to pledge support in the form of food and funds for inland transport and European governments have followed suit.

Administration spokesmen made it clear that, though deep differences with the Ethiopian government remained, the U.S. would act promptly and generously to meet the humanitarian need. This policy decision carried down the line and has resulted in greater harmony at both the headquarters and field levels between the U.S. government and the PVOs. For its part, the Ethiopian government was initially highly cooperative with donors and PVOs and has announced major reforms in agricultural policy which had long been advocated by the United States and other critics of the regime. Taken together, the response in 1987–88 seemed to show that many of the hard lessons that the previous famine response imposed had been learned and that in large measure humanitarian need had been clearly identified as the major priority, notwithstanding the existence of very real political problems. By April 1988, however, political and strategic priorities once again prevailed over humanitarian concerns as Ethiopia ordered some expatriate workers of international relief agencies out of its northern provinces when its army launched a counteroffensive against rebels in Eritrea. But CRS was able to count on its local church counterparts and continue its humanitarian relief operations without interruption.

The private agencies working in Ethiopia have tended to see the relief needs in a longer perspective. From the beginning of our activities, CRS has held that emergency measures like the distribution of food are part of a continuum which also includes efforts to promote recovery and rehabilitation among famine victims, such as the distribution of seeds and tools, provision of water and improved health care in affected areas. The ultimate goal, in this sense, is to help people return to productive life in conditions where they are less vulnerable to such disasters in the future. Given this point of view, there was an important difference of opinion with the United States and some other donors on how and over what period of time resources would be needed in Ethiopia. The differences were heightened in a dispute between the U.S. government and the private agencies over inland food transport costs, which carried elements of the conflicts operating at the political level. American officials attempted to put in place a policy that would have required private organizations operating food programs to pay 50 percent of inland transport costs. This policy, while ostensibly applicable throughout Africa, in fact came to be directed principally at feeding programs operating in government-controlled areas of Ethiopia. For an agency like CRS, which was distributing 225,000 tons of food, this would have meant that we would have exhausted all of our private resources in less than a year and that we would not have been able to undertake the $30 million recovery and rehabilitation program to which we had committed ourselves from private funds. Since the U.S. had indicated that it would not fund such measures, and other donor governments took much the same attitude, those activities would simply have gone undone, at a considerable cost in further suffering. In the event, the issue was resolved with the United States and, thanks to the unprecedented donations from the public CRS had received, we were able to proceed.

I have attempted to isolate some of the issues involved in the Ethiopian relief effort that seem to me to be most germane to this discussion. It goes without saying that I have not exhausted the subject. The response to the Ethiopian famine was a major undertaking, involving governments, international organizations, private agencies and hundreds of thousands of individuals who reacted with contributions and concern. The UN coordinator in Ethiopia, Kurt Janssen, called the relief operation one of the largest and most successful humanitarian responses in history. The size of the effort and number of difficulties involved caused innumerable problems. The relationship of the private agencies with governments must be seen in the wider context of what has been a highly complex and demanding effort. While important, it was a piece of a very elaborate mosaic and does not define by itself the whole of the relief operation. Having acknowledged that, I want now to attempt to draw some conclusions about that relationship as seen in Ethiopia and to make some comments on what lessons there may be for the humanitarian dimension in foreign policy.

The first thing that one must say about Ethiopia is that the relief effort was a success in the fundamental humanitarian sense that the millions who were at risk did not die and the suffering was greatly reduced. Today, the camps at Korem and Bati are no longer in existence; their one-time residents have returned to their lands. Pockets of hunger remain. Whatever the initial delays, whatever the conflicts that may have retarded action earlier, when the United States and the rest of the international community moved to intervene the impact was decisive. Thanks largely to aroused public opinion in the donor countries which reflected a deeply held moral position on the value of human life, formidable political obstacles were overcome and the necessary humanitarian response was made. In the midst of much confusion, heated rhetoric, and disparity of views, food and other supplies did reach those who needed them to live.

In mounting this effort in Ethiopia, the role of the Western donor governments, particularly the United States, was essential. The magnitude of the need being faced was such that only resources commanded by governments could have met it. No private agency or combination of private agencies could possibly have purchased, shipped, and moved inland the amounts of food that were required to head off the tragedy that was being played out in Ethiopia. The private organizations, to be sure, played a central role in ensuring that the necessary supplies reached those in need, but it was in large part the resources provided through governments that enabled those groups to respond as extensively as they were able to do. As we have seen, this relationship between the private agencies and the governments was often fraught with tensions, but its functioning was a necessary element in the relief effort.

Particularly in the early days, the response of the Western donor governments may have been reluctant, given the political antipathies that existed. There were, however, three principal factors which strongly encouraged such a response. The first is the relative prosperity enjoyed by these countries: they had the means at hand to provide the help required. Second, in each of these countries there is a humanitarian ethos, a general sense of shared values, a tradition of philanthropic activity, that was animated and given tremendous impetus by the media reports. Finally, in the Western democracies the societies and the institutions of government are open to the influence of public opinion and thus a popular moral consensus can, in such circumstances as prevailed in Ethiopia, set priorities that politics might otherwise preclude. My point here is that, while media attention certainly kindled the public conscience, there were grounds for receptivity to the message that was being conveyed on several different levels.

The partnership between governments and the private

agencies (and I am referring here primarily to the CRS relationship with the U.S. government) was beset by conflicts and tensions, often bitterly so. Whatever the strains, however, the partnership was effective. With the pledge of resources from governments, the private groups were able to set up a system of
distribution parallel to the Ethiopian government's and the two
together largely ensured that most of those in need would be
reached. On this operational level, though on a scale vastly larger
than they normally function, the private groups made a vital
contribution to the response. At the same time, the private agencies exercised an important advocacy function for the humanitarian principle which kept the issue in Ethiopia alive before
media attention was focused and, afterwards, served as a major
force for defining the kinds and levels of assistance that were
needed.

In many ways, Ethiopia has been an anomaly. The coinci-
dence of factors which served to stimulate the worldwide response that occurred will not soon be repeated and, of course, all
of us must hope that starvation on such a scale will not threaten
again. The experience of Ethiopia will nonetheless leave several
legacies for the future. Perhaps the most important of these is the
overwhelming support for humanitarian programs as part of
national policy objectives that it revealed or, more accurately,
reconfirmed. Policymakers will, I think, find it difficult to ignore
this fact as they confront such situations in the future. We cannot
take the matter for granted, however, or overlook the likelihood
that attempts will be made to turn this support for humanitarian
objectives to political ends, as seems to have happened in the
Central America debate. Without a defined and active constituency for foreign aid, public opinion is the ultimate guarantor of
the humanitarian principle as expressed in policy. The less visible
public concern is, the greater the temptation to compromise the
integrity of humanitarian programs. In this equation, the private
agencies will be important advocates and participants in the
process to ensure that the proper balance is maintained. That
means that the tensions between those agencies and the government will continue and, in some cases, intensify.

In the life of nations, as in the life of individuals, moral
action is based on choices which must be made every day, in
changing circumstance, and often with incomplete information

at hand. We can expect that many of those choices will present conflicts between what is advantageous or expedient and what we hold to be right in principle. At such times, we need to refer back to those basic values which guide our lives, direct our hopes, and keep whole our sense of integrity. I believe that we did that on the national level when we chose to respond to the suffering in Ethiopia. We cannot foresee what events in the future will again test our commitment as a moral nation. We can, however, trust that the values which we called upon in this instance will, if properly nurtured, endure and guide our path into the years ahead.

NOTES

1. The original formulation was Lord Palmerston's in a very different context. My paraphrase is meant to convey the usage that has evolved to justify various hard-line approaches to foreign policy more recently. Palmerston's words were: "We have no eternal allies, and no perpetual enemies. Our interests are eternal and perpetual, and it is our duty to follow." He was attempting to make the point in a debate in the House of Commons in 1848 that moral concerns were not necessarily incompatible with national interests, though his meaning has been much distorted in recent times. Jasper Ridley, *Lord Palmerston* (London: Constable, 1970), p. 334.

2. Daniel J. Boorstin, *The Americans: The Democratic Experience* (New York: Random House, 1973), p. 560, pp. 562-572.

3. Landrum R. Bolling with Craig Smith, *Private Foreign Aid* (Boulder, Colo.: Westview Press, 1982), p. 19.

4. Sidney E. Ahlstrom, *A Religious History of the American People* (New Haven and London: Yale University Press, 1974), p. 954.

5. Boorstin, *The Americans*, p. 574.

6. Catholic Relief Services Annual Reports, 1984 and 1985. Available on request from Catholic Relief Services, 1011 First Avenue, New York, N.Y. 10022.

7. U.S. General Accounting Office, *The United States Response to the Ethiopian Food Crisis*, "Report to the Honorable Byron L. Dorgan," House of Representatives, GAO/NSIAD-85-65, April 8, 1985. This is the fullest available examination of the difficulties involved in the early stages of the Ethiopian relief effort and the tensions that existed between the U.S. government and the private agencies at that time.

ETHIOPIAN FAMINE AND THE RELIEF AGENCIES

Jason W. Clay

Between October 1984, when the West became fully aware of the Ethiopian famine and January 1986, more money was raised, both publicly and privately, and funneled to Ethiopia than during any emergency humanitarian effort in history. The best evidence available suggests that the Ethiopian famine, like most other famines, was largely man-made. The context into which Western assistance was given, the problems that arose in attempts to deliver the assistance impartially, and consequently, the role the assistance played in maintaining and extending the famine all raise fundamental questions about the politicization of humanitarian assistance. This is not a new issue. Both famine and humanitarian assistance are often used as weapons. Famine is usually an indication that governments or elites are extracting too much food from the countryside with too little compensation to those producing it. Famine assistance, in turn, often gives power and international credibility to the groups that perpetrated the famine. This is true of both totalitarian and authoritarian states.

This essay first touches on the creation of famine by the Ethiopian government as well as the manipulation of food assistance by Western governments before and during the 1984–1985 Ethiopian famine. However, these brief discussions merely provide the context to describe and critique the role Western humanitarian agencies inadvertently played in maintaining and spreading the famine. Although the humanitarian task confronting such agencies was enormous, they responded inadequately and, in many instances, indefensibly. Prior to the declared 1987–

232

1988 famine in Ethiopia some agencies appeared to realize that they had made mistakes and were attempting to restructure their relief and development programs. But, with the media coverage of the new famine even these agencies retreated behind the policies of 1984–1986 which had been manipulated by Ethiopia. The following descriptions of specific problems that arose in the delivery of humanitarian assistance in Ethiopia are intended to encourage debate on such issues. The public has a right to know.

BACKGROUND TO THE FAMINE CRISIS

Ethiopia, perhaps the poorest country in the world, is nonetheless a strategic ally. Located at the geopolitical crossroad between Africa and the Middle East, North Africa and sub-Saharan Africa, Ethiopia is a key player in the superpower struggle for the region. When the United States refused to sell weapons to the Ethiopian government in the mid-1970s (due to human rights violations), Ethiopia turned to the Soviet Union, ending a longstanding alliance. Since that time U.S. officials have sought to reestablish ties to the country.

In late 1984, independent political observers and journalists speculated that the famine would allow the West, particularly the U.S., to win Ethiopia back; humanitarian assistance, they suggested, might succeed where diplomacy had failed.[1] This was not to be. Instead, Ethiopia took food from the West and continued to take weapons from the Soviets and their allies. In fact, Col. Mengistu Haile Miriam, Ethiopia's head of state, blamed the severity of the famine on the West's failure to respond to the crisis earlier.

There is evidence that the U.S. National Security Council (NSC) wanted the famine to occur in order to force Ethiopia to ally itself, once again, with the United States. The NSC had been aware of the impending Ethiopian famine since the early 1980s. At a 1982 meeting, in fact, the NSC decided to withhold food from Ethiopia even though it knew that the country was already suffering serious food shortages. According to one observer, the consensus of those present was to let the famine occur in the hopes of either destabilizing the regime or forcing it to make economic reforms.

Such politicization of food relief should surprise no observer of American foreign policy. Since the 1950s the provision and, in some cases, denial of food to third world governments has become an important weapon in the foreign assistance arsenal. Since its inception in the 1950s, "food for peace" was seen as a way to ensure political stability and security in individual countries or regions, thus adding to global security. Food shipments to such countries as Egypt and Iran allowed governments to keep urban food prices low and prevent unrest. Never mind that such assistance destroyed food production in those countries: the farmers there did not have sufficient clout and did not pose immediate threats to the state, as did urban residents or the military. Besides, food as a key aspect of foreign assistance allowed the United States not only to ignore domestic agricultural policies that resulted in huge surpluses but to further subsidize food grain production by making it available at concessionary rates throughout the world.

Although the United States eventually made some food available to U.S.-based agencies to distribute in Ethiopia in 1983, it did not respond to requests promptly and rarely gave the full quantities of grain requested. The reduction of food stocks in Ethiopia continued through 1984. Fred Cuny (this volume) suggests that most relief assistance arrived in late 1984 and early in 1985, *after* the death rate had already started to decline. Yet the Dergue, Ethiopia's ruling military junta, ignored the famine throughout the summer of 1984, not mentioning it in their own media and preventing foreign television crews from entering famine-affected areas until after the tenth-anniversary celebrations of the Ethiopian revolution in September 1984.

Regardless of one's views about the U.S. government's decision to allow food shortages in Ethiopia to go unmet, the United States did not create the food shortages. However, this question, "what caused the shortages?" is at the heart of the debate concerning the delivery of "appropriate" "humanitarian" assistance. At this late date it will be quite difficult to assess accurately why people were starving. Yet, this line of questioning was not adequately pursued by Western agencies trying to rush assistance to the region at the time. Ethiopian officials *asserted* that drought was the main cause of the famine, and occasionally insects and warfare played a role.[2] Westerners—diplomats, relief officials, and journalists—accepted these explanations *assuming* that they must be correct. In some cases specific policies were acknowledged to cause minor problems. Westerners saw the massive starvation but did not see the need to examine carefully its causes. How then could they legitimately claim that their help did not reinforce the causes? The answer is simple: they could not.

As the famine persisted, it appears that top Ethiopian officials were either embarrassed or unconcerned. Certainly they were unprepared to make policy changes that would alleviate the conditions which created it. Their priorities lay elsewhere. Famine provided the opportunity—a smokescreen of chaos—to intensify resettlement and villagization programs. Mengistu, for example, did not visit relief camps in Wollo or Tigray, the areas hardest hit by famine, until December 1984. However, in October, just after publicly acknowledging the famine, he toured the western and southwestern administrative regions to identify resettlement sites.

During the fall of 1984, at a meeting with Western diplomats, Ethiopia's foreign minister Goshu Wolde was arguing about whether Ethiopia would allow the West to deliver food to all famine victims regardless of whether they lived in government-held areas. Wolde, during the heat of the argument, declared that "food is an element in our strategy," against the insurgents.[3]

After it became apparent that food would not realign the Ethiopian regime, the U.S. government looked seriously at alternative groups (e.g., liberation fronts or their relief agencies) that, through humanitarian assistance, could be supported in their struggle against the government. Although the EPDA (Ethiopian People's Democratic Alliance) had received $500,000 worth of assistance per year from the US Central Intelligence Agency since 1984[4] they were apparently not effective. The Reagan administration then looked at the Tigrayan People's Liberation Front (TPLF) as a more acceptable alternative. Vice-President George Bush and M. Peter McPherson, head of the U.S. Agency for International Development (AID), visited Sudan to meet with representatives of the TPLF and REST (Relief Society of Tigray) in early 1985. In April 1985, however, the TPLF unveiled its Marxist platform, and at that point, the United States withdrew most of the support it had pledged.

From mid-1985 to the present, the United States appears to

have taken a "wait and see" attitude. After all, American citizens had demanded that their government send assistance to Ethiopian famine victims. The government began to do this, using U.S.-based agencies, primarily Catholic Relief Services (CRS) and World Vision, as the conduits. As a result of the famine U.S.based agencies and Americans in general, while still somewhat restricted, had more and freer access to rural areas in Ethiopia than at any time in the decade since the 1974 revolution. Who knew what these agencies might report.

From the outset Ethiopian officials suspected Western relief agencies, particularly those from the United States, of spying for their governments. Consequently Ethiopia placed strict conditions on the relief agencies' movements in the country, their presence in rural areas and, once on site, their movement into the surrounding countryside. In their haste to help, humanitarian agencies accepted numerous restrictions that adversely affected their ability to move freely, assess local conditions, and monitor the impact of their programs—in short, to deliver impartial assistance.[5] It appears that in their efforts to appease local officials, some agency personnel further curtailed their activities and even their discussions with the media and other outsiders.

The relationship between U.S.-based agencies working in Ethiopia and U.S. political interests in the area is undocumented and little known. While the relationship raises a number of interesting issues with important implications, it does not appear to be central to an adequate understanding of the politicization of humanitarian assistance during the famine. Although the United States certainly withheld assistance for some time in the early 1980s, once the food was given to U.S.-based agencies to distribute, few conditions were attached to its distribution. Three conditions, however, were aimed at reducing the Ethiopian government's ability to manipulate the assistance. These conditions are notable because similar stipulations were not placed on the distribution of the food the EEC (European Economic Commission) gave. First, the United States attempted to negotiate with Ethiopia an agreement that would allow its food relief to be distributed to famine victims regardless of whether they lived in government controlled areas.[6] Second, the United States stipulated that no U.S.-supplied assistance could be used to support resettlement. And third, the United States is required by law to ensure that its relief assistance to Ethiopia is not used for development. Had similar restrictions been applied by other governments, the 1987–1988 famine (in which more than seven million people are claimed to be at risk) would certainly be less severe.

Ethiopia's contribution to famine relief in the north consisted only of the salaries of the government's Relief and Rehabilitation Commission (RRC) officials detailed to the area and some equipment, much of which the West or international organizations had donated.[7] What developed was a division of labor—the West provided famine relief in the north and the Ethiopian government freed its resources for resettlement.

There were, of course, problems with this arrangement. Trucks, always in short supply in Ethiopia, were allocated to long-distance resettlement. Thus, although the west had donated many trucks to transport grain, after January 1985 the ports were never clear. In one incident alone, 13,000 tons of grain were destroyed in one downpour.[8] An MSF (Médecins sans Frontières, the French medical relief agency Doctors without Borders) estimate indicates that if in the first year the trucks used to move people had been used instead to move food, some 200,000 to 300,000 more tons of food could have been sent to the north for famine victims, 50 percent of the annual total food needs of the people in the area.[9] This apparently was not the government's priority. The artificial scarcity of trucks forced western governments to use air transport not only to supply remote regions but also Makelle, the administrative capital of Tigray, from October 1984 until mid-summer 1985.[10]

The Ethiopian government's politicization of humanitarian assistance during the 1985–1985 famine stems primarily from the relationship of its policies to the western agencies' programs. Some 90 to 95 percent of all western assistance went through government-held areas, including virtually all U.S. government assistance. It was this assistance that the Ethiopian government politicized by funneling it into its own existing programs.

The massive assistance effort in response to the Ethiopian famine came virtually entirely from the west.[11] Without doubt it saved many lives, although perhaps only a fraction of the numbers western agencies and governments claimed to have saved. For example, in early 1985, 7 million people were estimated to be at risk. Some relief, but not full rations, was reaching 2.5 to 3 million people. Later, revised World Food Program estimates "generously" pushed the estimate of food recipients to 3.5 and subsequently to 4 million people.[12]

Perhaps less well known or even understood by the agencies is the fact that the Ethiopian government has used so-called humanitarian assistance to reinforce the conditions that led to the famine. Furthermore, the government used humanitarian assistance in ways that extended the famine into formerly self-sufficient regions. Conservative calculations indicate that Western assistance contributed to conditions that have resulted in the deaths of 250,000 to 300,000 people since late 1984.[13] Although reliable data inside Ethiopia is difficult to obtain, considerable evidence is there for those willing to look for it. In addition, there is every indication that the 1987–1988 famine can be attributed in part to the role played by Western assistance in resettlement, villagization, and general population displacement.

Famines are man-made. The 1984–1985 Ethiopian famine was no exception. Research undertaken with famine victims indicates that the most significant causes of famine in Ethiopia were official government policies.[14] Policies, both agricultural and military, implemented since the late 1970s made it impossible for farmers to produce food for their families, let alone surpluses to sell. Inputs (improved seed, credit, fertilizer) were rarely available for private farmers, prices paid to farmers were low and, increasingly, marketing was controlled by the state-run Agricultural Marketing Committee.

Famine and famine assistance are political. The failure of most humanitarian agencies and governments to address this issue directly in Ethiopia resulted in a number of avoidable mistakes. In short, the help hurt. Most of the problems that have resulted from the delivery of Western humanitarian assistance to Ethiopia stem from four sources, all of which relate to the unwillingness of Western agencies and governments to insist on understanding the context in which the famine occurred and into which the assistance was delivered. The four problem areas stem from relief agencies' unwillingness to insist that they be allowed independently:

—to determine the causes of the famine,
—to assess the extent of the famine,

—to monitor the implementation and impact of their programs, and

—to evaluate the effectiveness of their programs at treating
the root causes of the famine.

These types of information would be needed to deliver appropriate assistance in any famine.

THE WEST'S RESPONSE TO THE FAMINE

The West's response to the Ethiopian famine was truly massive. The tremendous effort on the part of agencies, journalists,
civil servants, and entertainers, each doing what they could do to
reduce the suffering that moved them to act, should not be
belittled. Nor is that the intent of this essay. The effort was also
remarkable both for its technical logistics as well as for the well-
orchestrated cooperation between agencies, governments, and
international organizations. It was not only commendable that
the public wanted agencies and governments to rush assistance
to Ethiopia as quickly as possible in 1984, it was remarkable that
the agencies and governments could mount an effort of the massive scope required so quickly with relatively few problems. To a
large extent this was possible because agencies and governments
put politics, at one level at least, aside. United States AID director
McPherson said at the time, "A starving child knows no politics."
Such attitudes carried the day, sweeping all doubts before them.

By late 1984, however, concerns about the causes of the
famines as well as the Ethiopian government's programs ostensibly designed to eradicate it (e.g., resettlement and villagization)
had already begun to surface. Considerable documentation and
specific inquiries into the causes of famine were made public,[15]
and the information called into question the "natural causes"
explanation of the famine advanced by the Ethiopian government and accepted by Western governments and agencies. Agencies working in government-held areas for the most part either
echoed the government's explanations of the famine (drought
and prolonged soil degradation) or were silent, allowing them to
go unchallenged. Most agency personnel believed that an open
debate on the underlying causes of the Ethiopian famine would

lead to donor apathy and a reduction in the number and value of contributions, thus reducing their ability to assist the victims.

Many agency personnel, however, were anything but passive in their attempts to limit the debate concerning the causes of the Ethiopian famine. In public fora they attempted to discredit information that did not support the "natural causes" explanation of the famine. At one such meeting in the spring of 1986 sponsored by the Refugee Studies Program at Oxford University, the World Vision-U.K. representative insisted that research on the causes of the famine might be academically interesting, but it should not be undertaken. Although it might be an "ego booster" for the researchers, it would hurt Ethiopians. The same representative stated that it was "immoral" to publish such information.

At the same meeting, a representative of Oxfam-U.K. publicly contradicted a finding that mosques were not allowed in the new villages being created in eastern Ethiopia in 1985 and 1986. In private, the same person said that of course the new villages he had visited were model villages for Westerners to see and that he did not doubt that religious persecution occurred during villagization, particularly in villages off the main roads. This, incidently, is most villages. Western agencies will never be present in more than a few hundred of the 15,000 new villages already created or the 50,000 planned. They were present in even fewer of the 30,000 to 50,000 traditional villages that were destroyed in the past three years.

At a similar meeting of Canadian assistance organizations in September 1986, the head of the Irish agency Concern's operations in Ethiopia, which included work in resettlement sites, stated categorically that those who undertook research and whose findings discredited resettlement were "dangerous." From 1984 through 1986, Western agencies preferred to denounce researchers and their findings rather than confront the difficult issues that the research raised.

Unfortunately, such criticism by relief agencies did silence some critics directly; it silenced others indirectly by discrediting them or their findings. Sadly, the net effect of these efforts by many Western humanitarian agencies was to limit the debate on the Ethiopian famine precisely at a time when it should have been expanded, a time when an open debate could have improved the agencies' ability to understand the famine and respond to it.

By 1987 little had changed in this regard. On December 11 and 12, 1986 the Development NGOs' Liaison Committee to the European Communities (EC) met to discuss "The Situation and Possibilities for Aid in Ethiopia." The points of discussion on which the organizer, Dr. Hartmut Bauer (in a December 1, 1986 letter to all NGO committee members), thought all NGOs could agree included, among others, the following:

—Ethiopia continued to need the support of Western governments and agencies.
—Villagization and resettlement were undertaken with brutal methods and the programs will continue into the future.
—Resettlement was an opportunistic program that far exceeded the ecological necessities.
—Ethiopia relied on her allies for the transport of people in resettlement, but the program could not have been undertaken as it was without food from the West.

The same memo anticipated that the government would expect Western donors to supply food to resettle people. The predicament posed in the memo was that Western agencies, in their efforts to assist needy Ethiopians, would be forced to support, either directly or indirectly, government programs which would have devastating consequences. Thus, the memo concluded, the agencies were to avoid such problems, the memo recommended that they come to a general understanding about certain issues such as the voluntary participation of people in their programs, sufficient planning and preparation of programs before they are implemented and the minimum scientific investigation needed to insure that the help does not hurt. The memo went on to note that no single NGO could insure such conditions, so all would have to work together, along with their governments, on these points. Political clout from the respective governments, it was assumed, was needed to deliver the type of humanitarian assistance in Ethiopia that European agencies could find acceptable.

Not much headway was made at the December meeting. Instead the group decided to set up an ad hoc committee to discuss strategies for delivering humanitarian assistance in Ethiopia which all agencies could find acceptable. The ad hoc group held its first meeting on January 28, 1987. The points identified in the letter provided the agenda for the meeting. The agenda provided a useful format for an interesting and worthwhile discussion of future strategies for the agencies. In the subsequent meeting, however, the mood, as one of the participants reported, quickly shifted from an open discussion of Ethiopia's policies and how the agencies could avoid reinforcing them through their assistance, to expressions of grave concern about the disaster that would confront each NGO if the media began to report the link between Western assistance and agricultural collectivization policies in Ethiopia. The agencies' representatives declared that they would have to take a different tack immediately if the media became interested in the topic. All expressed central concern for continuing their presence in the country. They did not even discuss the strategies or leverage that the NGOs and their governments might implement to influence Ethiopia's policies.

Although some humanitarian agencies are now prepared to acknowledge, privately at least, the disastrous consequences of Ethiopia's famine-producing policies (particularly resettlement in the short term and villagization in the long term), they still do not acknowledge the need to examine the causes of the famine. This lack of recognition persists, nevertheless, in spite of indications of the government's role in the famines from 1984 to the present.

The research of some organizations as well as oblique reports in the media should have given the agencies pause even in 1984, certainly by 1985. It did not. In fact, without ever undertaking research of their own or supporting the research of others, agencies vehemently denied reports that implicated government policies as the underlying causes of the Ethiopian famine even though the reports came from the victims themselves.

Instead, during the fall of 1985 and continuing through the summer of 1986 Western humanitarian agencies tried to fan the flames of compassion by presenting the Ethiopian famine, in both the press and their public appeals, as a continuing natural disaster. By 1987–1988 a new famine was declared, a figure of seven million at risk was estimated, and the press, once again became interested. But the public had been become understandably skeptical.[16] Even in the fall of 1984, during the height of the publicity surrounding the famine, we interviewed by telephone the supervisors of the "1-800" telephone fund-raising operators for six of the largest U.S.-based relief agencies. They indicated that one-fifth to one-third of all callers wanted to know how the agencies proposed to avoid the politics of the famine. By the time the second and third round of fund-raising took place, extensive media coverage and the limited research that had been undertaken specifically concerning the causes of the famine led many potential donors to realize that, at best, the agencies were not telling the whole story. At worst, the agencies did not know what was happening in Ethiopia and therefore were not qualified to receive contributions.

The public's skepticism also resulted, in part at least, from the literature agencies working in Ethiopia published and distributed. Their public information and education packets were little more than self-serving fund-raising mailings. Most humanitarian agencies claim to have public education programs. A careful reading of most of their material on Ethiopia, however, indicates that the material is not an independent, careful assessment of the famine. Rather, the literature consisted of fund-raising appeals that repeated the standard, assumed causes of the famine and used descriptions of the agencies' existing programs to raise money for future work. Most important, the content was shaped by existing public awareness and did little to expand it.

The lack of confidence in the agencies' portrayal of the famine, not mere donor apathy, is, in 1988, at the heart of the difficulty in raising funds for famine victims not only in Ethiopia but in other parts of Africa as well. As a result of the problems arising from the West's response to Ethiopia—and following on the heels of similar problems encountered in Kampuchea—humanitarian agencies' ability to claim apolitical postures, much less deliver apolitical assistance, has been seriously impaired.

What led to this situation? It appears to have been the agencies' unwillingness to find out what caused the famine, or even if they undertook quiet investigations into the causes, their unwillingness to go public with that information either through the media or in their fund-raising efforts.

FROM RELIEF TO DEVELOPMENT

A separate but related problem arises when relief and humanitarian agencies shift their focus from relief to development assistance or see relief as a development tool. Increasingly, U.S.-based NGOs operating throughout the world, using both public and private funds, are "doing" development. In the U.S. the use of NGOs for local-level development began in the 1960s and 1970s due to hiring ceilings in government. Few relief agencies and not all nonprofit development agencies have sufficient internal expertise to undertake successful development work. Lutheran World Relief (LWR), which would be considered by some to be one of the more sensitive relief/development organizations, by its own admission does not fund research.[17] But how can such an agency possibly believe that it can solve problems if it does not assess what has caused them? The LWR is not alone in this regard. Most relief agencies apparently believe that research is expensive and takes a long time. It need not be either.

Cultural Survival's research on the causes of the Ethiopian famine is the largest and most systematic, replicable pieces of research yet undertaken on the topic.[18] The research cost less than $15,000, or less than .0001 of 1 percent of the more than $1.5 billion the West spent on famine assistance in Ethiopia from 1984–1986. The agencies' reluctance to undertake or fund research on the causes of the famine is difficult to understand, since most Western agencies and governments constantly give lip service to the need to attack the "root causes" of famine.

For Western agencies, both private and public, research on the impact of assistance during the famine was limited to monitoring the flow of grain from its point or origin to the point it left their hands. It might seem adequate to trace the path of Kansas wheat through its long journey into the hands of an Ethiopian famine victim;[19] but it is not. The context is crucial. The Ethiopian government used food as bait in a trap to force people to take part in "voluntary" programs.

Good intentions are not a sufficient foundation for good programs. Agencies' attempts to ignore the context of the Ethiopian famine by burying their heads in the sand and claiming political neutrality cannot be accepted. Finding out as much information as possible about a situation in which it is directly involved is an agency's only hope for remaining neutral. Sticking one's head in the sand is to take sides; it is a political act.

A sports analogy clarifies this point. In an athletic event

neither the contestants nor their respective followers are expected to be impartial. Referees, however, must remain neutral. They achieve this impartiality by not only thoroughly knowing the rules of the game but also, to the best of their ability, by watching the actions of all participants at all times. Only in this way can they remain neutral.

Each relief and development agency operating in Ethiopia, however, is political, each has its own agenda, albeit hidden, its own ideological leanings and its own assumptions about what constitutes appropriate relief and development activities. In short, agencies do not remain neutral. Unfortunately, few are aboveboard about these positions. This happens, apparently, for two reasons. First, it is rare that agencies' positions are clearly thought out. Second, agencies are afraid that donor giving will decrease as a result of such public disclosure and debate. In some of the smaller agencies an additional problem arises; programs can be traced to the agendas of specific individuals who do not even discuss their rationale, much less their overall agenda, with other staff.

All these issues aside, I am not suggesting that assistance should have been withheld from famine victims until assessments of the problems were undertaken. Rather, I am suggesting that agencies should have negotiated these conditions with the government so that as they began to provide relief assistance, they could also have begun the necessary work to understand the nature and the scope of the problem they hoped to alleviate. Even if such conditions could not have been negotiated with the Ethiopian government, each agency, as its understanding of the causes of the famine increased, could have modified its programs accordingly. Such research need not have been expensive. Doctors, nurses, and administrators are good observers.[20] Considerable information slips out in feeding centers, food distribution centers, villages, or refugee camps even from local officials, drivers, and residents of the area. However, someone has to collect this information and analyze it systematically to make it less impressionistic and as representative as possible. This did not happen in Ethiopia. Yet, it would have taken only one person per agency or even one for a number of like-minded agencies to have collected this information from all the agencies' personnel to determine if patterns could be discerned regarding the causes of famine, the abuses associated with resettlement or villagization, or the problems associated with the delivery of humanitarian assistance.

What would the agencies have seen if they had examined the conditions leading to famine in Ethiopia? How could such information have helped them to understand their own role in maintaining or extending those conditions? These questions can be answered best after reviewing the specifics of the Ethiopian case.

THE EXTENT OF THE FAMINE

If Western agencies had examined the situation closely, they would have found out, and might have shared with the world, how Ethiopia made its calculations of the "at risk" population. According to former RRC officials who were in charge not only of Ethiopia's famine relief agency but also the distribution of all relief assistance in the country, the calculations were based, by and large, on rainfall measurements and spot field checks taken at a few dozen points throughout the government-held regions of the country. According to these officials the government did not have access to the most severely affected areas. Yet, in this calculation, a 15 percent decline in rainfall, nationally, was assumed to indicate that 15 percent of the population would not have enough food. Such an equation not only incorrectly assumed a one-to-one relationship between rainfall and crop yields, it also assumed that there were never surpluses in any area of Ethiopia.

Furthermore, the final "at risk" calculation depended entirely on the total Ethiopian population. In the calculation the larger the population the greater the absolute number of people at risk and the greater the need for foreign assistance.[21] Therefore, the government claimed to have undertaken a census in the country in early 1984 even though it's own army could barely penetrate large, densely populated regions, including some of the areas most affected by famine. The government's census "showed" that 42 to 45 million people lived in the country. By comparison, the World Bank's estimate indicated that the population was 32 to 35 million people.[22] Subsequently, the population figure of 40 to 42 million and the rainfall shortage figure of 15 to 18 percent appear to have been negotiated and finally accepted for planning purposes. From these numbers, then, it was calculated that around seven million people were at risk.

By early 1986 the government indicated, again with no independent confirmation, that one million people died from the famine. It followed logically that six million of the people at risk had been saved during the crisis and the relief agencies were quick to claim credit.[23] During the crisis, how the number of famine victims was determined was never made public. None of the agencies or their governments appear to have been unduly concerned about the degree of error that might have been introduced in such a calculation, because their people on the ground could see so many people in need, so many sick and dying.

Many people were at risk during the famine. Thus, the point is not merely to show that the calculation might have been off by x or y percent, but rather to indicate that no one knew how large the population at risk was, where it lived, and whether it was increasing, decreasing, or regionally varying. The urgency of the moment as well as the horror and chaos the agencies witnessed each day conditioned them to be ready to believe each new report—100,000 people dying of starvation in this inaccessible region, 10,000 famine orphans in need of immediate assistance in that area, etc. The agencies were conditioned to ask where and how many, not why.[24]

THE CAUSES OF THE FAMINE

Researchers generally agree that government taxes and contributions from 1978 to the present (even from famine victims in the period 1984 to 1986) stripped peasant producers of the cushion (both grain and animals) that they needed to survive anticipated years of bad harvests. Even studies conducted by Ethiopian researchers in Wollo confirm these findings. Production was further reduced, both in famine areas and in surplus-producing areas, because farmers were required to perform unpaid days of labor on local militia and government officials' lands and on plots from which produce went to the government. During the height of the famine in 1984, the artificially low government price for food crops led many farmers to leave their crops in the field.

Joseph Collins, co-director of the Institute for Food and Development Policy, reported that on his drive north of Addis Ababa to the famine camps, his Ethiopian and Western travel companions pointed out numerous fields visible from the road that should have been harvested and that were going to waste because of the government's low price.[25] Even Ethiopia's much heralded early warning system to predict food deficits to prevent famines became part of the problem in the 1980s because it allowed the government to define, identify, and expropriate surpluses from peasant farmers who were accused of hoarding grain when in fact they were storing it for periods of scarcity. Many farmers learned to expect bad harvests every few years.

Government policies, both agricultural and military, played a major role in creating the famine. Even the "natural causes" of the famine advanced by the government had greater impact as a result of government policies. Victims reported that government programs caused delays in planting in both liberated areas by attacking during the planting season and in government-held areas by requiring forced labor during peak agricultural periods.[26] The delays in planting allowed pests to become established in fields while food crops were in their early, most vulnerable stages.[27] This allowed the pests to cause far more damage than they would have done otherwise. Likewise, government actions and policies that delayed planting in years when rains stopped early (1983 and 1984) intensified the effects of drought. Thus drought did not cause the conditions that resulted in the famine, rather it exacerbated them—it was the final straw.

The Impact of Western Assistance

Ethiopian officials viewed Western assistance as an essential element for the continuation of their policies and programs. Furthermore, many officials saw Western assistance as the best way to extend such programs as resettlement and villagization that had had official priority for years but which lacked sufficient funding. How then was the Western assistance manipulated to achieve these ends? In some cases the food and rations the West gave proved to be no more than transfer payments to the government. For example, all residents of Ethiopia were required to pay a famine tax—even famine victims. Nonfamine victims reported receiving food from CARE and using it to pay their required famine taxes, either in kind of by selling it and giving the cash to the government. Some former recipients of food rations indicated that in their areas the famine tax appeared to be pegged to the level of Western assistance individuals received.[28] These citations, as well as others that follow, are not intended to single out specific agencies for special criticism. Rather, it is these agencies about which we have received specific information; no doubt the practices reported are common to most agencies working in Ethiopia.

Self-sufficient peasant producers in many parts of Ethiopia were required to give grain contributions to the government even though they did not themselves produce a surplus. Some of these peasants reported that they sold cash crops in order to buy food from CARE in Hararghe, eastern Ethiopia.[29] Other peasants reported that they purchased food from Catholic Relief Services in northern Ethiopia.[30] They then fulfilled their required grain contributions to the government from these stocks. To the extent that this happened, it would have been far simpler if the U.S. government had merely handed over the food to the Ethiopian government at the port rather than transferring it to the U.S.-based agencies who gave or sold it to farmers who in turn gave it or it's value in cash to the Ethiopian government.

Delivering humanitarian assistance to famine victims in Ethiopia also involved a number of direct payments to the government—taxes, handling fees, airline tickets, accommodations, office rentals, etc. Although the total amount is not known, these direct payments do appear to have been insignificant. The government, for example, purchased with cash up to nine new airplanes for the state-run airlines.[31] In 1985, during the height of the famine, Ethiopia tripled its foreign currency reserves.[32] Famine assistance seems to have generated more income for the government than any other single source. In a normal year, by contrast, agricultural exports (mostly coffee) account for about 90 percent of Ethiopia's known foreign exchange earnings. In the past Ethiopia has spent most of its foreign reserves to purchase weapons and equipment needed to carry on wars in different parts of the country. However, in Ethiopia, as the government has recently demonstrated, food is also a weapon.

The delivery of relief assistance involved additional transfers of money, which also increased the Ethiopian government's cash reserves. Government-approved Ethiopians hired as translators, camp assistants, drivers, and assistants all earned foreign exchange for the government. "Famine tours" by the media, diplomats, agency personnel, and interested individuals not only generated money for the government inside the country, but also increased Ethiopian Air occupancy rates by 30 percent during the famine.[33]

Many agencies such as Save the Children-U.S./U.K., OxfamAmerica/U.K., CARE and Live Aid provided indirect support to the government through programs the government designed to reorganize agricultural production and rural life. In 1985, during the height of the famine, Western agencies purchased oxen that were distributed for cooperative production while the government exported 200,000 head of livestock, an export figure four times higher than the previous year.[34] The agencies also bought and distributed seeds and tools to and through local government organizations (peasant associations, and producers' service cooperatives) when the government was forcing people to cultivate crops, without compensation, that were destined for government warehouses and even nationalizing produce in some areas where Western agencies had distributed agricultural inputs.

Western agencies have given millions of dollars as well as personnel and material to work with children "separated" from their parents during the famine. Yet, some agencies acknowledge that during the resettlement program food was deliberately withheld from children until their parents "volunteered" to be separated and resettled, on average, 1,000 miles away. The government recently admitted that some 200,000 children were reunited with their parents more than a year after being "inadvertently" separated during resettlement.[35]

Our research indicates that as many as 300,000 to 400,000 children were separated as a result of resettlement. If only 200,000 were reunited with their parents, where are the rest? We will never know how many children died because they were separated from their parents. However, the separation of parents from their children must have played a role in the deaths of many children. In the absence of their families and in an increasingly malnourished state, many probably lost the will to live. In addition, eyewitnesses saw children beaten to death as they attempted to climb on departing trucks to stay with one or both parents. The separation, in many cases, was far from inadvertent; it was deliberate. This should surprise no one since the Ethiopian government commonly undertook resettlement from 1978 to 1984 after deliberately separating household heads from the rest of their families.[36]

Although few Western agencies or governments overtly supported resettlement, they did, in fact, indirectly support not only the program but also the separation of families, because the food they distributed was being used to force people to take part in the program. For example, in 1984 the government set up "orphanages" in each of Ethiopia's administrative regions. Many Western agencies provided assistance to these children, in some cases working in the institutions. Westerners in Ethiopia have speculated that they will be used to train a new cadre of supporters for the government.[37] International agencies such as UNICEF which gave millions of dollars directly to the government for programs with orphans and children separated from their parents are particularly susceptible to this type of manipulation. However, even smaller groups such as Save the Children-U.S., which began to receive massive donations for Ethiopian famine relief in late 1984 (due to the pictures of starving children) even though it was not operating in the country at the time, went to the government and asked officials to identify the areas of need where it could work.

Finally, Western humanitarian agencies allowed themselves to be manipulated in other ways. Refugees in Sudan reported that while in feeding centers in government-held northern areas, they had been given blankets by foreigners who came in white vehicles with red crosses on the sides. As soon as the foreigners left the camp, the blankets were confiscated. Likewise, MSF, the French-based humanitarian relief organization, reported that local authorities confiscated the blankets that it had brought to

Ethiopia to distribute to people in its centers. MSF was told that local officials did not want to make life too comfortable in the camp or famine victims would not agree to be resettled.[38]

FORCED RELOCATION IN ETHIOPIA AND WESTERN FAMINE ASSISTANCE

Two Ethiopian programs designed ostensibly to eliminate the famine and to provide better services to the rural population now appear to be the leading causes of starvation in Ethiopia.[39] Both programs, resettlement and villagization, move people from their homes into planned villages where the government can monitor residents' movements and activities. Both programs give the government control over labor through the immediate or eventual establishment of communal production systems as well as forced labor on government projects such as the building of roads. What farmers plant, as well as what is produced, is increasingly controlled by the state through local peasant associations. The overriding intent of these programs is twofold. They provide sufficient government-controlled supplies of food which guarantee the needs of the military and urban residents, the groups most likely to organize against the present government in the event of food shortages, and they give the government control of the rural population which might otherwise support one of the many liberation fronts in the country. Virtually every Western relief agency working in Ethiopia was either actively or passively involved in one or both of these programs.

Since 1978, government policies have undermined each of the major ethnic groups in the country by nationalizing lands and productive assets and using a divide and conquer strategy in which members of dissident groups are moved from their own areas onto the land or even into the villages of others. This systematic mixing and consequent destruction of the economic and social fabric of peoples within the country is intended, apparently, to create a strong central state upon which each community is dependent. The government has imposed, from the top down, local organizations (peasant associations), through which Western agencies providing relief or development assistance are required to work. Many peasant farmers view these "local" organizations correctly as reducing their communities' autonomy as well as their ability to feed themselves.[40]

Ethiopian policies aimed at increasing the power of the state over peasants producers laid the groundwork for the 1984–1985 famine. Yet, the famine clearly demonstrates that although the state has succeeded in rendering such communities dependent and unable to feed themselves, it cannot provide sufficient food for all those peasants no longer allowed to feed themselves. Ethiopia's first proposed solution to the starvation it was instrumental in creating was to resettle 1.85 million famine victims from northern areas to well-watered, "uninhabited" areas primarily in the southwestern administrative regions of Wollega, Illubabor, and Keffa. The government succeeding in resettling about one-third of this goal. Western humanitarian assistance and Eastern gasoline and transport vehicles were the key elements that allowed the Ethiopian government to undertake even the scaled-down version of the resettlement program.

RESETTLEMENT

The resettlement program the Ethiopian government is now pursuing with peasants from the northern administrative regions parallels the Amhara-led military expansion in the late nineteenth and early twentieth centuries which resulted in the extension of Abyssinia into the present-day Ethiopian empire. The incorporation of the "southern" 60 percent of Ethiopia's surface area into the Abyssinian-dominated empire has been accomplished mainly through the establishment of military garrisons, which evolved into trading centers and small cities and served as outposts for colonization of these areas by northerners loyal to the central government. Resettlement recreates these conditions.

This ongoing conquest and incorporation of southern regions that are inhabited by a number of distinct indigenous peoples, including the Oromo, who probably account for half of the country's population, has been referred to by a number of observers as "natural" (note the similarities to the present famine) and "spontaneous" migration. During the colonial expansion, one-third of all lands in the conquered areas were given to soldiers and officials who helped to conquer and later administer the new regions.

"Spontaneous" settlement became more systematic during the 1950s and 1960s when Ethiopia received some international encouragement for it. Since AID, World Bank, and FAO reports are often cited by Westerners and Ethiopians alike to justify the current government's resettlement programs, it is important to comment briefly on them. First, AID, the World Bank, and FAO rarely propose policy options that are not either already being seriously considered or implemented, albeit haphazardly, by the host government. Thus, it is likely that each of these three agencies had examined a number of policy options that they had identified with the government. As early as the 1950s and, more concertedly in the 1960s, the Ethiopian government attempted to attract foreign assistance from the West to fund colonization programs. Yet the previous government was consistently denied substantial funds for this purpose. Given that the government wanted massive assistance for colonization, it is significant that neither AID, the World Bank, nor FAO recommended massive colonization, certainly nothing even vaguely approaching the numbers moved during the 1984–1986 program or the ultimate goal of seven million identified by Mengistu. Each of these potential funding institutions, in fact, raised serious questions about Ethiopia's ability to undertake even limited, long-distance colonization. In their reports, they recommended first and foremost redistributing the population within the northern highlands (usually within fifty kilometers), a task that should have been possible under this government after it nationalized all lands. They also recommended rehabilitation programs in the northern highlands as the long-term solution to the problem that should receive most funds.

When viewing these reports, one must also take into account the prevailing assumptions of the day. In the 1960s and 1970s colonization had become an agricultural development panacea of the major development institutions. Colonization projects, especially in Latin America but also in south Asia and southeast Asia and, admittedly, to a lesser extent in Africa, were seen as politically acceptable solutions for solving problems of rural and even urban poverty because they did not require land reform or other structural changes. Instead, the projects called for moving of poor people from one area to another region where the indigenous residents, because of their isolation, were usually only nominally under the control of the central government and had even less power than those being moved. The record of massive, planned colonization programs undertaken around the world during this period is poor, *even* when participation was voluntary and the states involved were committed to adequate prior study and the provision of services to the colonists (see, e.g., Brazil). The environmental consequences alone of such projects have led AID, the World Bank, and FAO, among other funding agencies, to take a long and hard look at any colonization programs.

None of these three organizations could have supported the 1984-1986 program in Ethiopia. First, the program was for most part not voluntary and, if allowed, most residents of the resettlement sites would surely return to their homes. Second, the government had undertaken no studies that justified resettlement over other possibly less costly or less socially disruptive programs or that could have helped to avoid the immediate or long-term problems that resettlement posed for those moved, those resettled upon, or the local environment.[41] Third, the government had not budgeted any funds for the program until four months after it had begun and after more than 100,000 people had been captured and moved in the program.[42] Even then the appropriations were far less than necessary. For example, 60 percent of all the land cleared for planting was left barren because the clearing took place too late or the appropriate seed was not available.[43] Finally, agencies such as AID and the World Bank have policies that require them to determine, before funding, whether the projects being considered will have a negative impact either on the environment or on distinct tribal or ethnic groups occupying the project area.[44] For example, according to World Bank policy guidelines, if projects adversely affect either, they must be changed or not funded. If after a project has been approved and partially funded it is found to have negative effects either on the environment or the people indigenous to the project area, further funding is to be withheld until acceptable changes have been made.

The history of colonization in Ethiopia suggests that Amhara-dominated governments of the right and the left have attempted to use foreign assistance opportunistically to centralize their authority over the rest of the empire through massive colonization. Western organizations, following the government's wishes, have endorsed small, experimental colonization programs, but have recommended more enthusiastically resettlement programs and environmental rehabilitation programs in the northern highland areas.

The combined efforts of the present government as well as that of Haile Selassie to resettle northerners had resulted in the movement of approximately 250,000 people during the ten years before the intensification of the resettlement program in 1984. From 1974 to 1984, the present government provided early settlers with between 80 and 90 percent of all agricultural aid (seed, fertilizer, equipment, credit, extension).[45] Yet, according to Ethiopian researchers using government data, in ten years *none* of the 87 resettlement sites were self-sufficient in food production.[46] Thus, even the available "official" evidence indicates that resettlement is not an economically viable program. Agricultural rehabilitation programs in the northern administrative regions, on the other hand, funded by the FAO in government-held areas and by a small number of Western agencies in the liberated areas increase production immediately and significantly.[47]

In February and March 1985 Cultural Survival undertook its initial research on the famine. The objectives of the research were to investigate the causes of the famine and the impact of resettlement on those resettled as well as on the former inhabitants of the areas selected for the program. Members of the research team were not permitted into Ethiopia to undertake the research. Thus, the study was undertaken, by necessity, with recently arrived refugees in Sudan from the Ethiopian administrative regions of Tigray, Wollo, Wollega, and Illubabor. The findings were reported in *Politics and the Ethiopian Famine, 1984–1985*, authored by Bonnie Holcomb and myself. Subsequently, our findings were corroborated by a number of reports (e.g., Niggli, Steingraber, REST [Relief Society of Tigray], OLF [Oromo Liberation Front], MSF, WFP [World Food Program], numerous newspaper articles, and even reports from Ethiopia's RRC). No researcher in Sudan has found evidence to dispute the findings presented in the report. Comparable, systematic research is not allowed in Ethiopia.

Our research on those resettled from Wollo and Tigray indicates that important differences existed between the two groups. According to the RRC some 70 percent of all people taken for resettlement were from Wollo. Cultural Survival found that those "captured" (the term those resettled used) for resettlement from Wollo were, on average, less than twenty-five years old; 95 percent were Moslem Oromos. Only 18 percent were resettled with their entire family. Nearly two-thirds reported that their lands in Wollo were fertile. Whereas only 10 percent reported that their 1983 harvest had been their best production under this government, most reported that production had fallen short of their needs. However, those with livestock (77 percent) reported that they had more than 16 head of animals which they reported would have been sufficient to carry them through to the next harvest.

Those from Tigray who were interviewed, by contrast, averaged forty-three years of age and were all Coptic Christians. Only 8 percent were resettled with their entire families. Nearly two-thirds reported that their lands were fertile or average (the remainder were not asked the question). Nearly half reported that their 1983 harvest was their best under this government. Those who were allowed to harvest their crops in 1984 indicated that they had produced nearly 80 percent of their families' cereal needs and, in addition, had nearly twenty-three head of animals at the time they were resettled.

Nearly one-third of the farmers from Wollo reported that government policies were the primary cause of production declines in 1984. More than a third of those from Tigray reported that in their village, government troops had burned crops and houses, killed civilians or stolen oxen or other large animals, or both. One-quarter reported that the straw needed to feed oxen during the dry season was burned by the army.

None of those interviewed had volunteered for the resettlement program. The majority from Wollo (72.7 percent), unbeknownst to them, had been nominated for resettlement by their peasant association.[48] The remainder from Wollo were taken when they were traveling away from their homes.

Nearly one-third of those from Tigray were captured while working in their fields or when their village was surrounded by soldiers; about 40 percent were taken when they were traveling away from home (looking for family members that they presumed had been resettled, attending the local market, trading, or looking for work); and more than 18 percent had been advised by government representatives to go to a government-designated location—usually a food distribution center or meeting site—where they had subsequently been surrounded and taken for resettlement.

All those interviewed indicated that they had been guarded from the time they were captured for resettlement in their homelands until they had escaped from the resettlement sites to Sudan. Why guards were necessary in an allegedly voluntary program has never been explained.

Of those resettled from Wollo, more than 13 percent reported that they had been imprisoned since being taken for resettlement (the remainder were not asked the question). More than one quarter of those from Wollo reported that they were beaten, and an equal number witnessed beatings (the remainder were not asked the question). Nine percent reported seeing people killed who tried to escape from the resettlement program (the other 91 percent were not asked the question). Not everyone was asked these questions because we did not anticipate such overt human rights violations.

During the resettlement process—in the holding camps, during resettlement, or in the new resettlement sites—more than 60 percent of those from Tigray were imprisoned. More than half of those from Tigray reported being beaten since they were taken for resettlement. More than one-fifth witnessed people beaten to death during resettlement, whereas more than one in ten saw people killed when trying to escape from the program.

Many of those interviewed reported that death rates in the holding camps were quite high, but this question was not asked systematically of all those interviewed. An internal memo of the WFP indicates that death rates in two northern holding camps where people waited until they were resettled were quite high. MSF, calculating from that data, concluded that death rates in the holding centers are ten times higher than the death rates in the feeding centers in nearby areas.

Those interviewed reported that food was often stockpiled in the holding centers, particularly in Wollo, but that both food and water were deliberately withheld from those being resettled.

Those interviewed argued that this was done to make them weak and prevent them from escaping. Some 60 percent of those interviewed from Tigray and Wollo saw people die during the journey to the resettlement sites (the remainder were not asked the question).

All those interviewed reported that conditions in the resettlement sites were deplorable. Most sites had neither houses nor health facilities when the colonists arrived. Food supplies were erratic and never sufficient for individuals engaging in strenuous manual labor. Armed political cadres and militia forced camp residents to work ten hours per day, six and a half days per week. If the residents did not reach production goals cadre members had established, their food rations, already inadequate, were cut.

In the initial announcements of the resettlement program, apparently to allay the suspicions of the West, Ethiopia stated that household heads would be given ten hectares (twenty-five acres) each of land to farm individually; later the figure was reduced to two hectares. Cultural Survival's interviews indicated that none of those resettled received two hectares; some, but not most, received a garden plot of approximately .1 to .2 hectares.

Death rates associated with resettlement reported by refugees ranged upward from 33 per 10,000 people per day. These rates are extremely high given that, as a result of the selection process in the north, camp populations were comprised mostly of relatively healthy adults. Even if the most conservative estimate of the death rate (33 per 10,000 per day) is halved and then halved again (i.e., reduced by 75 percent), then 100,000 of the 500,000 resettled by August of 1985 had already died. The ICRC (International Committee of the Red Cross), in an internal report, estimated that 50,000 of those resettled had died in the sites by July 1985.[49]

Other corroboration of the high death rate comes from a number of sources. According to the RRC, some 525,000 people had been resettled by the end of August, 1985.[50] People were resettled by the tens of thousands from September 1985 until well into January 1986. If the rate of resettlement during this period was the same as during earlier months, then an additional 200,000 to 300,000 people were resettled in the fall of 1985 alone, bringing the total number of resettled people to somewhere between 740,000 and 840,000. Yet, in April 1986, the government claimed that by February only 540,000 people were in the resettlement sites.[51] What happened to the other 240,000 to 330,000 people?

In January 1986 reports from resettlement escapees in Damazine, Sudan indicated that whereas the death rate had declined somewhat, mortality in the camps was still high.[52] In fact, one recently arrived refugee in Damazine who was formerly employed by the RRC to supervise food distribution in the Wollega resettlement sites indicated that although RRC records stated that 300,000 people had been moved to the region between late 1984 and early 1986, only 250,000 people were receiving food. Since none of the resettlement sites were self-sufficient this indicates as many as 50,000 deaths. Furthermore, according to the former head of food distribution in the region, the figure of 250,000 includes previous settlers in the area who serve as armed militia in the resettlement camps as well as members of the Sudanese People's Liberation Movement, which, with the support of the Ethiopian government, is attempting to overthrow the Sudanese government. Again, most food distributed in the resettlement sites was provided by the EEC through the RRC.

One of the most serious aspects of resettlement, which has received the least international attention, is the impact of the program on the peoples previously living in the areas of resettlement. At least five distinct peoples—Anuak, Barta, Gitaan, Komo, and Oromo—have been displaced as a result of resettlement. Since resettlement began in the area in 1977, tens of thousands have fled as refugees to Sudan; even more have been displaced internally one or more times. For example, from December 1987 to January 1988 alone more than 5,000 people fled into southern Sudan. Displacement has generally resulted from military actions, government confiscation of lands for settlers, or fear of imprisonment resulting from an inability to pay required "voluntary" contributions to support the resettlement of colonists in the area.

Half of the people interviewed reported that the lands they and their families had cultivated traditionally had been confiscated for the settlers to use. This displacement began in 1977 and has continued to this day. Most people displaced in the area first moved to another more isolated, less fertile region to clear new lands or moved in with relatives in nearby areas. In either case, they were forced to move onto more marginal lands doing untold ecological destruction in the region, or into existing households where, as a result, more people had to be fed from the same area. Some of those evicted from their lands by the government had moved three times before deciding that they simply could not live in their homelands under this government and fled to Sudan.

The other half interviewed indicated that they had been forced to sell oxen or even seed in order to make required "voluntary" contributions to the resettlement program. Others reported giving from one-quarter to one half of all their possessions (oxen, plows, tables, chairs, kitchen utensils, agricultural tools) to those being settled "on top of them." Many local peasant associations had to build houses for the colonists and to provide food for them as well. In Illubabor, local Oromo were required to plow and cultivate for the newcomers. In some cases those being resettled were moved into the former residents' houses and were given crops in the fields that the former residents had cultivated. Those interviewed, both the former residents and resettlement escapees, insist that the program is creating famine in the areas of the settlement sites.

As mentioned earlier, none of the previous settlements in Ethiopia have become self-sufficient although some have existed for more than ten years. If resettlement is encouraged or allowed to continue with international support, then, based on past agricultural performance, the international community must be prepared to feed these people for more than ten years. Some speculate that soil fertility in the resettlement sites will decline long before then, so the prospects for continued food shortages in the sites appear, unfortunately, to be quite good.

Previous settlers in Wollega and Illubabor have been armed by the government and designated as special security forces to carry out search and seizure operations against the local populations. These forces confiscate coffee, grain, and manufactured goods, and are reportedly given free reign to arrest, punish, or kill persons considered "counterrevolutionary." In addition to a number of local informants in each region, settlers are increasingly installed in existing communities (called integrated settlements) where they constitute up to 25 percent of the population and serve as spies for the government.

Many previous as well as present resettlement sites are in

actual or potential areas of coffee production. To date, settlers are not being used to cultivate coffee, but rather to harvest or confiscate it from local producers so that the government controls the crop.

Deforestation and soil erosion in the northern highlands are frequently cited as two of the primary reasons for the resettlement program. Resettlement sites, however, could result in the clearing of 250,000 hectares of Ethiopia's remaining forests, causing the same environmental problems it is intended to correct.[53] Ethiopian forestry officials began to call for reforestation in some of the current resettlement sites as early as December 1984.[54]

In summarizing Cultural Survival's findings, each of which has been corroborated by the research of other organizations, the following points should be emphasized:

—Resettlement was, by and large, not voluntary.
—Families were separated, in many cases deliberately.
—Death rates were high in resettlement holding camps and sites, far higher, it appears, than in the feeding centers and famine-affected areas of the north.
—Resettlement became an important, perhaps the single most important, cause of mortality in Ethiopia in 1985.
—Resettlement was an expensive and risky "development" program, yet neither the Ethiopian government nor foreign donors evaluated the social or environmental costs of the program or compared its costs with alternative rehabilitation programs for the northern highlands.
—The rights of the previous residents in Wollega, Illubabor, and Keffa were ignored and resettlement uprooted tens of thousands.
—Resettlement caused famine in southwestern Ethiopia.
—Resettlement achieved at least two military objectives in the north. It allowed the government to remove young Moslem Oromos from Wollo who were seen as potential recruits for the TPLF as well as prosperous farmers from Tigray who were suspected of supporting the TPLF.
—In the south, settlers were collectivized and used as security forces against local inhabitants, leading to a militarization of the areas around the resettlement sites.

Ethiopian estimates indicate that the resettlement program costs approximately Eth $5,000 (U.S. $2,500) per settler. The Soviet Union and its allies provided gasoline and some of the vehicles used for transporting the settlers. Other vehicles which the West donated for delivering food, were used instead to transport settlers. To date, the direct financial burden of resettlement has been borne by residents of the areas receiving settlers, the USSR, the World Food Program (WFP), and the EEC.

The World Food Program and the European Economic Community have provided most of the food that is given to settlers. Prior to late 1984, the WFP had already been supplying food to Ethiopia for use in resettlement. This program increased in size from 1984 to 1986. In addition, the EEC gave considerable grain to the Ethiopian government for feeding famine victims but failed to specify that it not be used in resettlement. Sixty to eighty percent of the EEC grain went to warehouses south of Addis Ababa and, apparently, was distributed in resettlement sites in southwest Ethiopia.[55] According to the Ethiopian food distribution coordinator hired by the RRC to deliver food to resettlement sites in Wollega, recipients of the EEC and WFP food included militia and members of the Sudan Peoples Liberation (SPLA), an Ethiopian-supported organization attempting to overthrow the Sudanese government. The Italian government is funding resettlement sites directly, and the Canadian government gave just under $1 million to the Irish agency Concern for its work in seven sites in Wollega. In addition, Canadian, French, and German PVOs have funded resettlement sites themselves or have sent money to agencies working in them.

Resettlement began again in 1987 and 1988 at a rate of approximately 30,000 people per month, about half the rate in 1985. Although the West gave some direct assistance for resettlement, most governments and agencies considered the resettlement program too brutal and economically unsound to fund directly. Even so, Western assistance given in government-held areas in the north of Ethiopia indirectly supported the program.

Food given by the EEC and the WFP was certainly used in the northern holding centers where those to be resettled were kept until there were sufficient numbers to be transported or until transport could be arranged. Although Westerners were not generally allowed into the holding centers, spot checks undertak-

en by a WFP food monitor at two holding centers indicate that
death rates were so high that, if other centers were similar, as
many as 60,000 people could have died in the holding centers
before even being transported.[56]

Western food assistance also indirectly supported the government's resettlement efforts. The food was bait which the government used to capture people for resettlement. In some instances agencies were not allowed to travel in the countryside
surrounding their feeding centers. As villagers came to the centers (many had been told to go by government officials) they
were captured for resettlement by the army or militia. In other
instances, Western agencies (e.g., Save the Children-U.S. in Shoa
administrative region) were allowed to set up food distribution
programs only after the government's local quotas for resettlement had been filled. Peasant associations were not eligible to
receive food or other Western assistance until their quotas were
met. Thus, peasant association officials were quick to nominate
"volunteers" for resettlement. Food provided by Western agencies then, not only allowed the government to coerce people to
resettle; it also allowed local officials to consolidate their own
power by eliminating opponents. In addition, thousands of people were taken forcibly from Western-run feeding centers where
they had sought refuge. Some of these incidents were reported
in the press. Agencies known to be affected included MSF, Save
the Children, Oxfam, CRS, and World Vision.

Food and blankets (it was 30-35° F at night) reportedly
could not be distributed in some camps until people agreed to be
resettled. In some camps the Ethiopian government did not allow
children to receive food from Western agencies until their parents agreed to be resettled. MSF eventually left Ethiopia after an
estimated 6,000 children died in a camp where they had adequate materials for assistance but were not allowed to distribute
them because, according to government officials, a sufficient
number of adults had not agreed to be resettled.

VILLAGIZATION

For eight years, Ethiopia has pursued another policy, related
to resettlement, of incorporating peasant farmers into new vil-

lages where agricultural production will eventually be undertaken cooperatively. The process is known as villagization. Since 1979, efforts aimed at restructuring rural life through villagization were most successful and intense during periods of social and economic chaos which acted as smokescreens for the programs—for example, the aftermath of the war with Somalia (1979–1982) and the 1984–86 famine. At these times the provision of Western assistance, first humanitarian and then developmental, permitted the government to expand the villagization program.[57]

In 1985 the government announced that it would intensify its villagization program. According to the government, by 1994 (i.e., after ten years) the program would bring 32 million peasants together into central settlements that are to become producers' cooperatives. By early 1988 nearly 10 million people had been moved into 15,000 new villages. Some 30,000 to 50,000 traditional villages were destroyed in the process.[58] Thus, according to government estimates, by the end of 1987 some 25 percent of Ethiopia's rural population were living in new villages.[59]

Western relief agencies have played only a marginal role in the implementation of the villagization program. Once villages have been established, however, agencies have been invited to become key players. The government can never hope to provide services to the 50,000 new villages it expects to create by the early 1990s. In fact, the government has stated that all development assistance in new areas must now go through those new villages to make them more attractive to the people being moved into them. Agencies have been given the choice of funding through the producers' or service cooperatives or providing central water, social or health services to new villages. To date, Oxfam-America/U.K., Save the Children-U.S./U.K., Lutheran World Federation, World Vision, and CARE, among others, are known to be working in these new villages. Once again, Western assistance has become a carrot to make the move more palatable.

In the new villages, agencies (e.g., CARE in Hararghe province) have been asked to provide food to people who produced surpluses last year but whose crops were taken from them and who now are not allowed, because of forced labor programs, to devote enough time to cultivate their own crops. In addition, farmers spend up to five times as much time walking from their homes to the fields as they did before. Western agencies are being asked to fill the food shortages that have been deliberately created by the government in its efforts to gain control of agricultural production in the countryside. For example, the 1987–1988 famine is severe in parts of Bale and Hararghe that were the first areas villagized in Ethiopia.

Western agencies are providing assistance (seed, tools, and oxen) to local organizations that often use these inputs to produce crops that the state controls. Even in the cases where the inputs end up in the hands of individuals before the creation of new villages, the government has nationalized crops and oxen from the peasant producers when the new villages are constructed.

Although the villagization program is supposedly voluntary, a number of observers have openly questioned whether any program of this nature could be run on a voluntary basis in Ethiopia. The threat of violence and coercion have been used repeatedly. Again, the West has played a role. Western agency personnel have reported that in the eastern highlands of Hararghe, new irrigation systems, funded by Western agencies, capture water in areas where traditional villages were located. Villagers are then given the choice of remaining behind where they will have little or no water with which to irrigate their crops or moving to the plains.

Ethiopia's official position on villagization as well as its public pronouncements, internal directives, and even the record of an earlier version of the program in Bale administrative region from 1979 to 1984, clearly link the program with the creation of government-directed and controlled communal systems of agricultural production, locally called producers' cooperatives. Many Western diplomats and assistance agencies, however, cling to the belief that although villagization has proceeded at a rapid pace and coercion appears to have played a role in the program, there is no evidence of the creation of producers' cooperatives in 1985 and 1986. Yet, the Ethiopian press is full of such evidence.[60]

The most complete documentation concerning villagization in Ethiopia can be found in *The Spoils of Famine: Ethiopian Famine Policy and Peasant Agriculture*.[61] In that volume, I address in detail the history of villagization in Ethiopia as well as the systematic, coercive aspects of the program I discovered when inter-viewing refugees in Somalia who had fled their homes in eastern Ethiopia as a result of the program in 1985 and 1986.

Villagization has been implemented first in the major food surplus producing regions of the country and is apparently an attempt by the government to take control of agriculture produc-tion in these areas. In some surplus producing areas there are already food shortages. However, the true impact of the program will only become clear in five to ten or even twenty-five years when intense cultivation will have reduced soil fertility in the fields nearest the new villages, forcing people to cultivate more distant fields; when irrigation without adequate supplies of wa-ter has led to salinization of the soil, making it unfit for cultiva-tion; when fuel wood near the villages has been eliminated and it costs as much to cook a meal as to buy the food; and, most important, when population increases put a tremendous strain on the resources of the new villages, where population growth was never taken into account in the planning stages.

It is interesting to note in passing that three agencies work-ing in eastern Ethiopia in villagized areas—Oxfam, Save the Children-U.K., and CARE—were also working with Ethiopian refugees in Somalia who have fled the program. Yet, after the flight of some 50,000 refugees in the second wave (December 1985 to April 1986) they still had not bothered to systematically interview those in Somalia who had fled the very programs that they supported across the border.

CONCLUSION

The record indicates that during the Ethiopian famine of 1984–1986 Western humanitarian agencies collaborated with the government, both actively and passively, in programs that both intensified the famine and extended it to new areas. The agencies often-stated and legitimate fears of expulsion for speaking out about problems in Ethiopia do not explain their apparent willing-ness to take part in, even inadvertently, the manipulation of the famine to increase state control over the countryside. The Ethio-pian government manipulated the famine and international pub-lic opinion in order to wring money and food from the West which was used to establish a state-run rural economy. Ethiopia's intentions in this regard are a matter of public record. One can only conclude that the agencies were willing actors in the 1984–1985 tragedy and continue to be in the 1987–1988 instant replay.

Is it possible to give nonpolitical, humanitarian assistance? Probably not. However, the best way to remain neutral in such situations is to keep informed. This in no way implies that, given the same information, every agency would choose the same course of action. Each agency has its own political agenda, goals, and, in the case of some religious agencies, constraints from local counterparts. Still, a rigorously informed position would be the best way for each agency to achieve its own goals and at the same time serve the victims.

The agencies, however, have instead taken a rather lofty moral stance, ignoring the political implications of their own actions. Furthermore, many agencies have attempted to block the efforts of those researchers attempting to understand the intent and long-term impact of Ethiopia's programs, the same programs that Western agencies are being asked to support. In 1986, for example, I requested from Save the Children-U.S. information concerning the location of their programs in Ethiopia and in which of the sites new villages had been built. I did not ask for information about levels of funding or the specifics of the agency's programs. I merely wanted to test the hypothesis that in ethnically diverse areas, specific ethnic groups were being villagized before others. I explained why the issue was important and what implications it had for villagization throughout the country. Save the Children refused to provide the information, saying that it was too political. Likewise Oxfam America will not make internal documents publicly available even though they have already been leaked to those researchers favorably disposed to the programs Oxfam supports. These actions raise serious questions about such agencies. One might expect that agencies raising funds from the U.S. public and, in some cases, from the government, should be willing to divulge basic information. Their failure to do so might result in moves to regulate them or take away their tax-exempt status. Ultimately, however, the public must decide which courses of action are more appropriate. In 1988 they appear to be doing so by withholding their financial support.

Western humanitarian agencies are setting themselves up
for a fall. This fact, in and of itself, should not be our concern.
However, it is inevitable that not only will famine continue in
Ethiopia, but that similar emergencies will develop elsewhere.
The agencies' ability to meet these new demands will be im-
paired by the justifiable erosion of public trust that has resulted
from their collective response, first in Cambodia and now in
Ethiopia.

Will the agencies learn from their Ethiopian experiences so
that in future they can better serve the victims—not just governments or elite groups that persecute their own people? It seems
doubtful unless there is public pressure and perhaps even new
regulations for humanitarian agencies. The Oromo, the largest
single group in Ethiopia, have a saying that describes well Western relief agencies' response to the political dimensions of the
recent famine in Ethiopia, "You can't wake a person who's pre-
tending to be asleep."

NOTES

Since late 1984, researchers working with Cultural Survival have
conducted hundreds of interviews with Western government and humanitarian agency officials, former Ethiopian officials, journalists, and
refugees from Ethiopia. Many agreed to be interviewed on the condition that they not be cited. For that reason, many sources are not cited.
In any case, the issue is not to point a finger at either individuals or
organizations.

However, in a number of instances, organizations are cited for
having undertaken certain types of programs or for having assisted,
directly or indirectly, the government in its villagization and resettlement programs. These citations are included, not because these agencies are more guilty than others, but because Cultural Survival has
specific information about their activities. The programs and actions of
these organizations are representative, or perhaps even better than
many groups not cited. That is why their actions deserve close scrutiny.
Furthermore, it will be easier for future researchers to follow up the
lines of inquiry laid out in this article if they have more specific information about who did what, when.

1. Many Ethiopians apparently hoped that the famine would
force Mengistu to open up to the West. " 'This famine is a blessing in

disguise. . . .' I heard over and over again from articulate Ethiopians, many of them serving as officials. 'It forces Mengistu to open to the West. . . . It demonstrates the pointlessness of trying to follow a Russian economic mode. . . . It underscores Moscow's unwillingness to do anything to help Ethiopia,' " (Paul Henze, "Behind the Ethiopian Famine—Anatomy of a Revolution III," *Encounter,* September-October 1986, p. 31).

2. See, for example, Ethiopia's Relief and Rehabilitation Commission (RRC), "Drought Situation in Ethiopia and Assistance Requirements," October 1984; "Review of the Current Drought Situation in Ethiopia," December 1984; "Review of Drought Relief and Rehabilitation Activities for the Period December 1984-August 1985 and 1986 Assistance Requirements," October 1985; and Radio Addis Ababa, 9 February 1985.

According to Dawit Wolde-Giorgis, in an interview with the *New York Times,* the government's policies were as responsible as the drought for the famine of 1984–1985. "We called it a drought problem, but it was more of a policy problem. Drought only complicated the situation. If there is no change in our policies, there will always be millions of hungry people in Ethiopia" (cited in *African Report,* July-August 1986, p. 49). The Ethiopian government also blamed the famine on the West *New York Times,* December 12, 1984, and July 11, 1985; *Washington Post,* December 12, 1984, and *Boston Globe,* December 13, 1984).

3. David A. Korn, "Ethiopia: The Dilemma for the West," *World Today,* January 1986, p. 5.

4. The EPDA "has the appropriate right-wing credentials, but no military clout and virtually no following within Ethiopia," *Africa Report,* July-August 1986, p. 49.

5. Korn, note 3 above; Jason Clay "Help That Could Hurt," *Boston Globe,* December 17, 1984. Jason Clay, "Feeding the Hand that Bites," *Cultural Survival Quarterly* 10, no. 2 (1986): 1.

6. Korn, note 3 above, p. 5. The U.S.'s efforts were not altogether successful. On the first point they failed totally, a failure that continues to be important in 1988. On the second point, the U.S. was partially successful. No U.S.-provided food was used for resettlement directly, but much of it was used to lure people into feeding centers where they were captured for resettlement. On the third point the United States was more successful, only in early 1985 was famine assistance traded for seed to give farmers. It is interesting to note, however, that the government would have been willing to allow its farmers to forgo planting their crops had the U.S. not purchased the seed.

7. Ibid., p. 6.

8. Ibid.

9. Claude Malhuret, *Mass Deportations in Ethiopia*, Medicins sans Frontieres (MSF), 1985, p. 45, and Roni Brauman, president of MSF, personal communication. See also *New York Times*, January 21, 1985; *Washington Post*, May 2, 1985.

10. Korn, note 3 above, p. 6.

11. Ibid., p. 5. In fact, Ethiopia, in an attempt to make the two appear similar in scale, consistently reported the food assistance from the USSR and its allies in 100 kilogram units while reporting that from the West in tons.

During 1985, the percentage of foreign aid given through Ethiopia's RRC dropped from 75 percent to 25 percent *New African*, March 1986, p. 43). Radio Addis Ababa (June 18, 1986) reported that "It has been stated that 1.2 million metric tons of grain are required to satisfy the daily needs of a total of 6.4 million needy people in 1986. Donor organizations will contribute 70 percent of this amount while the Relief and Rehabilitation Commission [RRC] will provide 30 percent through the assistance it will receive both from within the country and abroad."

In 1988, the USSR pledged 250,000 metric tons of food to Ethiopia. It is not clear if they intend to deliver this assistance or if they are merely playing the pledge game. Where and how food assistance from the USSR would be used raises interesting questions.

12. "Of a population of 7 m believed in danger of starvation early in 1985, relief was reaching only between 2.5 m and 3 m—and not all of these were getting full rations" (Korn, note 3 above, p. 6). Later, the World Food Program estimated in May 1985 that the number of people reached with any assistance was 3.5 million (*New York Times*, May 17, 1985). One month later the figure was "adjusted" to 4.1 million (*New York Times*, June 16, 1985).

13. Calculations concerning the overall contribution of Western assistance to the life or death of Ethiopian famine victims are difficult to make. Statistics on deaths, in general, are hard to come by, particularly information concerning the circumstances under which deaths occurred. Therefore this calculation should be considered more an exercise than a precise measurement. Even as an exercise, however, the results are disconcerting.

If estimates of one million dead (an estimate many consider high) and if Fred Cuny's observation that the death rate had already started to decline before most Western assistance began to arrive beginning in January 1985 are accurate, then we can assume that at least half of all deaths occurred prior to the delivery of Western assistance. It follows, then, that most Western assistance was delivered when fewer than 500,000 people died. There is good evidence which suggests that resettlement could have contributed, directly or indirectly, to most of the deaths after January 1985, and resettlement could not have been undertaken without the promise, at least, of Western assistance.

Conservative estimates indicate that 100,000 people died in the resettlement sites by the summer of 1985. In addition to estimates associated with resettlement made by Cultural Survival, MSF, and the International Committee of the Red Cross, sources inside Irish Concern indicate that in late July 1985 John A. Finucane, Irish Concern's field director in Ethiopia, estimated that during the first three months from the time settlers were taken for resettlement some 25 percent died. Out of 500,000 resettled by early August, according to that estimate, 125,000 people would have died. Later Finucane was quoted in the *London Times* (October 24, 1985) as estimating that more than 700,000 people had been moved by early October. By January 1986 close to 800,000 would have been resettled, of which, if the conditions Finucane reported in July held, 200,000 (25%) could have died.

The *Christian Science Monitor* (May 22, 1986) reported that "A UN official confirmed that deaths have occurred among the 670,000 Ethiopians resettled from famine areas, but termed the 100,000 figure 'astronomical.' 'I haven't seen their [MSF's] figure confirmed publicly by any other organization,' said Paul Mitchell, of the Rome-based World Food Program." The *Monitor* failed to ask Mr. Mitchell to speculate about what happened to account for the difference between the 670,000 people the UN admits were moved (probably a low estimate) and the 545,000 the government claims are living in the sites.

Internal memos of the World Food Program indicate that death rates in the resettlement holding centers were so high that as many as 60,000 people could have died prior to transport.

Ethiopian officials indicate that 200,000 children were reunited with their parents in the resettlement sites between 1986 and 1987. What happened to the remainder of the children? Cultural Survival's research indicates that as many as 400,000 may have been separated from their parents. It is likely that forced separation of parents would cause the condition of already malnourished children to deteriorate rapidly.

MSF reported that 3,000 children died when they were not allowed to take care of them because not enough parents had signed up for resettlement. Was this unique to camps run by MSF?

Peasant associations in Wollo and Shoa were not allowed food assistance until they met their quota for resettlement. How many people in all died while they were waiting for the assistance from the West?

How many refugees died trying to leave Ethiopia to receive assistance? How many died as refugees in Somalia or Sudan, choosing exile and possible death rather than Western assistance delivered under the auspices of the Ethiopian government?

How many people in the north died for lack of food when trucks which could have been used to carry food to them were used instead to resettle people to the south. MSF estimated that 200,000 metric tons on food (half of the annual food needs of the north) could have been transported north with these trucks.

If, as Cuny suggests, the death rate had peaked prior to the influx of Western assistance, then it is at least possible that *most* deaths in Ethiopia (or of Ethiopians in Sudan and Somalia) after late 1984 occurred as a result of government programs that Western assistance made possible.

14. See Jason Clay and Bonnie Holcomb, *Politics and the Ethiopian Famine, 1984-85* (Cambridge, Mass.: Cultural Survival, 1986); Peter Niggli, "Ethiopia: Deportation and Forced Labor Camps—Doubtful Methods in the Struggle against Famine," *Berliner Missionswerk,* January 1986; Sandra Steingraber in Jason Clay et al., *The Spoils of Famine: Ethiopian Famine, Policy and Peasant Agriculture* (Cambridge, Mass.: Cultural Survival, 1988); Paul Keleman, "The Politics of the Famine in Ethiopia Eritrea," Manchester Sociology Occasional Papers no. 17, March 1985; REST, "Report on Interviews Conducted in Damazine Camp in the Blue Nile Province of Sudan with Tigrayan Refugees Who Have Escaped from Resettlement Camps in Southwest Ethiopia," January 1986; Jim Doble, "Resettlement in Ethiopia 1986," unpublished manuscript.

15. See note 14. Virtually every major newspaper in the West discussed man-made causes of the famine as did various television programs on each of the major U.S. public and private networks.

16. See, for example, David L. Guyer, president of Save the Children—U.S. "Keeping the Aid to Ethiopia Coming," *Christian Science Monitor,* June 18, 1986; John Hammock, "Aiding Peasant Production in Ethiopia," Oxfam America Special Report: Recovery in Africa, Winter 1986; and a mailing from Interfaith Hunger Appeal dated March 1987.

17. Numerous communications between Lutheran World Relief and Cultural Survival, including ones from Bob Cottingham, LWF program director for Africa, indicated the LWF could not fund research on the causes of famine in Ethiopia.

18. Cultural Survival's research was a systematic investigation into the causes of famine. While Cultural Survival was not allowed to undertake the research in Ethiopia, the team of three did interview three types of refugees. Those who fled to Sudan directly from famine affected areas of Tigray, those who were resettled from Wollo and Tigray and subsequently fled to southern Sudan, and finally, those residents of southwestern Ethiopia who were forced to leave their homes as a result of resettlement. Independent translators were hired and interviews were tape-recorded and retranslated to assure accuracy.

All interviewers used the same basic questionnaire so that information which was being collected simultaneously from different camps could be compared. The questionnaire included the same questions in a number of forms to check consistency of answers. Interviewees were randomly selected in each site to ensure that those interviewed represented the camp's population. Each interview took one to three hours (see Clay and Holcomb, note 14 above, chapter 3 for a full discussion of Cultural Survival's research methods).

19. Most of the U.S. government and agency assistance was traced from the United States to delivery to specific famine victims. This does not, however, illuminate the context in which the assistance was used. Carol Ashwood (an Oxfam–U.K. relief worker) said that Ethiopian authorities had deliberately denied Western grain to villagers to force them to move (Reuters London, December 1985, 1828). Many humanitarian agencies apparently did not understand how their food was being used. For example, David Guyer, president of Save the Children-U.S. indicated in a 1986 interview on CBS's morning news program that he was not even aware that Save the Children was not allowed to work in peasant associations until after a local quota for resettlement had been met. Save the Children, like all other Western agencies, is not allowed to begin programs in new areas until the residents have been moved into new villages.

Europeans made few attempts to monitor the impact of their assistance. European governments and the EEC gave food directly to the RRC, who, in turn, sent most of it to the resettlement sites (Malhuret, note 9 above, p. 42). Thus while most European governments did not approve of resettlement, their food was a key ingredient in the program.

20. Cultural Survival was asked by two agencies to discuss with them the types of information that they might be able to collect inside Ethiopia which could in turn be used to verify or reject the conditions reported by refugees in Sudan and Somalia. In one instance this included a discussion of specific questions that doctors and nurses could work into their discussion during routine examinations.

21. Population estimates in Ethiopia are more of an art than a science. Clay and Holcomb, note 14 above, pp. 214–15, review the reports of the numbers affected. The *Christian Science Monitor* (November 2, 1984) reported that "The government has just escalated two estimates: It says Ethiopia's population has jumped to 42 million and that the number of people registering for emergency food has gone from 6.4 million to 7.3 million." An article written later stated that "The number of famine victims . . . is now officially estimated at 7.7 million . . . the new figure replaces the previous government estimate of 6.5 to

8 million, which was considered too vague" *Boston Globe,* December 4, 1984. On April 14, 1985, USAID was reported to have estimated the number in need of assistance in northern Ethiopia at 2.3 million while the government put the figure at 7.7 million (*Washington Post*). Mengistu even went so far as to claim in August 1986 that sixteen million Ethiopians were affected by drought (*Der Spiegel,* August 18, 1986, pp. 140–45).

22. See, for example, the World Bank, *An Economic Justification for Rural Afforestation: The Case of Ethiopia,* August 1984, p. 8, where the total population in 1981–82 was listed as 32.55 million.

23. The Tinker-Wise report, "Ethiopia and Sudan One Year Later: Refugee and Famine Recovery Needs," mimeo, April 1986, has frequently been sited as a quasi-official assessment which proves that Western assistance saved six million Ethiopians. There are a number of qualifications that should apply to the report. First, contrary to frequent citations, the report was produced at the personal request of Senator Kennedy, not the U.S. Senate Judiciary Committee. Second, the two authors used government translators for interviews and did not tape-record the interviews. They talked with very few victims; only three in resettlement camps are quoted. There was no attempt to collect data in a replicable, i.e., a reliable, way. Finally, it is not clear what their qualifications and interests in the issue are. Jerry Tinker is a member of Senator Kennedy's staff, but there is no mention of his qualifications other than a brief visit in the fall of 1984. According to *Olsen's Agribusiness Report* 8, no. 1 (July 1986). John Wise is the export manager of ADM Milling Co. of Shawnee Mission, Kansas. This company exports food grain commodities from the United States and handles some grain both in the U.S. Food for Peace Programs and the P.L.-480 program.

24. According to expatriates in Bale in 1983 and 1984, World Vision flew grain into a region that is accessible only by plane or military convoy. The grain was then turned over to the RRC, who distributed it. According to these observers, World Vision neither attempted to find out the causes of starvation in the region nor to monitor the actual distribution of grain by the RRC. Since 1978 food has been used as a weapon in Bale, where people have been systematically displaced by the military, collected into new villages, and then fed with internationally provided grain (see Clay in Clay et al., note 14 above). This was, in fact, where villagization was first undertaken in Ethiopia.

25. Joseph Collins, personal communication.

26. Clay and Holcomb, note 14 above, p. 192.

27. Ibid.

28. See Jason Clay, "Famine and Western Assistance in Ethiopia," invited paper presented at the 85th annual American Anthropological

Association meeting, 4 December 1986, in Philadelphia. Also see Clay in Clay et al, note 14 above.

29. See Clay in Clay et al., note 14 above.

30. CRS acknowledges that it sells food assistance to recover some of its costs, even in Ethiopia, but it denies selling food to famine victims *Newsweek*, August 26, 1985).

31. See *African Business*, July 1984, November 1986, and May 1988.

32. According to Blaine Harden *International Herald Tribune*, December 3, 1985) Ethiopia's foreign exchange reserves increased from $41 million in the last quarter of 1984 to $152 million for the first quarter of 1985. At the end of 1985 the reserves stood at $147.8 million *Africa South of the Sahara*, 1987: 436). By mid-1986 Ethiopia's currency reserves stood at $266 million *June Afrique*, October 15, 1986).

33. *African Business*, May 1986, p. 33.

34. Radio Addis Ababa.

35. *New York Times*, March 5, 1987.

36. See Clay in Clay et al., note 14 above.

37. The *International Herald Tribune* carried a more complete version of the same story than did the *New York Times*, March 5, 1987. The *International Herald Tribune* article, in addition to indicating that orphans are taught the Amharic language and Coptic Christianity (although neither the language nor the religion was that of many of the parents), mentioned that the orphanage discussed in the piece is next to the local center where political cadres are trained.

38. Malhuret, note 9 above, p. 45, and Roni Brauman, MSF, personal communication.

39. See Clay and Holcomb, note 14 above; *Africa Report*, March-April 1986; Clay et al., note above; Clay, 1986, note 28 above; Malhuret, note 9 above, and Malhuret and Brauman, personal communication.

40. See Clay and Holcomb, note 14 above; Clay, 1986, note 28 above; Holcomb in Clay et al., note 14 above.

41. *Boston Globe*, December 13, 1984; *New York Times*, January 21, 1985; and *New York Times*, March 26, 1985. Clay and Holcomb, note 14 above; Steingraber in Clay et al., note 14 above.

42. Radio Addis Ababa.

43. Mengistu also reported (Radio Addis Ababa, September 2, 1985) that in the resettlement sites alone 7.5 percent of Ethiopia's remaining forest would be cleared for planting in 1985-86.

44. See the World Bank publication, *Tribal Peoples and Economic Development: Human Ecologic Considerations*, May 1982.

45. Eshetu Chole and Teshome Mulat, "Land Settlement in Ethio-

pia—A Review of Developments," unpublished paper, December 1984.

46. Ibid.

47. See Oxfam–U.K.'s assessment of their rehabilitation work in Karen Twining, "Food for the Future—Soil Conservation in Tigray," mimeo, July 1984; see also John Bennett et al., "Tigray 1984: An Investigation," January 1984.

48. Clay and Holcomb, note 14 above.

49. In addition to Clay and Holcomb's estimates, these figures were all arrived at independently by MSF, Irish Concern, U.S. AID, ICRC (see also note 13 and David Blundy, the *Times*, November 3, 1985).

50. RRC, "Review of Drought Relief . . ." October 1985 (note 2 above), 1985, p. 15.

51. Radio Addis Ababa, April 1986.

52. See Steingraber in Clay et al., Niggli in Clay et al.; REST, note 14 above.

53. See Steingraber in Clay et al., Sandra Steingraber is currently in Sudan investigating, once again, the environmental consequences of resettlement in Ethiopia both in southwest Ethiopia and on Sudan.

54. *Christian Science Monitor,* December 19, 1984.

55. Roni Brauman, personal communication.

56. See John J. Mitchell internal report (August/September 1985, dated November 6, 1985) to the World Food Program.

57. See Clay in Clay et al., and Niggli in Clay et al.

58. See Clay in Clay et al.

59. *New York Times*, March 11, 1987; Clay in Clay et al.

60. In fact, I devote a whole chapter to the evidence. See Clay in Clay et al., *The Spoils of Famine,* note 14 above.

61. Studies conducted inside Ethiopia include John M. Cohen and Nils-Ivar Isaksson, *Villagization in the Arsi Region of Ethiopia,* International Rural Development Centre, Uppsala, February 1987, and Angela Roberts, "Report of Villagization in Oxfam America Assisted Project Areas in Hararghe Province, Ethiopia," (June 1986). Roberts' report, while cited by many generally supportive of villagization, has not been made available to others.

POLITICS AND FAMINE RELIEF

Frederick C. Cuny

The unprecedented public response to the Ethiopian Famine of 1984–85 will undoubtedly elicit many books and articles. Already many authors are focusing on the work of the relief agencies, the political environment in which the counter-famine operations took place, and the personal and human impact of famine victims and relief workers alike. Most writers give glowing praise to the relief agencies and the tireless efforts of the workers, credit the major donors, especially the U.S., with acting in the spirit of humanitarian concern, and fault the Ethiopian government for most of the ills and failures of the operation. Yet few of the writers have looked beyond the self-serving reports of the international relief agencies or the statistical data that is available.

Most writers place the beginning of the famine in 1984. However, famine warnings were being given as early as 1980. A famine warning system using indicators established after the famine of the early 1970s, the government of Ethiopia, and no less than seven international agencies monitored the situation that was developing. Not only was the crisis predicted, the problems were very well known by 1983. The first warning was given by the Ethiopian government's famine warning system which, for some reason, no one wanted to believe. These first appeals were issued in 1981 and were triggered by the falling prices of livestock—a well-known famine warning indicator—and the declining rainfall. The international community said the indicators were "too spotty."

Cattle prices and rainfall were not the only measures used by the government to monitor the deteriorating situation. They did nutrition studies (one in 1981, a second in 1982, and a third in 1984) which accurately pinpointed what the problems were and where they were occurring. They also monitored the price of basic grains in the markets (although they were not able to reach some of the areas in Eritrea, Tigray, and parts of Wollo where fierce civil wars were being fought).

In the country, the international relief agencies could see what was happening. Catholic Relief Services made independent evaluations of the situation in their operational areas. Famine research groups, such as the highly respected Famine Research Unit of the Ross Institute, came in and made evaluations that were available to anybody who was interested. On the basis of these assessments, private agencies began to make requests to the major donors for increased food support, with Catholic Relief Services, (CRS) being the first. In 1983, CRS made a request to the U.S. government for food for famine relief under Title II of the Food for Peace Program. It was not granted. Other agencies also made requests to their food donors for emergency food, and again the donors were silent.

Why did the donors ignore the warnings and the early appeals for food? What happened was a result of many factors: politics, history, and the weaknesses of the international relief system. Combined, the result was that the relief agencies were not able, and in some cases were not permitted, to raise the money needed to respond to the famine at the time it was still manageable, or to prevent the spread of famine to other areas.

Famine is not new to Ethiopia; there have been many major famines reported as far back as two centuries ago. The most recent was in the early 1970s, which may have been, in many ways, as large as the one just experienced. The mishandling of that disaster toppled the government of Haile Selassie.

It has been popular to blame the famine on the political system and what are seen to be disruptive economic policies of the Ethiopian government. However, famines in Ethiopia are a result of many factors including environmental degradation, overpopulation, and a major change in microclimate in many of the major food-producing regions. No one is on sound ground when saying that it was due strictly to political causes. For example, the decline in the amount of ground cover (that is, trees and vegetation) in Ethiopia since the turn of the century is incredible. There are studies showing that forests covered much of the area that was famine-struck, with ground cover reaching sometimes 70 to 75 percent of the area. Today those areas are almost totally denuded. The rate of deforestation accelerated greatly in the 1970s because fossil fuels, such as kerosene, became prohibitively expensive and people were forced to turn to firewood for most home fuel needs. These problems occurred long before the present government came into power.

Most of the causes of famine are systemic to Ethiopia and have existed for a long time. They may have been accelerated or heightened by the present government, but it certainly can't be blamed for everything.

Because of the enormous amount of aid that went into Ethiopia, it is assumed that the assistance saved millions who were on the brink of starvation. Yet that is hard to prove. As a matter of logistics, food aid often takes about four to six months to reach its destination from the time it is ordered to the time it arrives on site. Massive international assistance did not begin until after the airing of the BBC/NBC news stories and the groundswell of public support in November and December 1984. Thus the food did not begin to arrive in large enough quantities to make a difference until April 1985. Although some exceptions must be noted, by the time most of the aid began to arrive, the death rates were already falling and many of the people who had come to relief camps were beginning to return to their villages. Even the refugees who had fled to Sudan were returning in large numbers as early as March. Thus, for all the effort, the vast amounts of international aid cannot really be shown with any degree of accuracy to have had much impact. Yes, lives were saved, but by and large they were the residuals; the majority of those who were going to die had done so by the time the aid arrived at food distribution centers. How many lives were saved cannot be quantified, and neither can the number of lives that would have been saved had the food arrived six months earlier; but it is clear that it would have been many more. Perhaps the better question is: had the international system responded in 1981, how many lives would have been saved?

Many of the problems are systemic; they are a result of the weaknesses of the international relief system that has evolved in the postcolonial period. For example, the "system" doesn't have built-in mechanisms that release food into a country when a problem is first developing. Most agencies have to wait until they can show a starving baby on TV in order to raise the funds they need for relief operations. By then it is too late—remember, it takes almost six months to get food to the areas.

One may ask how can we get it there faster. Can't we fly it? Not realistically. It's a question of costs. A C-130 transport plane can carry about twenty tons of cargo (about a truckload of food) and that is only on short hops. On a 500-mile flight, the fuel costs alone are enormous. For every ten tons of food, it will require ten tons of fuel. On longer, intercontinental flights, the cargo load will have to be reduced so the plane can carry more fuel. Then the economics look even more prohibitive. At present fuel prices, an agency could buy a truck for every 500-mile flight of a C-130. The cost per meal becomes just too expensive and the relief agency that chooses this method will soon be out of business. The only economical ways to ship food are by sea, railway, and truck, which take months.

One way to speed the delivery would be to buy and swap grains at sea, and to some extent this is done. However, there are no permanent systems to do so, though it has been proposed for over twenty years to set up a system for emergency situations. Instead of having an institutionalized "wheeler dealer" speeding the delivery of commodities, we basically have to rely on a few governments with food surpluses to provide the food and to arrange transportation (sometimes competing with each other for ships).

Where do the world's humanitarian agencies get the food? The EEC and some of the European countries are food donors, but the vast majority of the food comes from one major donor— the United States. We not only give food bilaterally—from country to country—we also supply the lion's share of the food to the World Food Program. Much of the food provided by private relief agencies is given to them by the U.S. government. Even a portion of the food given by some other countries originates in the U.S. It is swapped, rebagged, and sent overseas.

In the case of Ethiopia, the relations between that country and the U.S. were a major factor in the long delays in procuring sufficient food to counter the growing famine. The present U.S. government has poor relations with Ethiopia (there is no ambassador) and opposes many of the political and economic policies of the Marxist government. Some writers have praised the fact that the U.S. provided more than half the food that was sent to Ethiopia during the famine, noting that it was given in spite of the poor relations between the two countries. The former Administrator of the U.S. Agency for International Development, Peter McPherson, is often quoted as saying "a starving child knows no politics." He said this after NBC ran the shots of dying children in relief camps and after public pressure forced the U.S. to take action. In fact, as noted earlier, the U.S. had consistently turned down requests for aid prior to the public awakening to the crisis. Top government political strategists discussed the issue as early as 1982 and decided that food needs would be a means of putting pressure on Ethiopia to change policies that were unpopular with Washington.

That policy remained constant throughout the relief operations, despite what appeared to be a wellspring of "purely humanitarian aid." For example, food aid was permitted to meet relief needs but not reconstruction or rehabilitation needs. In other words, food could be used to save people but not to permit them to avoid another famine the next year. If one looks closely at the amounts of food that were approved, it is clear that the U.S. provided just enough food to bring the food level in the country back to its prefamine level, a food-deficit situation large enough to cause widespread, chronic malnutrition. Never was enough food aid permitted for the country to overcome the deficit and store enough food to hold even a small surplus against future shortfalls. As a result, the country was forced to depend on food aid for the near future. Some apologists for the administration argue that other donors could have made up the difference; but the U.S., as *the* major donor, was in a position to lobby the others to keep within the levels desired by the U.S. or, failing to gain universal compliance, could simply reduce its commitment if others tried to exceed the specified level. All other donors combined couldn't make up the U.S. portion.

While the relief agencies and the donors are universally praised, the Ethiopian government has been roundly criticized. Some criticism is justified, but many of the comments are misleading and don't reflect the situation accurately. For example, the government was criticized for mishandling the influx of food at the ports. While it is true that the ports were a mess to begin with, the situation was sorted out in a relatively short time and, in the main, the operation was fairly smooth. Furthermore, the amount of theft was minimal. In operations in nearby countries, sometimes 30 percent or more of the food disappeared; in Ethiopia, the amount was insignificant.

The Ethiopians have been criticized for exporting livestock during the famine. Critics argue that the animals should have been used to feed the people. However, it is not unusual in famines to find food exports. Why? Most of the exports are foods not consumed locally. Most of the cattle that were exported were breeding stock; the animals could have been eaten but it was better to export the beef and earn the foreign exchange. It must also be remembered that, value for value, grains are better than beef and logistically much easier to move. Distributing beef would not have practical, and anyway few of the famine victims were regular meat-eaters.

It is ironic that in food-dependent countries, food is exported, but when a country is so destitute that massive free food is imported regularly, it often happens that even grains are exported to earn hard currency. In neighboring Sudan, during the famine relief operations that occurred at the same time, sorghum was being exported while it was being imported for famine victims. To knock Ethiopia for exporting livestock is to ignore the inequities that are common throughout the famine-prone African regions. And it must also be remembered that the Ethiopian government was forced to use its hard currency reserves to purchase food on the international market, because food import limits set by the donors only provided enough food to raise the supply to the normal deficit level. Ethiopia had to sell what it could.

Ethiopia was also criticized for spending money on arms during the period. How much Ethiopia actually spent in terms of hard currency on weaponry is debatable. Their major supplier is the Soviet Union and a secondary source is Cuba. Much of the military aid provided by the Soviet Union to Ethiopia is given free, not sold. How much they spend on other weapons, which they can buy on the international market is hard to determine. But whatever the cost, it must be remembered that the country is fighting major conflicts in Eritrea, Tigray, Wollo, and Hararghe; no country stops fighting a civil war to fight a famine. We may not agree with the causes but we have to be realistic about their priorities.

It must also be pointed out that the West is not in a good position to lecture anyone on arms expenditures. During the famine, Band Aid, USA for Africa, and the international voluntary agencies raised a total of almost 80 million dollars. As large as that amount is, it will not buy the wings on one B-1 bomber.

The internal policies of the Ethiopian government were also criticized. Many critics have claimed that the resettlement and villagization programs of the government both fostered famine conditions and diverted much-needed resources and energies away from vital relief operations. The resettlement program was designed to relocate a large portion of the population in the overpopulated famine regions to the sparsely populated zones of the southwest. The northern populations, who were among the populations targeted for resettlement, claimed that it was an effort to depopulate the region and thus deprive the guerrillas of their base of support.

Resettlement is not a new concept in Ethiopia. (An interesting fact is that it was originally planned and supported by USAID during the Haile Selassie regime.) Resettlement programs exist in other countries, often supported by the U.S. government. Resettlement is common all over Africa.

Whatever the reasons for the resettlement program, in practice it has been handled badly. It was done brutally. While the program was supposed to be voluntary, the government imposed quotas on the officials responsible for the moves. In many places the persons in charge were nothing more than party hacks worried about meeting the quotas. (If you don't meet your quota in a repressive system, you lose your job.) People were picked up without warning, put on transports, and sent hundreds of kilometers from their homes and, often, families. There is no doubt that execution of the program has been a disaster. It is a sophisticated program carried out by unsophisticated people who were big men with guns. But there is no question that the program, were it carried out on a voluntary basis, could be a partial solution to the growing cycle of declining food production, overpopulation, and hunger for many people in the country.

Villagization in Ethiopia is another heavily criticized program. The government began the process of moving people from small individual plots to centralized villages in the early 1980s. The announced motive was to be able to more efficiently provide basic services such as water, sanitation, and electricity. Another reason was to free up additional land for cultivation. Since most peasant farmers live on plots of less than one acre, moving their homes off of arable land to a central location would free up to 20 percent of the land area.

Villagization schemes are common throughout the third world. Mexico began such a system (called the *ejido* system) after their revolution. Villagization has been supported by organizations as conservative as the World Bank. So why is villagization in Ethiopia so controversial? In many socialist countries, villagization has preceded collectivization of the agricultural production and, more disturbing, has been used as a means of extending control over rural people. But the truth is, the program was probably criticized more because it was being carried out by a socialist country than because of any disruption to the agricultural system that it may have caused. There is no hard evidence to say one way or the other whether the program had a negative effect on overall food production in the country. True, production was down; but was that a result of villagization, or of the drought? The figures are inconclusive. Villagization, in fact, may actually meet some of its objectives. In studies carried out during an evaluation of villagization in Hararghe, consultants to CRS found that creation of the new villages may have actually freed up as much as 25 percent of the land in some valleys. The villages are usually located on sites that are difficult to farm and where it would be easy to supply services. For that reason, the jury is still out on villagization.

Some critics of Ethiopia say that the donors should have insisted that villagization and resettlement be stopped as a condition for food aid. The major donors did make it clear they disapproved of the schemes (and eventually the relocation program was temporarily suspended). However, both programs are so ingrained in the Ethiopian development plans that it is likely the programs would have continued whether or not donors provided food.

Some writers have suggested that the relief agencies and the donors, by failing to insist on restraints on the resettlement and villagization programs and to force major changes in agricultural policies, may have extended the famine. That is a doubtful pro-position. As already discussed, the relief operations appear to have begun at a time when the famine was already abating, so it is doubtful that their assistance or the way in which it was offered had any effect either way.

That is not to say that the agencies do not merit a review. The voluntary agencies are as much a part of the problem as they are a part of the solution. Few of them were properly prepared for the famine, and many of those that were there waited until the last moment before sounding the alarm. Early warning is not just a government function; it is the responsibility of all.

The problem is that many of the international agencies are very amateurish. Only a few engage in disaster preparedness and training programs. (Many don't even have professional li-braries.) Many do not conduct in-depth evaluations of their ef-forts. Almost none do any real research. The famine relief agen-cies don't contribute to agricultural research and they don't gen-erally look at the cause and effect relationships of food aid. Some relief agencies do not participate in international conferences on drought and desertification, famine and food relief, and other technical meetings. Only a small number have participated in the emergency management training programs that are conducted around the world. Emergency management skills are often poor. Few use standard approaches or programs and, as a result, there is heavy duplication and overlap in relief operations. Profession-alism and real coordination simply don't exist yet. The relief agencies, be they private or part of the UN system, are very much a part of the problem. They are very well-intentioned, but are just beginning to see the need for increased understanding of the impact of their programs on the people they are intended to benefit.

We have to take a hard look at the relief system and try to find out why it doesn't work in order to make the necessary improvements. To begin with, we must recognize that there is really no such thing as apolitical or truly humanitarian aid. Take, for example, the American food aid program. The main purpose of food aid is not to help people in the third world; it is to help maintain the subsidies for American farmers. By giving grains overseas, each year the farmers can sell more grains to the U.S. government. That is why arguments that the food aid is having a negative impact on local markets, is creating disincentives to production, and may actually be increasing hunger, have not raised much interest or concern in the U.S. Congress. (Distributing free food is not the only problem the food program causes. The Title I program, which gives food to governments to sell, has sold so much food in some African countries that the governments are holding vast quantities of food that they can't commit to projects; if they release it, it will have the same effect as printing more money: it will cause massive inflation.)

Second, we must understand that technical improvements will only result in limited improvements in the system. Today, there is much emphasis on improving famine early warning systems. Famine early warning is certainly a beginning, but it is not the end. What is really needed is to improve decision-making. We have to factor in, where we can, the political choices. We have to look at the way the aid system is set up. We have to question the very values implicit in the food programs as they are set up. And finally, we have to come up with some new approaches to preventing and mitigating food crises. Unless we can overcome the political and economic restraints, the system will continue to falter in crisis.

In summary, we must recognize that in disasters there are often no best choices, only "least worse" choices.

RESCUING ETHIOPIA'S BLACK JEWS

Bruce Nichols

By the mid-1980s an estimated 700,000 to one million Ethiopian refugees had fled civil war, forced resettlement, and famine at home and settled throughout the arid, poverty-stricken wastes of eastern Sudan. There, with limited assistance from the United Nations High Commissioner for Refugees and a handful of Western voluntary agencies (few private agencies were encouraged to come by the graft-ridden and suspicious Sudanese government), the refugees did what they could to survive. The American government strongly supported refugee assistance programs there as an adjunct to its foreign aid to Sudan, but the level of aid provided was barely enough to keep the aided refugees alive.

In late 1984 and early 1985, stories began to appear in the press concerning an extraordinary rescue operation designed to single out a small group of these refugees for special attention. Those refugees, members of a small tribe of Ethiopians known as Falasha (or outcasts), were black Jews, and their fate was of special interest to members of the American Jewish community and of the Israeli government. Within several months, and under the most complex political constraints imaginable, thousands had been removed from their temporary homes in Sudan and resettled abroad, mostly in Israel. Of some three million Ethiopian refugees scattered throughout the Horn of Africa, how had such lavish attention come to be directed toward their fate?

This essay examines the political background of this operation in the context of humanitarian goals in U.S. foreign policy. Without the direct intervention of the American government many of these Falasha would likely have perished in eastern Sudan, but it was not an intervention that the U.S. government openly sought. In a remarkable way, the Falasha rescue operation demonstrates several dimensions of humanitarianism discussed in this book: the spoken or unspoken centrality of humanitarian philosophies, the importance of cooperation between private and public authorities, and the degree to which humanitarian practice, by favoring some and excluding others, both meets and falls short of many of its own highest ideals.

COSMOPOLITAN VERSUS COMMUNAL IDEALS

We have defined humanitarian relief as the provision of assistance to victims of natural or political disasters. Yet humanitarian claims to special political attention rest also on two controversial doctrines that describe humanitarian "neutrality." The first of these holds that humanitarian assistance must be administered in a nondiscriminatory fashion, specifically, "without any adverse distinction founded on sex, race, nationality, religion, political opinions or other similar criteria." Second, humanitarian actions should be guided impartially on the basis of need rather than by political ends. This doctrine is at the heart of all claims to the apolitical nature of humanitarian relief, including its neutral, non-ideological character.[1] Without such claims humanitarian action would be indistinguishable from partisan political activism, especially in politically unstable settings.

Such standards, rooted in common sense and in international humanitarian law, correspond to the sorts of norms Henry Shue argues for in his essay in this volume. They are comprehensive, universal, and cosmopolitan, and while no government (certainly not the United States) has accepted them as legally binding obligations, they represent legitimate international aspirations as articulated by governments in the twentieth century. While no other set of ideals can adequately protect humanitarian operations, these norms are hardly an accurate description of humanitarian practice. They were contradicted by the very specificity of the Falasha operation, which given the scope of the overall refugee needs in Sudan, was both discriminatory and highly political. Nonetheless, it was hailed as one of the great humanitarian triumphs of the decade in the press and by various political leaders. How is this contradiction to be explained?

In our world humanitarian practice is still much closer to the reality described by Rogers Smith in his discussion of the role of communitarian and national goals in setting policy. While assent to broad goals and norms is easy, people and groups still act largely on the basis of interests, and those interests carry into the humanitarian realm as well. Because morality and national interests are not always the same, Smith argues, one must in practice be subordinated to the other. In the case of the Falasha rescue, the national interests of the United States were subordinated to the moral claims and national interests of Israel, as well as to a set of interests eventually judged vital by the American Jewish community.

Even in the realm of humanitarian action, choices must be made, choices that fall short of the impartiality of broadly defined humanitarian goals. In turn, those cosmopolitan and somewhat abstract goals have gained most of their "practical content" from what Smith calls "more concrete moral traditions that give arguments as to what constitutes human worth, what degrades it, and why." The communal sense of urgency that propelled American Jewish activists into the Falasha rescue did not arise from an abstract sense of justice applicable to all, but was deeply embedded in the traditions and history of the Jews. To quote Smith again,

> If we ask ourselves . . . why we want justice, why we find certain inequalities degrading, I think our answers will inevitably involve arguments about why human life is worthy, that is to say, why it is morally good. For it is the qualities that give worth to human life that make its degradation morally wrong. . . . Hence our sense of the right will not be found to be analytically prior to a sense of the human good. It will rather be dependent upon some such sense. Of course, notions of the qualities that make for human worth are controversial . . . in the long run we cannot avoid those controversies by keeping our assumptions about what they are implicit and professing to be neutral on the question. If these points are correct, then it will usually be clearest to argue directly in terms of our moral goals and purposes, indicating why we think they sustain and advance human qualities we value, and what they imply for justice. Moral requirements would then be presented as flowing directly from our pursuit of our sense of appropriate human ends; they would not appear as outside and above our aims and interest, but rather as integral to their realization.[2]

An understanding of Jewish communal mandates, and of the determination of Jews to act on them, goes much further toward explaining how the Falasha were singled out among the hundreds of thousands of refugees in eastern Sudan than broad abstractions about humanitarian justice. This episode is valuable in helping us understand some of the ways that private-sector humanitarian goals are accommodated in U.S. foreign policy today.

THE LAW OF RETURN: A POLITICAL AND RELIGIOUS MANDATE

Israel has consistently required an expanding Jewish population, yet for more than ten years there has been a net emigration of Israel's Jewish population. This has meant renewed emphasis on the Law of Return, or *aliyah*. While the political significance of an expanding (or contracting) Jewish population in Israel is obvious today, its religious meaning was also newly emphasized in the late 1970s by a variety of national and religious authorities involved in the migration process. While most other refugee flows emerged specifically in the face of religious or political persecution at home, the actual process of migration to Israel was itself charged with independent religious meaning: Jews would find their true homeland by making the *aliyah*, a message Israeli leaders broadcast to Jews dispersed around the world.

In contemporary refugee work there is no adequate parallel to U.S./Israeli cooperation in the modern Jewish *aliyah*. From the founding of Israel the United States has played a critical role in financing this migration. As Israel emerged as America's strongest ally in the Middle East there were strong secular and strategic reasons for the U.S. government assisting in a process considered central to Israel's survival. In the case of the airlift of Ethiopian Jews to Israel, however, there is little evidence that the United States wanted close identification with the process. Nevertheless as the situation developed the government had few options but to allow minority interests within the Jewish community to determine its policy.

In a set of clandestine operations conducted from 1978 to 1984 involving the U.S. government, U.S. Jewish agencies, Israel, and Sudan, the international refugee operations in the eastern region of the Sudan were used as the cover for moving Ethiopian Jews to Israel. The American Jewish community was no stranger to the illegal movement of Jews across international borders; Operation Moses, as the Israeli part of the Falasha airlift was known, found its spiritual ancestry in the illegal movement of Jews to Palestine prior to the founding of Israel. The movement of the Falashas was in this sense nothing new; even before World War I American Jews had supported international efforts to save the lives, even entire communities, of endangered Jews. When possible these movements had been legal; when not, not. The Falasha effort was among the most controversial and dangerous, hence the secrecy surrounding its details. In the end, when the operation collapsed under international publicity in 1985, it was only the intervention of State Department officials, Vice President Bush and the Central Intelligence Agency that saved the lives of the Falasha still stranded in eastern Sudan.

According to Isaiah 11:11-12,

> And it shall come to pass in that day, that the Lord shall set his hand again the second time to recover the remnant of his people, which shall be left, from Assyria, and from Egypt, and from Pathros, and from Cush, and from Elam, and from Shinar, and from Hamath, and from the islands of the sea. And he shall set up an ensign for the nations, and shall assemble the outcasts of Israel, and gather together the dispersed of Judah from the four corners of the earth.

The Cushites were the remnant outpost of Jews living in Ethiopia, at the far reach of the world Isaiah might have known. It had not gone unnoticed among modern Jews that Isaiah included Cushites in the *aliyah*. The Cushites were identified as early as the tenth chapter of Genesis as the sons of Ham, himself a son of Noah. The most ancient legend held that they were the offspring of Solomon and the Queen of Sheba. In New Testament times Philip the apostle had encountered an Ethiopian, presumably of Jewish background, in the Gaza desert on his way to worship at the temple in Jerusalem. He was treasurer in the court of Queen Candace—a name, incidentally, also applied to the Queen of Sheba in Ethiopian legends.

In the United States committees organized to assist the Falasha in Africa existed prior to 1940, but there was little consideration given to their removal to Palestine. Even after Israel was founded in 1948, efforts to aid the Falasha were limited to relief and rehabilitation in Ethiopia, conducted under the auspices of the Jewish PVO known as the Organization for Rehabilitation and Training (ORT), the American Jewish Joint Distribution Committee and smaller groups with specialized concerns. Only in the 1970s was it possible for Israel and other Jewish communities to address the question of the Falasha coming to Israel.

Several factors combined to press the urgency of operations directed at moving them from Ethiopia. In 1973 the chief rabbi of Israel's Sephardic (or Oriental) Jews declared that the Falasha were indeed to be recognized as Jews and hence eligible for inclusion in the *aliyah* under Israel's "sublime symbol of self-help," the 1950 Law of Return. In 1975 he was joined in this opinion by the chief rabbi of the Ashkenazi (or European) Jews.[3] As a result of the Yom Kippur War, Israel and Ethiopia broke diplomatic relations, eliminating an official channel for providing assistance to the Falasha. By 1976, the future of the Falasha, as of other sizable Jewish communities outside Israel, was inevitably measured against the need to expand the shrinking Jewish population of Israel. To Jewish activists concerned specifically for the Falasha, these factors all pointed to a rescue operation.

From the beginning controversy dogged their efforts. The American Jewish community was split over the proper approach to the Ethiopian Jews. Black, mostly illiterate, and living in a premodern agricultural setting, the Falasha practiced a preTalmudic Judaism that would be foreign even within the orthodox Jewish communities of Israel. Furthermore, staging an actual rescue operation in Sudan was complex. There, as in the large majority of black Africa, blacks eager to maintain good relations with the Arab population of North Africa became vocally anti-Israel after the 1973 war. Some black leaders were willing to blame the general problem of African refugees on "Zionism" and covert Israeli political operations.[4] In the Sudan, under Gen. Gafar Nimiery, Arab-language newspapers in Khartoum occasionally ran excerpts from the bogus *Protocols of the Elders of Zion*, an anti-Semitic document that originated in Russia and was promoted by Henry Ford in the early part of the century. Government officials in the United States were skeptical about Jewish claims that the Falasha were receiving especially harsh treatment. State Department evaluations of the human rights situation in Ethiopia in the early 1980s argued that while human rights were distinctly limited under the Marxist regime of Col. Haile-Mariam Mengistu, evidence that the Falasha were singled out for persecution was lacking.[5]

Mainline Jewish agencies, while not openly agreeing with State Department assessments, sought a moderating approach, suggesting that while emigration to Israel was the most desirable solution in the long run, short-term political complications argued for the establishment of assistance programs in Ethiopia. In 1974 the American Jewish Joint Distribution Committee began a small assistance program that provided $25,000 per year.[6] Such evaluations and limited assistance were challenged by Falasha activists in the U.S., who alleged that the Ethiopian Jews had been targeted as traitors, removed from their land, placed in ghettolike situations, and had their schools and synagogues closed. In July 1981 the regional governor of Gondar, the province where most of the Falasha lived, ordered the longterm programs of the international Jewish Organization for Rehabilitation and Training (ORT) closed. This meant that ORT operations involving wells, roads, farming aids, and sanitation, as well as support for the work of twenty-five synagogues, were brought to a halt.[7]

American Falasha activists turned to Israeli officials for assistance in their efforts to establish an Ethiopian *aliyah.* There had been hesitation in official Israeli circles, but the election of Menachem Begin as prime minister in 1977 augured well for more attention to the situation. The earliest efforts of the Israelis were tied to diplomatic efforts to buy the freedom of the Falasha to emigrate. In August of 1977 sixty Jews were taken to Israel as part of a deal with the Ethiopian government, and another sixty-one followed later in the year. But an admission by Moshe Dayan in February 1978 that the Israelis had been selling arms to the Ethiopians raised the clear possibility that the movement of the Falasha had been tied to the arms deals. This spelled the end of negotiated agreements between the Israelis and the Ethiopians.[8]

Following Dayan's announcement in early 1978, American Jews presented new plans for a Falasha *aliyah* to officials of the Begin government. As with previous movements of Jewish refugees, there were two essential matters to be addressed: rescue from abroad and absorption inside Israel. The rescue operation involved a variety of private Jewish groups. And there was no doubt that it was risky: it meant bringing Jewish civilians as well as agents of Mossad, the Israeli intelligence branch, to Sudan. The Falasha were told that they would be taken to Israel if they were willing to travel across the border into Sudan and wait temporarily in camps already filled with hundreds of thousands of Ethiopian and Eritrean refugees. The wider flow of refugees provided a cover for the movement of Jews in a country overtly hostile to their presence. Once the rescue portion of the operation was over and the Falasha reached Israel, responsibility for their absorption would shift to the Jewish Agency, the governmental arm of the Zionist movement that had been assisting Jews to settle in Palestine and Israel since 1922.

THE OPERATION BEGINS

There was nothing simple about the operation, which eventually began in Sudan in 1978. People with Israeli passports were not officially permitted inside Sudan, and official hostility toward Jews was well known. Had word leaked out to the Muslim Brotherhood in eastern Sudan that Israelis and Americans were transporting black Jews as part of the refugee operation, there might well have been serious civil disturbances. As it was, Sudanese officials in the state security, whose cooperation was required so that the operation could proceed, were paid large sums of cash, from both private and government sources, reputedly running into the millions of dollars.

There were remarkably few American voluntary agencies in eastern Sudan, due in part to the Sudanese government. Where dozens of agencies had flocked to help in a comparable refugee problem in nearby Somalia, only a handful of private agencies worked in Sudan. In the region of Gedaref, where the Falasha were being quietly held in camps, the International Rescue Committee worked on a contract with the State Department; the indigenous Sudanese agencies Sudanaid (Catholic) and the relief arm of the largely Protestant Sudan Council of Churches functioned in the camps with support from American and European counterparts. By 1983 CARE was working on water and reforestation projects, and a small independent U.S. Catholic organization, Lalamba, had left its Ethiopian work and followed the refugees across the border, reestablishing its efforts in Sudan with a State Department grant. Agencies were staffed by a few American expatriates; virtually all were under thirty and unaware of the Ethiopian Jews' presence in the masses of refugees.

The larger refugee operation was superintended by the Sudanese Commissioner for Refugees and the UNHCR, which staffed a sub-office in Gedaref. If many voluntary agencies were unaware of the early stages of the Falasha situation, the UNHCR could not make such a claim. In the beginning, according to UN sources, a standard route was established: Falasha were moved in buses to Khartoum, where they were met and superintended by Israeli Mossad agents working from a house in the city. When circumstances allowed, they were placed on chartered flights from the Khartoum airport for Israel. Despite lax security in Sudan, there was no way that a movement involving the transport of hundreds of Ethiopians inland remained other than an open secret. Those Falasha sent in the early busloads were reportedly disguised as Italian tourists, complete with makeup, clothes, and toys for the children; from that point on, UN officials familiar with the operation referred to the Falashas as "the Italian cases." The UNHCR could not officially support an operation that singled out a group of refugees for special attention. After all, the UNHCR as an institution officially embodies the cosmopolitan humanitarian ideals of nondiscriminatory and apolitical dealings with refugees. Yet the agency was powerless to halt the movement of Falashas.

By 1980 Falasha activists in the American Association for Ethiopian Jews (AAEJ) in the United States saw a correlation between the numbers of Falasha reaching Israel and the amount of pressure the AAEJ was willing to bring to bear at any given time on the matter; in other words, they doubted Israel's commitment to establishing a strong Ethiopian *aliyah*. This situation was as unacceptable to the AAEJ and their supporters as the increasingly vocal efforts of the AAEJ were to the leaders of the American Jewish establishment. Therefore an establishment effort was made to supplement the AAEJ's approach by forming a Committee on Ethiopian Jewry within the National Jewish Community Relations Advisory Council. Prior to this move, no organizational structure promoting the cause of the Falasha had existed; the AAEJ had served that function for twenty-five years, but its methods were increasingly unacceptable to more moderate Jewish leaders.[9]

Little has been said about the role of the U.S. government in the Falasha operation. In the early years, officials would have liked nothing more than to see the whole operation go away; it was a headache in their relations with the Sudanese, the Israelis, and the Ethiopians. But in 1980 a significant legislative development in Washington, the Refugee Act of 1980, made possible the next step of the operation in Sudan. Before 1981, the United States had not conducted a single refugee resettlement program in Africa. There were several reasons for this, despite the growing masses of refugees throughout the continent. First, it was the stated desire of Africans that refugee problems be handled at home. The Organization of African Unity had drafted a refugee convention in 1969 stating that refugee problems were "a source of friction among many Member States" and that "all the problems of our continent must be solved . . . in the African context."[10] Many African states were wary of resettlement programs which, necessarily selective in who they chose, siphoned off the educated Africans to the west. The African nations wanted to avoid such a "brain drain." Second, African refugee problems generated little political urgency for U.S. strategists; Soviet Jews or Vietnamese or Afghan refugees received far more attention and support. It was easier to provide limited support for local settlement and assistance, and hope that the problems could be resolved by Africans in the long run.

In 1981, however, some members of Congress argued that the lack of U.S. resettlement programs in Africa represented a racist approach to the continent's refugee problems. Under the new Refugee Act it seemed appropriate to institute a program that demonstrated American efforts to reach evenhanded solutions to the world refugee problem. In a notable example of domestic U.S. politics taking priority over the wishes of other nations, the State Department later that year undertook its first and only African resettlement program. It was based it in Gedaref, Sudan.

Two refugee camps near Gedaref held most of the Falasha that reached Sudan. From those camps Falasha were moved secretly to Israel by several escape routes. Some followed the routes established by Israeli intelligence officials through Khartoum. Some were taken to Sudan's coastline on the Red Sea, where they were met by boats and taken to Israel. Some were smuggled out to the south via Kenya; others were flown to South Africa on servant visas. Others were moved directly through the resettlement program of the U.S. government, so that by the end of 1983 some 5,700 Falasha had reached Israel.

Unable to halt the operation, U.S. officials had apparently adopted the "if you can't beat 'em, join 'em" approach, yet even this was done in an atmosphere of secrecy quite apart from the aboveboard resettlement effort openly sanctioned by Congress. Voluntary agency officials in Gedaref were for the most part unaware of the complexities of the operation going on around them, even unaware that several of the agencies had hired Falasha sympathizers from among the refugee population. As part of the resettlement effort the U.S. government financed education classes that taught English and elementary cultural background to refugees selected for resettlement. And as Africans had feared, it was common for refugees selected to have a certain level of skills; many had held professional positions in Ethiopia, others spoke decent English or had been staff workers with the voluntary agencies in the region. By late 1982, however, agency workers suddenly encountered entire classes of refugees who not only spoke no English, but had no professional skills or other background suitable for resettlement in the United States. They were in fact peasants and farmers: unknown to the agency workers, they were Falasha. At the same time, Sudanese officials and others responsible for supervising the movement of Ethiopians scheduled for resettlement in the United States noticed that they were often receiving two different sets of official listings of refugees, or that special efforts were being made to secure places for residents from the camps where Falasha were staying. Some going out under the U.S. resettlement program were indeed going to the United States; others, once they were out of Sudan, were transfered to planes to Israel.

One of the factors behind this stepped-up movement of Falasha to Israel was the increasing political activism of the Falasha supporters in the United States. Officials of the AAEJ frequently visited absorption camps in Israel, and were not happy with what they found. Indeed, they launched attacks against the director of the Jewish Agency in Israel for the alleged restrictions placed on Falasha once they reached Israel. The AAEJ believed the Jewish Agency was only willing to work with the Falasha problem as far as the establishment Jewish leadership in the United States was willing to push. The Jewish Agency could exercise control over the flow of Falasha by stating that absorption camps were full, or by claiming that excessive publicity by AAEJ leaders was creating a political problem. Indeed, in line with the collusion of AAEJ saw between the Jewish Agency and U.S. Jewish leadership, the United Jewish Appeal, the clearinghouse for all international funding raised in the U.S. Jewish community, circulated a confidential memorandum that (following most views in the U.S. State Department) suggested that the AAEJ's work was amateurish and endangering the lives of those involved in rescue efforts. In protest against efforts by Jewish leaders in the United States and Israel to clamp down on their efforts, the AAEJ withdrew from the Committee on Ethiopian Jewry, which had been established in 1980 as an effort to moderate its efforts. To AAEJ leaders, Jewish and governmental leadership had fallen into the same pattern as those who responded to Hitler by claiming that nothing more could, under the circumstances, be done.

The AAEJ and its fellow activists held a single trump card in this standoff: as long as Falasha kept appearing in eastern Sudan, the pressure could be kept up on authorities to do something. And despite the political wrangling going on in Israel and in the United States, the Falasha kept coming. Thousands—the majority of those still left in Ethiopia—had reached eastern Sudan by early 1984. In ill health, frightened, and unsure of the arrangements that awaited them, they had been persuaded that the dangerous trip across Ethiopia and the uncertain wait in Sudan were worth the chance to reach Israel. In 1983 several secret airlifts, one plane at a time, took place in the desert scrubland near the Falasha camps. As word of the secret operation spread, the possibility of quietly shipping the Falasha overland to Khartoum as part of the regular transport of refugees being resettled in the United States evaporated. Remarkably, however, local Moslem militants had apparently still not heard of the black Jews in their midst. Some time remained, but the measures needed were becoming more drastic, and the political clout of interested governments—particularly the United States—was increasingly needed to overcome hostility within the Sudanese government. In March 1984 nomads spotted the landing of a plane—a Hercules C-130 American transport—and news of this unannounced landing in the desert (also near the Falasha camps) spread quickly. So quickly was official involvement spreading, in fact, that after years of silence over what had previously been a matter of concern only within the Jewish community, the *New York Times* abruptly ran an editorial stating that "the plight of the Falasha ought to be on Ethiopia's agenda."[11]

A Swedish nurse working in the camps visited the American embassy in Khartoum in June 1984, asking if something could be done to get the Falasha out of the camps. The constant stream of Jewish refugee activists, many espousing a "Lone Ranger" style, had been a part of the embassy's life for years. The previous year, an individual calling himself "Jack Charity" had simply gathered a small group of Falasha and headed south, hoping that UNHCR workers would help him cross the border with Kenya. Another couple had descended on Gedaref, full of news of what the outside world was doing for the Falasha. As a result refugees were left terrified and unsure of who it was they were supposed to be dealing with. The U.S. embassy refugee coordinator correctly perceived that such individuals had no functional sense of the complexity and danger they were courting in a country as volatile as Sudan. They were doing little to address the overall problem, which in 1984 amounted to moving some 12,000 Jews out of the country, a multi-million-dollar operation.

NEW PRESSURES MOUNT

Despite continued resistance in the Israeli Jewish Agency to a stepped-up movement of Falasha, some humanitarian solution to the problem was needed. The Falasha in Sudan were so frightened that most refused to leave their huts in camps; packed tightly together, disease spread; they refused to eat, and death rates mounted steadily. State Department funds were made available to send food specifically to Falasha camps. Jewish activists in the United States, including an official in the office of the U.S. Coordinator for Refugee Affairs, pressed for action, but in Sudan officials "wanted something straightforward that would not create an embarrassing situation for the Government of Sudan."[12]

The UNHCR was also in a difficult situation. Its previous representative in Gedaref had heard of the Falasha and taken a personal interest in the situation. His assistant, an Ethiopian, was caught by Sudanese security officers providing assistance to the Falasha and jailed. Since the UNHCR was forbidden from showing preference for one refugee group over another, the incident was cause for serious embarrassment. Its Gedaref agent was quickly posted elsewhere and replaced by an American who was willing to help secure an American solution to the Falasha problem.

Jews and others impatient with the mixed messages coming from Israel revived pressure tactics. In a remarkable article on the op-ed page of the *New York Times* of September 15, 1984, a Falasha activist spilled the political dimensions of the situation to a world that still hardly knew the Falasha existed, let alone the complications over their fate in Israel, Sudan, or the American Jewish community. "At least 1,300 black Ethiopian Jews, mostly children, have died in refugee camps outside Ethiopia," he wrote, carefully avoiding any mention of Sudan. He directed criticism against then Prime Minister Yitzak Shamir, and other Israeli "bureaucrats" who were impeding a solution. From May to June, "not only were none rescued by Israel but also all major Jewish organizations, including the World Jewish Congress and Joint Distribution Committee, chose not to provide any financial, medical, or food aid. . . . What is needed, without further delay . . . is a massive rescue airlift from the camps and from Ethiopia. This will occur only if it is demanded in Israel and abroad."

The call was heard. By early fall 1984 the U.S. embassy had decided that no solution would be found without the active support of sympathetic and powerful members of the Sudanese government. The vice president, Gen. Omar Tayeb, agreed to provide assistance as long as the CIA was involved. This condition was officially turned down flat by Washington. The embassy refugee coordinator was to be in charge; he was the man who best understood the situation on the ground. In October he went to Geneva, ostensibly for the annual meeting of the Executive Committee of the UNHCR. There he held meetings with State Department officials and representatives of the Jewish Agency and the Israeli government. Sudanese officials charged with facilitating the coming airlift were also in Geneva and kept informed. Operation Moses was falling into place. Finances of the operation were to be channeled through the U.S. embassy, and in this regard he later insisted on two frankly incredible claims: that no bribes changed hands, and that no U.S. government money was spent on the effort.

OPERATION MOSES

On November 20, 1984 he and his co-workers in the Israeli Mossad had arranged for four buses to gather outside one of the Falasha camps, where some 250 Falasha boarded and were whisked off to the Khartoum airport, about a seven-hour drive. They were met there by a Belgian charter plane, and the first Operation Moses flight soon took off for Israel. This pattern continued for nearly seven weeks as thousands of Falasha were finally allowed to reach their destination. In a press account December 10, Reagan administration officials denied that the United States had had any involvement in the ongoing airlift, which by then, some three weeks into Operation Moses, had illegally moved some 3,000 Falasha to Israel. Diplomatic, governmental, and Jewish sources told reporters at the time that the airlift was taking place "as a result of the famine in Ethiopia." It was claimed that U.S. involvement was limited to $15 million that had been allocated for the absorption of the refugees inside Israel.[13] The same week, an article in the Washington *Jewish Week* quoted the chairman of the Jewish Agency as saying that Israel was experiencing "a sudden jump in immigration, far beyond the figures we projected for this and the coming year." The remark was made at a fund-raising dinner in New York; he was unaware that it would appear in the press. After this, there was a journalistic silence for the remainder of the year. Nothing had directly implicated the Sudan, and the operation continued; it was scheduled to run through January 17.[14]

It came to an abrupt halt January 3 after an Israeli official published an interview in an Israeli magazine acknowledging that the operation was underway. When the outside press picked up this official confirmation of Israeli involvement in the effort, Israeli censors temporarily gave up efforts at controlling any governmental acknowledgements of the airlift (a news blackout on the airlift in Israel followed shortly). At a news conference an official of the Foreign Ministry said, "When the time will come, it will be our honor to disclose the people and the governments who helped." In Sudan, meanwhile, the predictable happened: an embarrassed Sudanese government halted the flights. In Ethiopia, the government denounced the airlift as "illegal trafficking" in Ethiopian citizens and a "gross interference" in the internal affairs of Ethiopia. It claimed that the Sudanese had been offered money to draw them into a conspiracy with unnamed "foreign powers."[15]

There was little doubt that internal political debates over the Falasha in Israel had brought about the premature publicity on the operation. "It is my plea," said Israeli President Chaim Hertzog on January 7, "that we do not make this splendid rescue of Ethiopian Jewry into an ugly chapter of accusation and slanders leveled by political groups against each other."[16] It was more a matter of keeping the existing deep political divisions out of the press than preventing unprecedented slanders in the future. The Jewish Agency and others in Israel stood accused of racism and, even worse: of abandoning the Zionist promise that all Jews without exception had a home in Israel. Until the United States government formally entered the picture, the uncoordinated private rescue operations had created provocative and dangerous conditions for participants and for the refugees in Sudan, not to mention trouble caused for the Reagan administration in its relations with the Nimiery government. U.S. diplomats were often furious in private over the rescue mission mounted by Jewish activists. (As late as the fall of 1984, a State Department official directly involved in the Falasha affair maintained that the Falasha had not been singled out for persecution within Ethiopia).

Two further question remained. The premature halt of Operation Moses left hundreds of Falasha still stranded in Sudan;

estimates ranged from 900 to 4,000.[17] What was to happen to them now that publicity had destroyed the secret airlift? Secondly, what was happening to the Falasha once they reached Israel? It was the second question that next drew the attention of the press, when the United States protested to Israeli officials later in the month about reports that Falasha were being settled in the Israeli-occupied West Bank. This policy had been in place well before Operation Moses, though Israeli officials were now quick to claim that the fact that one processing center in the West Bank was handling Falasha did not mean that they would be permanently settled in that area. The U.S. government was on record as opposing Israeli settlement policies in the West Bank, and the use of U.S. economic aid to Israel for absorption costs of new immigrants was forbidden in the occupied territories. News that the Falasha were being sent to the front lines of the West Bank was more than the United States would tolerate.[18]

Israel still needed American help in addressing the matter of the Falasha still stranded in Sudan. Contrary to the embassy's claim that the U.S. financial role in Operation Moses was limited to the congressionally mandated absorption costs in Israel, the New York Times claimed that the costs of the charter flights by the Belgian Trans Europrean Airways "were paid for by Israel with money received from America."[19] Israel was simply in no financial position to handle the exorbitant costs of the operation, and it would need to return to the United States for aid in reaching the Falasha remaining in Sudan.

In March 1985 Vice President Bush visited Sudan with a sizable entourage. There he conducted meetings with President Nimiery, who agreed to allow the United States to airlift the remaining Falasha out of the country, provided that no Israeli planes were involved in the operation and that the refugees were given visas to countries other than Israel. Once the Sudanese leader had given his approval, the CIA was called in to manage the operation. Though CIA officials frequently take interest in refugee flows, it is unusual for them to administer a program directly, as was the case in the final rescue operation. Some eight hundred Falasha were flown out on C-130 Hercules transports between March 12 and March 23. The operation was paid for by CIA funds from U.S. refugee allocations.[20] Thus Washington's earlier insistence that the CIA not be involved was openly abandoned.

As far as the U.S. government was concerned, the affair was closed. The embassy's refugee coordinator, his life reportedly threatened by Arabs outraged by the Falasha movement, was hurriedly sent home from the Sudan in late March. On April 6 a coup toppled Nimiery's government; the new military rulers of Sudan announced later that month that senior Sudanese officials who had participated in Operation Mosses would be placed on trial. The trials were televised on evening television in Khartoum for weeks. In November several voluntary agencies suspected of participating in the Falasha operation were expelled from the Sudan. Far from controlling the situation, the Reagan administration had been placed in the unenviable position of pulling Israel out of a tight spot. It had been placed there by the outspoken and persistent efforts of an activist minority in the Jewish community. The AAEJ pursued its politics of intervention and created a tragic set of events it could no longer shield or manage. The AAEJ and its supporters believed religiously in the *aliyah*, particularly its relevance to the Falasha. That belief led them to international political intrigues that in the end demonstrated that the *aliyah* could take precedence over the political and diplomatic interests of any government that stood in its way, including the Israeli government. The London-based *Economist* sided with the Falasha and their managers, stating that they properly "got the benefit of permissable discrimination."[21] And the attitudes of American and Israeli activists toward political constraints were dismissive, not unlike those of church sanctuary workers helping Central Americans who had come to the United States to escape civil strife at home.

In order to achieve the final rescue of the Falasha, however, the Jewish community in Israel and the United States stood together (those who still had objections had made their weight felt by exposing the operation prematurely). Caught in the pressures of deciding what would become of several thousand Jews stranded in a hostile Muslim environment, reluctant establishment leaders among American Jews faced a choice of abandoning their fellow Jews—an intolerable choice—or bringing their weight to bear on behalf of U.S. government intervention. That intervention, coming as it did during a renewed Sudanese civil war, contributed directly to political instabilities that resulted in the collapse of Nimiery's government.

IMPLICATIONS FOR HUMANITARIANISM AND U.S. FOREIGN POLICY

With the growth of democracy has come an expanded role for privately sponsored humanitarian goals in foreign policy. This has been the case in the United States and in most Western European countries, with many voluntary agencies in these countries working actively with local affiliates in countries where humanitarian needs are great. It is hard to imagine, for instance, operations such as the movement of Falasha or immense famine relief campaigns playing a role in nineteenth-century statecraft, but at the end of the twentieth century such humanitarian involvement between private and public authorities is common. Yet as the examples and analysis found in this book indicate, no common definition of humanitarianism exists that can be automatically applied to the relief needs we have surveyed. Cosmopolitan and universal aspirations were established between the 1920s and the 1950s, but much of the growth of humanitarian practice, as in the example cited here, has grown not from those aspirations per se, but rather from communal, religious, and nationalists goals extending far into the past, often predating both international humanitarian standards and the current system of nation-states.[22]

The Falasha operation illustrates several dimensions of humanitarian practice today. It certainly meets the fundamental criterion that the focus be on delivery of assistance to victims of natural or political disasters. In order to make this claim credible, however, both private and public authorities had to be involved. Any definition of humanitarian neutrality that envisions a political "space" so protected that it would be free of governmental participation must be ruled out as impractical. Private Falasha activists required the collusion of at least three governments to accomplish their goals: the United States, Israel, and Sudan. Governments represent national interests; how, then, can their participation in humanitarian efforts be said to pursue a humanitarian "neutrality"? The same question must also be addressed to the private sector, in this instance Jewish groups who focused their attention on a few thousand Falasha amidst a sea of nearly a million refugees in eastern Sudan alone.

I believe the answer to this question is that the combination of international, national, and communal, often religious goals in the service of needy victims comes as close to tempering purely national or purely sectarian ends as we can hope for in this world. Consider, for instance, that following World War II, church-related voluntary agencies were routinely expected to work primarily with their co-religionists abroad. While such ties remain, the provision of assistance today increasingly goes to people in need regardless of their religious affiliation. Similar universalizing trends have appeared in Jewish relief agencies in recent years. While pure neutrality is unlikely to appear in international politics, the evolving system of cooperation between private, national, and international authorities has clearly created an arena where progress can be made, and where human needs can be met.

Is humanitarianism practice "apolitical"? Clearly not, certainly not in the case of the Falasha, where human needs—in this case their desire to escape persecution and deprivation and move to Israel—were met only to the extent that they overlapped with the political and religious interests of American Jews and the Israeli government. Neither American, Sudanese, nor Ethiopian authorities are likely to see the humanitarian rationale of the Falasha operation in the same light as the Jewish groups. Larry Minear has called for a "new professionalism" as the best approach for meeting new political pressures on PVOs.[23] What can be argued is that human needs—the meeting of which, after all, is the purpose of humanitarianism—are given greater protection in such operations than they might have been under purely *realpolitik* strategies. Any movement toward broader political neutrality that protects the rights of even some of the downtrodden and powerless must be counted as a step in the right direction. This is surely what the *Economist* meant by saying the Falasha "got the benefit of permissible discrimination."

Humanitarian goals in their purest universal and cosmopolitan forms take life most strongly not in private or public agencies, but in international bodies such as the UNHCR, the World Food Program, the International Committee of the Red

Cross and others that have been created to cement the international machinery of humanitarian practice among nations. As is clear from this analysis and from other chapters in this book, however, these bodies have no independent powers to enforce humanitarian standards. On many occasions they have provided signal contributions toward such ends, but their powers and their standards of humanitarian practice are often outweighed, in this case by the collaborative efforts of private individuals, communities, and governments.

In this particular instance, in fact, we see striking instances of both Henry Shue's universal humanitarian standards and the communal and national standards found in Rogers Smith's analysis of the same terrain. It is the former, however, as embodied in the weak, almost nonexistent role of the UNHCR in enforcing uniform standards of refugee care, that gives way to the latter, as found in the interests of the American Jewish community, Israel, and reluctantly in this case, the American government, in moving the Falasha to Israel. When those communal and national goals were pursued in the complex politics of the Horn of Africa, they could be met only by surreptitious and extralegal means involving covert operations, bribery, and open discrimination. While Churchill may have overstated the case when he claimed that truth requires a bodyguard of lies, it is often true that governments do. And it is these same governments that are required to carry out humanitarian actions.

In concert with private voluntary agencies and international humanitarian organizations, democratic governments such as the United States have formed the political backbone of modern humanitarian practice. Each of these sources contributes its own definition of morally good ends and of the proper means of pursuing them. In some cases those definitions overlap; in others, the presence of several thousand endangered refugees in desert camps and a handful of advocates in Washington and elsewhere can wring consensus where none previously existed. What must be seen today is that despite the limitations and historical contingencies institutions at the private, governmental, and intergovernmental levels bring to their tasks and to their differing views of the justice of their causes, their combined efforts have built a new (if fragile) dimension to the conduct of American foreign policy in the world today, a dimension committed to maintaining a focus on the needs of the victims. When all is said and done, this remains one of the signal moral and political accomplishments of U.S. foreign policy in the twentieth century.

NOTES

1. See, respectively, First Geneva Convention of 1949, Articles 12 and 18, and Fourth Geneva Convention of 1949, Articles 59-63 (for the text of these passages see *UN Treaty Series* 75: 1ff.); Additional Protocol II Article 18(2) (for the text of the treaty see *American Journal of International Law* 72 (1978):457). The United States has signed but has not ratified the additional protocols.

A similar listing of the components of humanitarian doctrine may be found in the Basic Principles of the Red Cross as adopted at the 20th International Conference of the Red Cross, Vienna, October 1965. They include humanity, impartiality, neutrality, independence, voluntary service, unity, and universality.

2. See Smith's paper in this volume, pp. 46, 47.

3. Leon Wieseltier, "Brothers and Keepers," *New Republic,* February 11, 1985. Roberta Fahn Reisman, "The Falashas," February 1982 (unpublished paper), p. 1.

4. See for instance Damas Deng, "Root Causes of the Refugee Phenomenon in Africa," presented at a Government of Sudan seminar on refugees, Khartoum, September 1982.

5. Personal interviews with U.S. embassy officials, Khartoum, January-August 1983.

6. "The Falasha Jews of Ethiopia" (New York: Council of Jewish Federation and Welfare Funds, January 1976).

7. Reisman, p. 2.

8. Charles T. Powers, "Ethiopian Jews: Exodus of a Tribe," *Los Angeles Times,* July 7, 1985.

9. Reisman, p. 4.

10. "OAU Convention of 10 September 1969 governing the specific aspects of refugee problems in Africa," in *Collection of International Instruments Concerning Refugees,* 2nd ed. (Geneva: UNHCR, 1979), pp. 193-200.

11. "Exodus for a Twice-Lost Tribe" (editorial), *New York Times,* March 3, 1984.

12. Powers, "Ethiopian Jews."

13. "Airlift to Israel is Reported Taking Thousands of Jews From Ethiopia," *New York Times,* December 11, 1984.

14. "L' 'Epopee Heroique' des Falachas," *Le Monde Diplomatique*, February 1985, p. 6.

15. "Disclosure of Secret Airlift Opens Rift at Israeli Agency," *New York Times*, January 5, 1985.

16. "Peres Vows Israel Will Finish Rescue," *New York Times*, January 8, 1985.

17. Charles T. Powers, "A New Life in Israel for Ethiopians," *Los Angeles Times*, July 8, 1985. "Sudan Blames Ethiopia for the Airlift to Israel," *New York Times*, January 8, 1985.

18. "Ethiopian Jews Said to Resettle on West Bank," *New York Times*, January 18, 1985.

19. Ibid.

20. "Sudan Lets U.S. Fly 800 Ethiopian Jews to Israeli Refuge," *New York Times*, March 24, 1985.

21. "Exodus from Ethiopia," *Economist*, January 12, 1985.

22. For a full study see J. Bruce Nichols, *The Uneasy Alliance: Religion, Refugees, and U.S. Foreign Policy* (New York: Oxford University Press, 1988).

23. Larry Minear, *Helping People in an Age of Conflict* (New York: American Council for Voluntary International Action [InterAction], 1988).

CONTRIBUTORS

JASON W. CLAY is an anthropologist and director of research at Cultural Survival, a human rights development assistance and advocacy organization that works with indigenous peoples. He is co-author of *Politics and the Ethiopian Famine* (1985) and *The Spoils of Famine: Ethiopian Famine Policy and Peasant Agriculture* (1988), both published by Cultural Survival.

FREDERICK C. CUNY is the founder and chairman of INTERTECT, a professional disaster management consulting firm based in Dallas, Texas. An acknowledged expert on relief issues in both natural disasters and refugee emergencies, he is the author of numerous publications and training materials including *Refugee Camps and Camp Planning: The State of the Art* and *Disasters and Development.*

DAVID P. FORSYTHE is a political scientist at the University of Nebraska who writes on human rights and humanitarian affairs. His 1988 book *Human Rights and U.S. Foreign Policy: Congress Reconsidered* won the Manning J. Dauer Prize.

LOWELL W. LIVEZEY is an administrator and lecturer at the Woodrow Wilson School of Public and International Affairs, Princeton University. His monograph *Nongovernmental Organizations and the Ideas of Human Rights* was published in 1987 by the Center of International Studies at Princeton.

311

GIL LOESCHER (Co-Editor) is associate professor of government and international studies at the University of Notre Dame. Co-author with John Scanlan of *Calculated Kindness: Refugees and America's Half-Open Door* (Free Press, 1986), a study of postwar American refugee policy, he is currently at work on a Twentieth Century Fund study of international cooperation and the management of refugee problems.

PETER MACALISTER-SMITH is a jurist and senior editor at the Max Planck Institute for Comparative Public Law and International Law, Heidelberg, Federal Republic of Germany. He is a member of the editorial committee of the *Encyclopedia of Public International Law* and the author of *International Humanitarian Assistance* (Dordrecht: Martinus Nijhoff, 1985)

MICHAEL MCCONNELL is a minister in the United Church of Christ and a member of the Chicago Religious Task Force on Central America. With Rennie Golden, he is the co-author of *Sanctuary: The New Underground Railroad* (Orbis, 1986). He has been active in the sanctuary movement.

DORIS MEISSNER has been a senior associate at the Carnegie Endowment for International Peace since 1986. Previously, she served as Acting Commissioner and Executive Associate Commissioner, U.S. Immigration and Naturalization Service (1981–85); Deputy Associate Attorney General and Executive Director, Cabinet Committee on Illegal Aliens (1973–80); and Executive Director, National Women's Political Caucus (1971–72).

BRUCE NICHOLS (Co-Editor) is director of education and studies at the Carnegie Council on Ethics and International Affairs, New York. He is the author of *The Uneasy Alliance: Religion, Refugee Work and U.S. Foreign Policy* (Oxford University Press, 1988).

LAWRENCE PEZZULLO has served as executive director of Catholic Relief Services since 1984. Previously he was a career foreign service official, and was U.S. ambassador to Nicaragua under the Carter Administration.

SYDNEY H. SCHANBERG joined *Newsday* in 1986 as associate editor and columnist after twenty-six years with the *New York Times*. He is the author of *The Death and Life of Dith Pran,* on which the film *The Killing Fields* was based. He won the Pulitzer Prize in 1975 for his reporting from Cambodia.

HENRY SHUE became the first director of Cornell University's program on Ethics and Public Life in 1987. He spent the previous decade at the Center for Philosophy and Public Policy of the University of Maryland. In addition to his book *Basic Rights* (Princeton, 1980), he had co-edited *Food Policy* and *Boundaries.*

ROGERS M. SMITH teaches political science at Yale University. He is the author of *Liberalism and American Constitutional Law* (Harvard, 1985) and co-author (with Peter H. Shuck) of *Citizenship Without Consent.* He is currently completing a book entitled *Civic Ideals: Conceptions of Citizenship in American Public Law.*

BIBLIOGRAPHY

Aga Khan, Sadruddin. *Legal Problems Related to Refugees and Displaced Persons.* The Hague: Academy of International Law, 1976.

————. *Study on Human Rights and Massive Exoduses.* ECOSOC doc.E/CN 4/1503, 1981.

————. "Towards a Humanitarian World Order." *Third World Affairs,* 1985, 105-23.

Baldwin, David A. *Foreign Aid and American Foreign Policy: A Documentary Analysis.* New York: Praeger, 1966.

Bau, Ignatius. *This Ground Is Holy.* New York: Paulist Press, 1985

Beitz, Charles. *Political Theory and International Relations.* Princeton: Princeton University Press, 1979.

Bolling, Landrum, and Smith, Craig. *Private Foreign Aid: U.S. Philanthropy and Development.* Boulder, Colo.: Westview Press, 1982.

Bramwell, Anna, ed. *Refugees in the Age of Total War.* London: Unwin Hyman, 1988.

Brewer, Kathleen, and Taran, Patrick A. *Manual for Refugee Sponsorship.* New York: Church World Service, Immigration and Refugee Program, 1982.

Brown, Francis J., ed. *Refugees.* Special Issue of the *Annals of the American Academy of Political and Social Science,* 203 (1936).

Brown, Peter, and Maclean, Douglas, eds. *Human Rights and U.S. Foreign Policy.* Lexington, Mass.: D.C. Heath, 1979.

Brown, Peter, and Shue, Henry, eds. *Boundaries: National Autonomy and Its Limits.* Totowa, N.J.: Rowman and Littlefield, 1981.

Bull, Hedley. *The Anarchical Society: A Study of Order in World Politics.* London: Macmillan, 1977.

Butterfield, Herbert, and Wight, Martin, eds. *Diplomatic Investigations.* London: George Allen & Unwin, 1966.

Clay, Jason, and Holcomb, Bonnie. *Politics and the Ethiopian Famine, 1984-1985.* Cambridge, Mass.: Cultural Survival, 1985.

Cogswell, James G. *No Place Left to Call Home.* New York: Friendship Press, 1983.

Coordinator for Refugee Affairs (U.S. Department of State). "An Edited Transcript of a Conference on Ethical Issues and Moral Principles in U.S. Refugee Policy." Washington, D.C.: Meridian House International, March 23-24, 1983.

————. "A Summary of the Conference on Ethical Issues and Moral Principles in U.S. Refugee Policy." Washington, D.C.: Meridian House International, March 23-24, 1983.

Curti, Merle. *American Philanthropy Abroad: A History*. New Brunswick, N.J.: Rutgers University Press, 1963.

Daedalus 112 (1983), no. 4. Special issue on human rights.

Dinnerstein, Leonard. *America and the Survivors of the Holocaust, 1941-1945*. New York: Columbia University Press, 1982.

Donnelly, Jack. "International Human Rights: A Regime Analysis." *International Organization* 40 (Summer 1985), 249-70.

Douglas, H. Eugene. "The Problems of Refugees in a Strategic Perspective." *Strategic Review*, Fall 1982.

Dowty, Alan. *Closed Borders*. New Haven, Conn.: Yale University Press, 1987.

D'Souza, Frances, and Crisp, Jeff. *The Refugee Dilemma*. Minority Rights Group Report no. 43. London: Minority Rights Group, February 1985.

Falk, Richard. A. *Human Rights and State Sovereignty*. New York: Holms and Meier, 1981.

Ferris, Elizabeth G. *Central American Refugees and the Politics of Protection*. New York: Praeger, 1987.

———. "The Politics of Asylum: Mexico and the Central American Refugees." *Journal of InterAmerican Studies and World Affairs* 26 (August 1984), 357-84.

———,ed. *Refugees and World Politics*. New York: Praeger, 1985.

Forsythe, David P. *Humanitarian Politics: The International Committee of the Red Cross*. Baltimore: Johns Hopkins University Press, 1977.

———. "Humanizing American Foreign Policy: Non-Profit Lobbying and Human Rights." PONPO Working Paper 12. New Haven, Conn.: Program on Non-Profit Organizations, Institution for Social and Policy Studies, Yale University, n.d.

———. "The United Nations and Human Rights, 1945-1985." *Political Science Quarterly* 100 (Summer 1985), 249-70.

Friedman, Ray. "The Role of Non-Profit Organizations in Foreign Aid: A Literature Survey." PONPO Working Paper 32. New Haven, Conn.: Program on Non-Profit Organizations, Institution for Social and Policy Studies, Yale Universtiy, n.d.

Gallagher, Dennis, ed. "Refugees: Issues and Directions." *International Migration Review* 20 (Summer 1986).

Gallagher, Dennis; Forbes, Susan, and Fagen, Patricia Weiss. *Of Special Humanitarian Concern: U.S. Refugee Admissions since Passage of the Refugee Act*. Washington, D.C.: Refugee Policy Group, 1985.

General Accounting Office. "International Assistance to Refugees in Africa Can Be Improved." GAO/ID 83-2. Washington, D.C.: December 29, 1982.

———. "Private Sector Involvement in the Agency for International Development's Programs." GAO/ID 82-47. Washington, D.C.: August 16, 1982.

Golden, Renny, and McConnell, Michael. "Sanctuary: Choosing Sides." *Christianity and Crisis* 43, 2 (February 21, 1983).

———. *Sanctuary: The New Underground Railroad*. Maryknoll, N.Y.: Orbis Books, 1986.

Goodwin-Gill, Guy S. *The Refugee in International Law*. Oxford: Clarendon Press, 1983.

Gordenker, Leon. *Refugees in International Politics*. London: Croom Helm, 1987.

Gorman, Robert. "Coping with the African Refugee Problem: Reflections on the Role of Private Voluntary Organization Assistance." *Issue: A Journal of Africanist Opinion* 12 (Spring-Summer 1982), 35-40.

———. *Private Voluntary Organizations as Agents of Development*. Boulder, Colo.: Westview Press, 1984.

Grahl-Madsen, Atle. *The Status of Refugees in International Law*. 2 vols. Leiden: A. W. Sijthoff, 1966, 1972.

———. *Territorial Asylum*. Dobbs Ferry, N.Y.: Oceana Publications, 1980.

Grant, Bruce. *The Boat People*. London: Penguin Books, 1979.

Hansen, Art, and Oliver-Smith, Anthony, eds. *Involuntary Migration and Resettlement: The Problems and Responses of Dislocated Peoples*. Boulder, Colo.: Westview Press, 1982.

Hanson, Christopher T. "Behind the Paper Curtain: Asylum Policy v. Asylum Practice." *New York University Review of Law and Social Change* 7 (Winter 1978), 107-141.

Harrell-Bond, Barbara E. "Humanitarianism in a Straightjacket." *African Affairs* 84, 1 (January 1985).

———. *Imposing Aid: Emerging Assistance to Refugees*. New York: Oxford University Press, 1986.

Hehir, J. Bryan. "The Struggle in Central America: A View from the Church." *Foreign Policy* 43 (Summer 1981).

Helton, Arthur. "Political Asylum under the 1980 Refugee Act: An Unfulfilled Promise." *University of Michigan Journal of Law Reform* 17 (1984), 243.

Hewlett, Sylvia Ann. "Coping with Illegal Immigrants." *Foreign Affairs* 60 (Winter 1981-1982), 358-78.

Hirschman, Albert O. *Exit, Voice, and Loyalty: Responses to Decline in Firms, Organizations, and States*. Cambridge, Mass.: Harvard University Press, 1970.

Hoffman, Stanley. *Duties Beyond Borders*. Syracuse, N.Y.: Syracuse University Press, 1981.

Holborn, Louise. *The International Refugee Organization: A Specialized Agency of the United Nations, Its History and Work, 1942-52*. London: Oxford University Press, 1956.

———. *Refugees, a Problem of Our Time: The Work of the United Nations High Commissioner for Refugees*. 2 vols. Metuchen, N.J.: Scarecrow Press, 1975.

Hoskins, Lewis M. "Voluntary Agencies and Foundations in International Aid." *The Annals of the American Academy of Political and Social Science* 329 (May 1960).

Hostetter, Doug, and McIntyre, Michael. "The Politics of Charity." *Christian Century* 91, 31 (September 1974).

Hull, Elizabeth. *Without Justice for All*. Westport, Conn.: Greenwood Press, 1985.

International Bibliography of Refugee Literature. Geneva: International Refugee Integration Resource Center, 1985.

Jorstad, Eric. "Sanctuary for Refugees: A Statement on Public Policy." *Christian Century* 101, 9 (March 14,1984).

Karadawi, Ahmed. "Constraints on Assistance to Refugees: Some Observations from the Sudan." *World Development* 11, 6 (1983).

Keely, Charles B. *Global Refugee Policy: The Case for a Development-Oriented Strategy.* New York: The Population Council, Inc., 1981.

Kent, Randolph. *The Anatomy of Disaster Relief: The International Network in Action.* London: Pinter Publishers, 1987.

Keohane, Robert O., and Nye, Joseph S., Jr. *Power and Independence.* Boston: Little Brown, 1977.

———, eds. *Transnational Relations and World Politics.* Cambridge, Mass.: Harvard University Press, 1972.

Kommers, Donald P., and Loescher, Gilbert D., eds. *Human Rights and American Foreign Policy.* Notre Dame, Ind.: University of Notre Dame Press, 1979.

Krasner, Stephen D., ed. *International Regimes.* Ithaca, N.Y.: Cornell University Press, 1983.

Kritz, Mary M., ed. *U.S. Immigration and Refugee Policy: Global and Domestic Issues.* Lexington, Mass., D.C. Heath, 1983.

Kuper, Leo. *Genocide: Its Political Uses in the Twentieth Century.* New Haven, Conn.: Yale University Press, 1981.

———. *The Prevention of Genocide.* New Haven, Conn.: Yale University Press, 1985.

Levenstein, Aaron. *Escape to Freedom: The Story of the International Rescue Committee.* Westport, Conn.: Greenwood Press, 1983.

Levy, Deborah M. *Transnational Legal Problems of Refugees: 1982 Michigan Yearbook of International Legal Studies.* New York: Clark Boardman, 1982.

Lichtenberg, Judith. "Moral Boundaries and National Boundaries; A Cosmopolitan View." Working Paper NB-4, University of Maryland Center for Philosophy and Public Policy, College Park, Md., 13 August 1980.

Lissner, Jorgen. *The Politics of Altruism: A Study of the Political Behavior of Voluntary Development Agencies.* Geneva: Lutheran World Federation, 1977.

Livezey, Lowell W. "Nongovernmental Organizations and the Ideas of Human Rights." Monograph, Woodrow Wilson School of Public and International Affairs, Princeton University, 1988.

Loescher, Gil, and Monahan, Laila, eds. *Refugees and International Relations.* Oxford: Clarendon Books, 1989.

Loescher, Gil, and Scanlan, John. *Calculated Kindness: Refugees and America's Half-Open Door.* New York: Free Press, and London: Macmillan, 1986.

———. *Human Rights, Power Politics, and the International Refugee Regime: The Case of U.S. Treatment of Caribbean Basin Refugees.* Princeton, N.J.: Princeton University Center for International Studies, World Order Studies Occasional Paper Series, No. 14, 1985.

———. "Human Rights, U.S. Foreign Policy, and Haitian Refugees." *Journal of Inter-American Studies and World Affairs* 26 (August 1984), 313-56.

———, eds. *The Global Refugee Problem: U.S. and World Response.* Beverly Hills, Calif., and London: Sage Publications, 1983.

Macalister-Smith, Peter. *International Humanitarian Assistance: Disaster Relief Actions in International Law and Organization*. Dordrecht: Martinus Nijhoff, 1985.

Mason, Linda, and Brown, Roger. *Rice, Rivalry, and Politics*. Notre Dame, Ind.: University of Notre Dame Press, 1983.

Meyer, Anne. *Annotated Bibliography on Sanctuary*. Champaign, Ill.: Urbana Ecumenical Committee on Sanctuary, 1986.

Moorhead, Wright, ed. *Rights and Obligations in North-South Relations*. London: Macmillan, 1986.

Nardin, Terry. *Law, Morality and the Relations of States*. Princeton, N.J.: Princeton University Press, 1983.

Newland, Kathleen. *Refugees: The New International Politics of Displacement*. Worldwatch Paper 43. Washington, D.C.: Worldwatch Institute, March 1981.

Nichols, Bruce. *The Uneasy Alliance: Religion, Refugee Work, and U.S. Foreign Policy*. New York: Oxford University Press, 1988.

————. "Favor in the Wilderness: Sanctuary Politics and the Shaping of American Refugee Policy." *Refugee Issues: British Refugee Council, Queen Elizabeth House Working Papers on Refugees* 2, 4 (August 1986).

————. "Rubberband Humanitarianism." *Ethics and International Affairs* 1 (1987).

Nickle, James W. "Human Rights and the Rights of Aliens." Working Paper N-3, College Park, Md.: University of Maryland Center for Philosophy and Public Policy, 30 July 1980.

Orbach, William W. *The American Movement to Aid Soviet Jews*. Amherst, Mass.: University of Massachusetts Press, 1979.

The Other Side 19, 3 (March 1983). Philadelphia: Jubilee, Inc. (Issue devoted to survey of work of private relief and development agencies.)

Pettman, Ralph. *Moral Claims in World Affairs*. London: Croom Helm, 1979.

"Postwar Catholic Relief: An Interview with Bishop Edward E. Swanstrom." *Newsletter on Church and State Abroad* 4. New York: Council on Church and State Abroad, May 1984.

Refugee Policy Group. *The U.S.-Based Refugee Field: An Organizational Analysis*. Washington, D.C.: Refugee Policy Group, April 1982.

Refugees: The Dynamics of Displacement. A Report for the Independent Commission on International Humanitarian Issues (ICHJ). London: Zed Books, 1986.

Reimers, David M. *Still the Golden Door: The Third World Comes to America*. New York: Columbia University Press, 1985.

Reiss, Elizabeth Clark. *The American Council of Voluntary Agencies for Foreign Service: Four Monographs*. New York: American Council for Voluntary Agencies, 1986.

Ringland, Arthur C. "The Organization of Private Voluntary Foreign Aid, 1939-1953." *Department of State Bulletin* 30 (March 15, 1954).

Rose-Ackerman, Susan. "Do Government Grants to Charity Reduce Private Donations?" PONPO Working Paper 13. New Haven, Conn.: Program on

Non-Profit Organizations, Institute for Social and Policy Studies, Yale University, March 1980.

Rose, Peter I. "The Business of Caring: Refugee Workers and Voluntary Agencies." *Refugee Reports* 4 (1981), 1-6.

———. "The Politics and Morality of U.S. Refugee Policy." *Center Magazine,* September-October 1985, 2-14.

Scanlan, John A., and Loescher, G. D. "Mass Asylum and Human Rights in American Foreign Policy." *Political Science Quarterly* 97 (Spring 1982), 39-56.

Schmidt, Elizabeth; Blewett, Jane, and Henriot, Peter. *Religious Private Voluntary Organizations and the Question of Government Funding* (final report). Ossining, N.Y.: Orbis Books, 1981.

Seeking Safe Haven: A Congregational Guide to Helping Central American Refugees in the United States. Published jointly by the American Friends Service Commitee, Philadelphia; Church World Service, New York; Inter-Religious Task Force on El Salvador and Central America, New York; and Lutheran Immigration and Refugee Service, New York, 1983.

Shawcross, William. *The Quality of Mercy: Cambodia, the Holocaust and Modern Conscience.* New York: Simon and Schuster, 1984.

Shue, Henry. *Basic Rights: Subsistence, Affluence, and U.S. Foreign Policy.* Princeton, N.J.: Princeton University Press, 1980.

Simpson, John Hope. *The Refugee Problem.* London: Oxford University Press, 1939.

Smith, Michael Joseph. *Realist Thought from Weber to Kissinger.* Baton Rouge, La.: Louisiana State University Press, 1986.

Smyser, William R. "Refugees: A Never-Ending Story." *Foreign Affairs* 64 (Fall 1985), 154-68.

———. *Refugees: Extended Exile.* New York: Praeger, 1987.

Sobel, Lester A., ed. *Refugees: A World Report, 1979.* New York: Facts on File, 1980.

Spragens, Joel, and Charney, J. *Embargo: Implications of the U.S. Humanitarian Embargo in Vietnam and Kampuchea.* Boston: Oxfam, 1985.

Stein, Barry, and Tomasi, Sylvano, eds. "Refugees Today." *International Migration Review* 15 (Spring-Summer 1981), 331-93.

Stewart, Barbara McDonald. *United States Government Policy on Refugees from Nazism, 1933-1940.* New York: Garland Publishing, 1982.

Stoessinger, John. *The Refugee in the World Community.* Minneapolis: University of Minnesota Press, 1956.

Teitelbaum, Michael S., "Immigration, Refugees, and Foreign Policy." *International Organization* 38 (Summer 1984), 429-50.

———. "Right vs. Right: Immigration and Refugee Policy in the United States." *Foreign Affairs* 59 (Autumn 1980), 21-59.

Thompson, Kenneth W., ed. *Ethics and International Relations.* New Brunswick, N.J.: Transaction Books, 1985.

———. *Moral Dimensions of American Foreign Policy.* New Brunswick, N.J.: Transaction Books, 1984.

Tomaso, Lydio F. *In Defense of the Alien*. New York: Center for Migration Studies, annual since 1983.

Tucker, Robert. *The Inequality of Nations*. New York: Basic Books, 1977.

United Nations High Commissioner for Refugees. *Handbook on Procedures and Criteria for Determining Refugee Status under the 1951 Convention and the 1967 Protocol Relating to the Status of Refugees*. Geneva: UNHCR, 1979.

United States Congress, Senate Committee on the Judiciary. "Humanitarian Problems of Southeast Asia, 1977-78." 95th Congress, 2nd Session, March 1978.

United States Department of State. *World Refugee Report*. A Report Submitted to Congress as Part of the Consultation on Refugee Admissions to the United States. Washington, D.C.: Bureau for Refugee Programs, 1986.

Vincent, R. J. *Human Rights and International Relations*. Cambridge: Cambridge University Press, 1986.

Wain, Barry. *The Refused*. New York: Simon and Schuster, 1981.

Walzer, Michael. *Just and Unjust Wars*. New York: Basic Books, 1977.

———. "Political Action: The Problem of Dirty Hands." *Philosophy and Public Affairs*, Winter 1973.

Winkler, Elizabeth. "Voluntary Agencies and Government Policy." *International Migration Review* 15, 1-2 (Spring-Summer 1981).

Wolfers, Arnold. *Discord and Collaboration*. Baltimore: Johns Hopkins Press, 1962.

Wyman, David S. *The Abandonment of the Jews: America and the Holocaust, 1941-45*. New York: Pantheon, 1985.

———. *Paper Walls: America and the Refugee Crisis, 1938-41*. Amherst: University of Massachusetts Press, 1968.

Zolberg, Aristide; Suhrke, Astri, and Aguayo, Sergio. *Escape from Violence: Globalized Social Conflict and the Refugee Crisis in the Developing World*. New York: Oxford University Press, 1989.

Zucker, Norman L., and Zucker, Naomi Flink. *The Guarded Gate: The Reality of American Refugee Policy*. San Diego: Harcourt Brace Jovanovich, 1987.